THE BIG BOOK OF
WEEKEND CRAFTS

THE BIG BOOK OF
WEEKEND CRAFTS

Over **90** step-by-step projects

General Editor: **Ruth Hamilton**

NH
NEW
HOLLAND

Published in 2005 by
New Holland Publishers (UK) Ltd
London o Cape Town o Sydney o Auckland
www.newhollandpublishers.com

Garfield House, 86-88 Edgware Road
London W2 2EA
United Kingdom

80 McKenzie Street
Cape Town 8001
South Africa

14 Aquatic Drive
Frenchs Forest, NSW 2086
Australia

218 Lake Road
Northcote, Auckland
New Zealand

ISBN 1 84330 771 5

1 3 5 7 9 10 8 6 4 2

Printed by Times Offset, Malaysia

CONTENTS

GENERAL INTRODUCTION

There is nothing more enjoyable than spending a weekend being creative and this book is packed full of exciting projects to help you do just that.

We have brought together advice on materials and equipment and all the information you need on techniques to get you started along with stylish designs for projects. You can learn how to make your own greetings cards, candles and mosaics as well as how to paint glassware and ceramics.

Whether you are a beginner interested in trying out a new craft or a craft-lover looking for new ideas and inspirations, the projects in the book are simple to make and take hardly any time to complete.

The fabulous designs are perfect for gift ideas or just for brightening up your own home and there is enough here to keep you busy for many a weekend! And if you feel inspired by the projects there are plenty of galleries to give you some fresh ideas and get you thinking about creating your own designs.

So, whether you choose to make a handmade card, produce a gorgeous candle, create a fun mosaic or paint some lovely glass and ceramic pieces, have a great crafting weekend!

MAKING CARDS

Jain Suckling

INTRODUCTION

Everybody loves to go to the letterbox to see if the postman has been round and if any surprises are in store! There is nothing nicer than receiving a bunch of cards on a birthday or other special occasion, and in amongst those cards a specially designed, handmade one has great significance – someone has taken the time and trouble to create a small work of art.

Making and sending cards is a lovely way to keep in touch and show people you care. There is no excuse for not finding a reason! There is always a birthday, wedding, christening or engagement coming up, a new baby on the way; perhaps a friend is moving house or has just passed their driving test. You may want to send a "Sorry" card to someone to apologise for a misdemeanour or say "thank you" for a good turn. Invitations are special if they are handmade and can be adapted for all occasions that involve a party! And there are, of course, the annual cultural festivals and celebrations: Christmas, Easter, Mother's Day, Father's Day and Thanksgiving.

Valentine's Day is my favourite day of the year – it lends itself to all manner of cards with lots of hearts and love poems and all things sparkly and wonderful! You can also invent your own occasion. Perhaps someone has cooked you a lovely meal and you want to make a food related "thanks for dinner" card.

Handmade cards are far too pretty to put away. You can store them in a specially made memento box, stick them to your pin-board, frame them or simply leave them on the mantle-piece forever!

The idea of making a handmade card originates from Victorian times, before mass-produced, printed cards were available and when it was the only form of conveying your best wishes on someone's special event. Styles and techniques have changed over the years and this book attempts to show modern, sophisticated and contemporary projects using bright, strong colours, fun and unusual textures, and a variety of collage ideas alongside traditional methods.

I hope this book will be a useful tool to springboard some ideas. Remember, a card is a very individual thing – feel free to adapt the ideas in this book to add a distinctly personal touch for your friends and family.

Make cards that appeal to your sense of texture and design. Love and passion should inspire them! Making cards can be an addictive hobby – once you start you will not want to stop. After reading the projects, attempt the ones you will enjoy making. You may discover you already have lots of the bits and pieces required to make your chosen card at home, but make sure you have everything you need before you begin.

Cardmaking is very versatile as it uses so many different media: paper and card, fabric, paint, dried flowers and favourite photographs. The beach, the countryside, your garden, Aunt Flo's sewing box, haberdashery stores, car boot sales, charity shops, craft fairs – all these are great places to source and collect unusual bits and pieces. At last you can stop feeling guilty about being one of life's hoarders!

If you are unsure of a technique, refer to the "Getting started" chapter at the front of this section. Then let your imagination run riot and enjoy yourself!

Iain Sinclair

GETTING STARTED

This chapter describes the tools and explains the general techniques used to make the cards in this book. Check that you have all the materials and tools you require before you begin so you don't get frustrated half way through! Once you have mastered a few of the projects, you will want to be creative and adapt things as you would like, happily using the materials and paper you have available, as well as the exciting paraphernalia that you will find everywhere once you start looking! Keep a special "card" box and as you discover things, store them in the box so when you want to begin making cards, you have all your treasures in one place.

BASIC EQUIPMENT

Paper shops and craft shops will stock most of the materials used in the projects. The basic tools and equipment to begin making cards are listed in detail below, but be sure to check the list of materials needed for specific cards before you start.

• **Paper and Cardboard:** When buying paper and card the abbreviations "mic" and "gsm" refer to various thicknesses and weights of the papers and cardboards. The abbreviation "mic" is used when describing thickness and is short for microns, i.e. 1000 microns equals 1 mm. The abbreviation "gsm" is used when describing the weight and is short for grams per square metre, i.e. a piece of 100 gsm paper measuring 1 m² weighs 100 grams. A good weight to use is 230-260 gsm as this will be easy to fold and will not be too flimsy.

• **Handmade papers:** ① Handmade papers are widely available in good stationery shops, artists' supply and crafts shops. There is a huge variety of colours and textures available, and you can also choose between paper with inclusions or without, and translucent or opaque paper. Of course you can also make your own handmade paper.

• **Funky papers:** ② Holographic card, metallic effect paper and card, textured and corrugated card and a range of other materials can be obtained from general and specialist stationery shops and artists' suppliers. Glitter-effect papers sometimes have a self-adhesive backing. Some high-street chains also offer pre-packaged selections of funky papers and card.

• **Paper sizes:** Standard sizes used in this book are A4 (210 x 297 mm/ 8¼ x 11¹¹⁄₁₆ in) and A5 (148 x 210 mm/ 5¹³⁄₁₆ x 8¼ in). A5, folded in half, gives you the standard size greetings card to fit a C6 envelope. Sheets of paper and card can be bought in larger sizes (A1 or A2) from specialist paper suppliers and cut to suit your requirements.

• **Cutting mat:** If you use cardboard, it retains score marks from a craft knife or scalpel, so you will need to change the blade frequently for accuracy. Using a cutting mat is much easier as it self-

②

blade on a craft knife can cut into the surface of a plastic ruler and ruin your work. A paper guillotine is also useful, but not essential.

• **PVA adhesive:** This is a strong glue which forms a permanent bond when used on paper and board. It dries leaving a transparent finish.

• **Spray adhesive:** This is commonly used for sticking paper to paper or board as it has the great virtue of sticking firmly. Repositioning can be possible for up to 30 seconds after

④

seals so your craft knife will not get stuck in previous score marks. The cutting mat allows the blade to sink into the material while cutting through the paper or card.

• **Craft knife:** A good, sharp craft knife is essential to keep your cut edges neat, so you may need to change your blade frequently. This also eliminates torn edges resulting from cutting paper with a blunt knife. Most craft knives come with blades which you can snap off when they become blunt. Scalpels can also be used – these are very sharp, so be very careful and have a supply of spare blades to hand if you are going to be doing a lot of cutting. It is very important to take great care when cutting – never cut towards your body. Have plasters handy just in case!

• **Scissors:** Do not use scissors reserved for cutting fabric on paper or card as the paper will blunt the blades. It is handy to have a couple of different sizes of scissors – a large pair for general work and a small pair, like nail scissors, for fiddly detail. Pattern-edge scissors can create amazing effects. Be careful when lining up the pattern from cut to cut ③. A pair of scissors with a smaller pattern can be used for details and a larger pattern for dramatic results.

• **Rulers:** A set square is essential, especially for cutting accurate right angles ④. A metal ruler is a good edge to cut against. If you haven't got one it will be worth investing in one, as the

③

bonding two surfaces. Always protect the area surrounding the paper or object you are spraying with some new paper. Spraying into a box is a good way of protecting surfaces. Remember to use in a well ventilated room and carefully read the instructions on the can!

• **All-purpose clear adhesive:** This is a strong cement-like adhesive for sticking objects together. It is ideal for mixed media and fabric and dries leaving a transparent finish.

• **Glue sticks:** You can buy glue sticks with a fine tip which can be useful for writing. Glitter or embossing powder can be sprinkled over the glue.

• **Glitter glue:** This also comes in different thicknesses and many different colours. A fine tip applicator makes it easy to write out greetings ⑤.

• **Tape:** Cellophane tape, masking tape, doubled-sided tape, magic tape, sticky fixers and foam pads are all useful. Double-sided tape can be used instead of glue for more lightweight craft materials. Masking tape can be useful when spraying glue on specific areas of a card or blocking out certain colours when colouring. Sticky fixing foam pads can be used as an adhesive and also create a three-dimensional effect.

• **Cotton buds:** These are very handy for applying glue to small or fiddly items.

• **Tweezers:** Use tweezers to pick up small items such as quilled elements.

• **Sewing equipment:** Different size needles are useful for a variety of sewing effects. Threads can also be bought in different thicknesses. A thimble is handy for protecting your thumb or fingers when sewing through thick card.

• **Pencils:** Pencils must be kept sharp for accurate marking. An HB pencil is a good hard pencil for marking edges to be cut – use a softer pencil, such as a 2B, if you think you are going to make mistakes and need to rub the line out. A good eraser is also useful for this reason.

BASIC TECHNIQUES

CUTTING AND SCORING

You will need a craft knife, steel ruler and cutting mat to score or cut medium-weight cardboard or thick paper. Cut the card to the desired size using a set square and rule to insure the corners are square. On the outside of the cardboard measure the centre line where the card will fold and mark with a pencil. Make sure the pencil mark is parallel to the edge, or the card will not fold properly. Using the metal ruler and craft knife, lightly score over the pencil line but make sure only to score the top layer of the cardboard with your craft knife ①.

CUTTING A WINDOW

Use a ruler to measure the centre of the front of the card and mark lightly with a pencil. Then, using a set square, mark out where you wish to have the window, using the centre mark as a guide. Check the window is centred correctly by using a ruler to measure from the edge of the card to the edge of the window.

With the card opened flat on a cutting mat, carefully cut out the window using a ruler and sharp craft knife. Move the card around when cutting each edge so you are always cutting parallel to (never towards) your body. Cut with the window on the inside of the rule so you can see where the pencil lines begin and end. Take care not to extend the cuts beyond the corners of the window ②.

TORN EDGES

An attractive finish to your card or the design within your card is a torn edge, which is a characteristic of many handmade and water-colour papers. To achieve this effect, measure and mark with a pencil where you wish the torn edge to be. Fold the paper over along this line so that you have a crease to work with. Firmly hold down the ruler against the crease and tear the paper by pulling away or towards you. Do a little at a time and press the ruler down firmly to avoid ripping the paper where you don't want it to tear ③.

❺

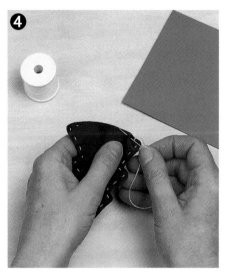

MOUNTING A DESIGN

First you must make sure your design is cut square. Using a ruler and pencil, measure on the card where the design will go. Mark the corners so that you can register the glued design quickly and avoid messy edges. Position the top edge of the design on the card and press the design down towards you to avoid any creases or air bubbles. Leave to dry in a safe place.

RUNNING STITCH

Bring the needle and thread through to the right side, then insert the needle further along the material in a straight line parallel to the edge. Leave a smaller gap on the wrong side before bring the thread up on the right side again and repeat the process to create a running stitch ④.

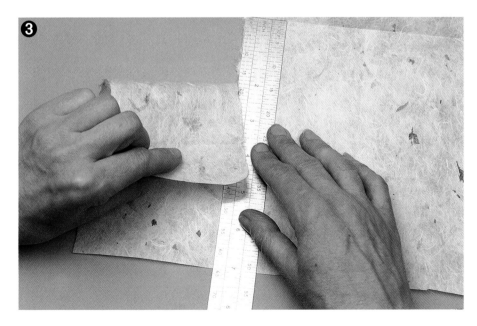

MAKING AN ENVELOPE

You can make special envelopes to fit your handmade cards in whatever media you wish, from beautiful coloured card to paper bags! Draw a plan before marking up your final piece. Use a pencil to mark the inside of the envelope. When measuring and marking the flaps, make dotted lines to indicate fold lines (or score lines if you are using card). You can also use the templates on pages 78 and 79, or disassemble an envelope of a suitable shape and size and use as a pattern.

Method:
Measure your handmade card and add 2.5 cm (1 in) to height and width. This

5

6

will be the base size of your envelope as it needs to be slightly bigger than the actual card for it to fit comfortably. Add a bottom flap which is three quarters of the basic height plus 2.5 cm (1 in). The top flap should be a quarter of the basic height plus 2.5 cm (1 in). Side flaps need to be 3 cm (1¼ in). All flaps should be tapered slightly. Mark the fold lines with a pencil and either fold or score using a rule and craft knife. Fold in the side flaps, apply glue to the edges of the bottom flap and fold it over on top of the side flaps. Fold down the top flap and use double-sided tape to seal the envelope before you send it ⑤.

PRESSING FLOWERS

At least two weeks in advance of making your card, press all the flowers, leaves and petals you wish to use in a heavy book between sheets of blotting paper or smooth tissue paper and leave to dry in a warm, dark and dry place. To avoid mould use less succulent flowers.

STAMPING AND EMBOSSING

Stamps can be bought in all shapes and sizes from shops or by mail order from specialist stamp manufacturers. Ink pads come in all the colours of the rainbow as well as in gold, silver and bronze. Special embossing ink pads can be used in conjunction with embossing powder to create a raised effect when the embossing powder is heated to melting point. When using stamps for decorating a card, make sure they are evenly covered with stamping ink ⑥.

AGEING

Use a heavy weight paper such as water colour paper. Wet the paper with a little water, then place two or three used tea bags on to the paper so the tea stains it. Coffee granules can also be used to stain. Use a wet paint brush to squash them into the areas you want to appear aged, or use a dry stencil brush to rub the granules into the paper.

COLLECTIBLES

Get collecting! Lace, shells, coins, old photographs and postcards, stamps, buttons, ribbons, raffia, feathers and much more can be found in flea markets, haberdashery shops or even your home. Keep things in labelled envelopes where necessary to make life easier. Similarly, make a file for magazine cuttings, wrapping paper and pieces of handmade paper ⑦.

GLITTER AND CONFETTI

Glitter stars, confetti in a variety of shapes from champagne glasses and numbers to Easter bunnies and angels,

bindis and holographic and glitter stickers are available from many stationery and card shops and are ideal for use in fabulous shaker cards or simply to sprinkle into the envelope for a special surprise ⑧!

GIFT TAGS

If you have leftover card, fabric, paper or other material from making a card, why not create a matching gift tag? You can also adapt elements of many of the projects in this book to a much smaller format and use them as gift tags.

DECORATING ENVELOPES

You can personalize envelopes in many ways: make one yourself from beautiful textured, handmade paper; wax-seal your envelopes; wrap the finished card and envelope in contrasting tissue or crepe paper and tie with gold cord; or embellish your envelope flap with small decorative elements from the card inside ⑨.

PACKING AND PADDING

At our studio we get hundreds of cards per week through the post and courier companies. Often the outside packaging gets damaged, so it is important to ensure all the goods we receive and send to shops are carefully padded to avoid damage. Nothing is more heartbreaking than to make a beautiful card and then to find it was broken on arrival at its destination. Gift-wrap your creation with tissue paper or cellophane to make it extra special, then send in a padded or stiff-backed envelope.

❼

❽

❾

HANDY HINTS BEFORE YOU BEGIN

Be kind to yourself – if all goes wrong, just try again!

~

The designs are only a basic guide – you can adapt most cards to suit a specific occasion.

~

Give yourself enough time to see a project through easily. Don't try to rush things – enjoy the process.

~

Be proud of your creations! If they turn out well you may want to suggest to the lucky recipient that they frame your card or stick it on the cover of an album.

~

If you regularly send cards to the same people you may want to make a special memento box for them.

~

Be adventurous – the beauty of handmade cards is that you can personalize them for the individual who is receiving them – whether they like cats, tulips, chocolate or whatever! You may like to use photographs and quirky sayings – something which will make the card unusual and unique.

~

Remember, children love to get in on the action! Encourage them to use their imagination – Father's Day, Mother's Day, Christmas, birthdays and thank you cards for Granny are all great opportunities for hands-on creativity!

~

Make sure there is no glue showing on your finished cards, as this makes them look cheap and messy.

~

If you have gone to lots of trouble to make a special card, you must remember to pack it properly if you send it through the post. Use a padded bag and bubble wrap. Perhaps wrap the card in nice tissue paper and tie a bow with some pretty braid: a gift in itself.

~

Finally, keep things simple. Don't clutter up your card with too many things and stick to a theme. Be adventurous with colour but, again, don't overdo it with too many combinations on one card. If in doubt – leave it out!

~

PROJECTS AND GALLERIES
FOR MAKING CARDS

EMBOSSED HEART

Pink, red and gold – the luscious colours of love! Embossing powder is available in many different colours and creates a stunning effect. Whispy handmade paper, red and holographic gold card and the lace effect of the embossed pattern make a splendid card to send to someone you really adore.

FUNKY ECLECTICA

1 Using the embossing stamp pad, stamp your design onto one half of the red card. Immediately sprinkle some gold embossing powder over the image before the ink dries, and shake off the excess powder back into its container. Heat the image from the underside over a toaster or use the embossing heat gun until the powder has melted. You will see this happen almost immediately. If the gold powder is not melting, your heat source is not hot enough.

YOU WILL NEED

Embossing stamp pad (tinted)
Rose stamp design
Red card, A4
Gold embossing powder
Embossing heat gun or toaster
Template (page 72)
Spray adhesive
Gold card, A5
Pink handmade paper, A4
Ruler
Pencil
Craft knife
Scissors with pattern edge
Greetings card blank, 250 gsm, 14 x 14 cm (5½ x 5½ in)
All-purpose glue
Plastic jewel

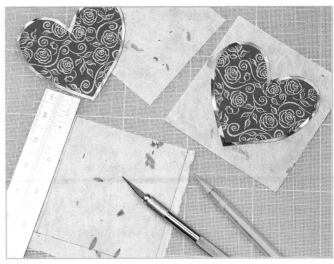

2 Using the template on page 72, cut out a heart shape from the embossed card. Apply spray adhesive to the back and stick onto the gold card. Now cut around the heart shape, leaving a 0.5 cm (¼ in) gold border.

3 Cut out a square of the handmade pink paper approximately 0.5 cm – 1 cm (¼ – ⅜ in) larger than the heart at its widest points. Apply spray adhesive to the back of the heart shape and stick centrally onto the pink paper square.

4 Cut out a square from the remaining red card, ensuring it is 1 cm (⅜ in) larger all around than the pink square. Use the scissors to achieve a patterned edge. Apply spray adhesive to the back of the pink paper square and stick centrally onto the red card.

5 Finally, cut out another piece of pink handmade paper slightly larger than your greetings card blank. Apply spray adhesive to the pink paper and stick onto the card blank, then trim along the edge to the size of the card blank.

6 Apply spray adhesive to the back of your collage and position on the card. Add the final touch to the embossed heart by glueing a plastic jewel to the top of the heart with all-purpose glue.

STENCILLED CUPID

Stencilling is easier than drawing – stencil your chosen image and nobody will believe that such a professional and unique effect was created by you! The cupid is a great alternative to a heart for this sophisticated love card, and the antiquing effect makes it that much more special.

FUNKY ECLECTICA

1 Using a permanent ink pen, trace the outlines of the cupid template from page 72 onto a sheet of mylar. Trace the bow separately as this will be worked in a different colour.

2 Place the mylar onto the picture glass. When the heat pen is hot, trace over the design, then carefully push out the shape with your fingers. Alternatively, if your design is not too complicated, it can be cut out with a craft knife. You can also use a pre-cut stencil.

3 Spray the reverse of the stencil with a light, even coat of stencil mount, wait a few seconds allowing it to become tacky and blot onto a spare piece of paper to remove any excess glue. Place the stencil in position on your watercolour paper. Shake a small amount of blue stencil paint into the lid or pour into a dish. Dab the brush into the paint and work the paint into the bristles of the brush in a circular motion on a piece of kitchen paper to disperse the colour evenly. With the almost dry brush, colour the stencil. Slowly build up the colours, using a circular or a stippling motion. Remove the stencil carefully and reposition it to work the bow in purple, using a clean brush.

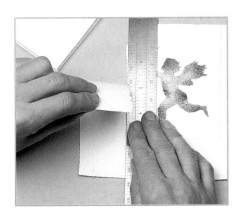

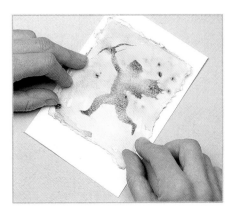

4 With a pencil, mark a rectangle close to the cupid on the water-colour paper, leaving approx. 0.5 cm (¼ in) from either side and approx. 1 cm (⅜ in) from top and bottom of the design. Position the ruler on the pencilled lines, put pressure onto the ruler with one hand and with the other pull the corner of the paper towards you to achieve a torn edge.

5 Lightly dampen the paper with a sponge, then gentle shake a small amount of coffee granules on top. Using a clean stencil brush, work the granules into the paper, leaving some granules undissolved. Place a couple of used tea bags on top and leave for half an hour to stain the paper, then remove the tea bags and dry with a hairdryer or leave to dry naturally.

6 When the paper is completely dry, lightly spray the reverse with spray adhesive. Wait for 10 – 15 seconds, then position on the greetings card blank. Place under a couple of heavy books until the adhesive is dry.

NINE ROSE PETAL HEARTS

The number nine signifies "forever" or "eternity" in Chinese culture and is considered auspicious for the celebration of birthdays and friendship, and red roses are a traditional western gift of love, making this a perfect Valentine's Day card.

ARTIST: CHIU MEI AU-YEUNG

1 Two weeks in advance, press the rose petals between blotting paper in the pages of a heavy book and leave to dry in a warm, dark and dry place.

YOU WILL NEED

9 pressed red rose petals

9 sheets mulberry paper in pink, lilac, purple, dark green, turquoise, earth green, yellow, orange, dark orange

Cocktail sticks

PVA glue

Textured white card, 250 gsm, A5, folded in half

Scissors

--- TIP ---

The torn paper squares should butt up against each other, but do not overlap them or the separate colours will not stand out so well.

24

2 Measure and fold a 3 cm (1¼ in) square on one of the sheets of mulberry paper, then tear along the folds to make a rough-edged square. Repeat with each of the different colours.

3 Using a cocktail stick, apply glue to the back of one of the squares of mulberry paper and stick it to the top left-hand corner of the front of the folded white card about 1 cm (⅜ in) from each edge. Stick down the rest of the squares close to each other to form a 9 x 9 cm (3½ x 3½ in) multicolour square.

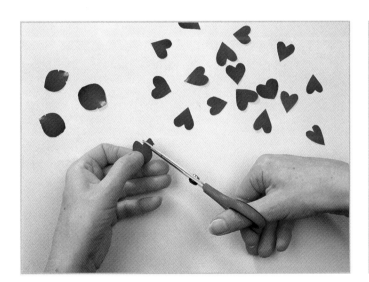

4 Using the scissors, cut each pressed rose petal into a heart shape to fit the 3 cm (1¼ in) squares of paper.

5 Apply glue to the back of the petal and stick to the middle of the top left coloured square. Repeat until all the squares are filled.

LOVE GALLERY

Gold swirly heart
A simple gold and red heart
on plain blue makes a
charming design.
Rowena Burton

Wire flower
Tracey's inimitable style is reflected here
in a wire flower on paper and gold net
with a pearl center and raffled edge.
Tracey Anne Turner

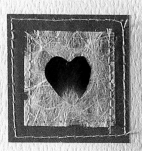

Gold frame petal
A machine-stitched gold border is an
attractive setting for this petal cut into
a heart shape and placed on gorgeous,
textured white paper.
Nadia Moncrieff

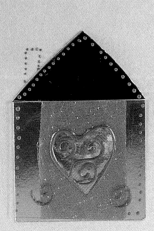

House of love
This happy house made from a simple, graphic
silver board cut-out is decorated with fabric pen
and glitter-effect fabric. *Lucy Thomas*

Perfect pansy
A pressed flower pansy, a patterned edge and good use
of simple colour combinations make this embossed
gold card a pleasure to behold! *Funky Eclectica*

Wooden daisy

The favourite daisy in yet another style.
Wood, painted spring yellow, frames it
beautifully with a ribbon detail.
RaRa

Mother's day

Purple ribbon adds a rich finish to this
antique-effect old favourite family
photograph. An ideal birthday or
Mother's day card. *Anke Ueberberg*

Sparkly heart

Sparkly fabric, craft paper, silver board
and swirls of glitter pen make this
unusual layered card ideal for a
romantic gesture! *Lucy Thomas*

Daring damask

Shining effect damask paper and fabric
pen were used to make this stylish and
sensual romantic card. *Kathryn Ferrier*

Silver heart

A card for any occasion related to
the heart! A kiln-fired clay heart, cleverly
textured and painted silver. *Zoe Ryan at Biscuit*

27

BOUQUET OF TULIPS

Perfect for a birthday, for Mother's Day, as a "Thank You" card, or simply to say "Hello", this exquisite and colourful paper and wire collage card shows the time and care taken to make it and will convey your love and friendship to the happy recipient.

ARTIST: TRACEY ANNE TURNER

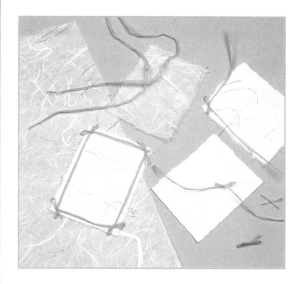

1 Tear a 9 x 7 cm (3½ x 2¾ in) rectangle out of the white cartridge paper and out of the white handmade paper, then glue together. Take two 25 cm (9¾ in) lengths of raffia and tie a bow near the centre of each, then glue the bows down on the inside edge of the handmade paper at opposite corners. Trim the excess lengths of raffia to fit the card and glue down. Make two separate bows from the left-over raffia and glue those down in the remaining corners. Put to one side.

YOU WILL NEED

White cartridge paper, A4
White handmade paper, A4
All-purpose glue
4 lengths of raffia, 25 cm (9¾ in) long
Scissors
Yellow handmade paper, A4
White organza, 10 x 10 cm (4 x 4 in)
Template (page 72)
Pencils in pink, blue, purple, orange, yellow and green
Craft knife or scissors
Gold plated jewellery wire, diameter 0.4 mm
Pliers
Blue ribbon, approx. 20 cm (8 in) long
Length of small pearls, 20 cm (8 in)
Small leaves from the garden
Yellow card, 250 gsm, A5, folded in half
Yellow envelope, C6

2 Draw two 8 x 5 cm (3⅛ x 2 in) rectangles onto the yellow handmade paper and cut out. Cut the corners off one of the rectangles to create a kite shape. From the second rectangle, cut a triangular shape to fit the lower part of the kite shape.

Apply a thin line of glue on the long edges of the triangle and glue in place on the kite shape. For extra decoration, cut an organza triangle slightly larger than the yellow handmade paper triangle. Place over the lower part of the kite shape, then fold and glue down the overlap on the back of the kite shape.

3 Draw 14 tulip heads and stalks onto the cartridge paper, using the template on page 72. Colour in six pink, two blue, two yellow, two purple and two orange tulip heads with the pencils. Colour the tulip stalks green and cut out the tulips. Make four or five golden swirls out of the jewellery wire using the pliers and tie a blue bow out of the ribbon. Cut one length of two pearls and one length of three pearls. Collect some tiny leaves from the garden or cut small leaf shapes out of a larger leaf.

4 Glue the kite shape onto the white rectangle made in step 1. Glue the flowers inside the pocket of the kite and add individual pearls, leaves and wire swirls. Glue the ribbon bow and the two lengths of pearls at the bottom of the bouquet and decorate with a single pink flower and two leaves, then glue the collage onto the front of the yellow greetings card blank.

5 For extra decoration on the back of the card, tear a 4.5 cm x 3.5 cm (1¾ x 1⅜ in) rectangle out of the cartridge paper and white handmade paper, glue together, glue one pink tulip and two leaves to the centre and decorate the edge with raffia as before. Glue to the back of the card.

6 For the envelope, tear a 2 x 2 cm (¾ x ¾ in) square out of the cartridge paper and white handmade paper, glue together, decorate with a tulip head and two small leaves and glue onto the flap of the envelope.

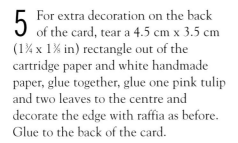

NET AND WEDDING CONFETTI

Think of a wedding and your first thoughts might be confetti, rings and the bride's veil. This collage combines all these elements to make a beautiful card to keep, vividly reminiscent of the big day for the happy couple!

ARTIST: AMANDA CAINES

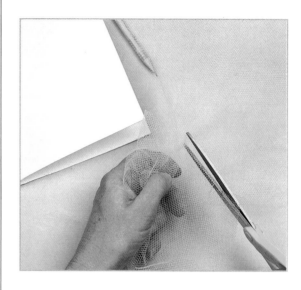

1 Fold and cut the white card to the desired size, using the ruler and craft knife. Cut the net fabric to approximately twice the size of the card to allow for gathering.

YOU WILL NEED

White card, 250 gsm, 15 x 30 cm (6 x 12 in) or as desired
Ruler
Craft knife
Cutting mat
Cream or pink net
Clear all-purpose adhesive
Scissors
2 imitation gold wedding rings (available through most party and bridal catering shops)
Spatula
PVA glue
Box of gold stars
Confetti
Box of gold bell decoration

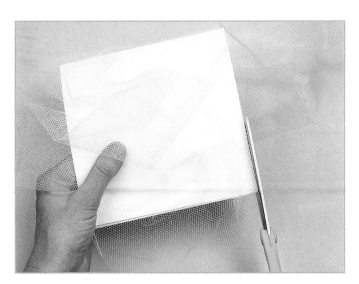

2 Spread clear glue all over the card. Gather the net fabric and gently press it in place on the card until the glue is dry. Trim off the excess net from around the edges, taking care not to cut into the card.

3 Interlock the wedding rings or place them side by side. Dot with glue using a spatula and place on top of the net in the middle of the card. Hold in place until the glue is dry.

4 Dot a little PVA glue on the back of the confetti pieces. Place them, glue side down, on the net, so that it looks as though they have been loosely scattered onto the net.

5 Glue stars and gold bells in place in the same way, spacing them evenly to give a balanced composition. Present in a silver, gold or brightly coloured envelope.

WEDDING GALLERY

Glorious stitching
Left: Gold Chinese leaf paper, orange tissue and a pressed primrose flower, edged with machine stitching, make a special spring wedding card.
Nadia Moncrieff

Embossed metal
An interesting alternative for the modern bride and groom: embossed aluminium metal can be left silver or sprayed with gold car paint as in our example.
Funky Eclectica

Cake congratulations
Subtle craft papers with petals and delicate stitching on the cake make a beautiful card. *Dawn Ireland*

Unique organza
Gold braid and divine embroidered material mounted onto board for a 3-D effect recreate the splendour of the special day. *Kate Twelvetrees*

Delicate decoupage
A pretty example of decoupage using bright colours and strong images for some old-fashioned romance.
Amanda Caines

Holographic heaven
The large card format lends itself to the strong silver holographic materials. A great example of simple yet effective design. *Kate Horeman*

Eastern flavour
The oblong format, bright pink card, mixed glitter colours, gold paper and a beaded Indian bindi make this an exotic and interesting wedding card.
Caroline Dent

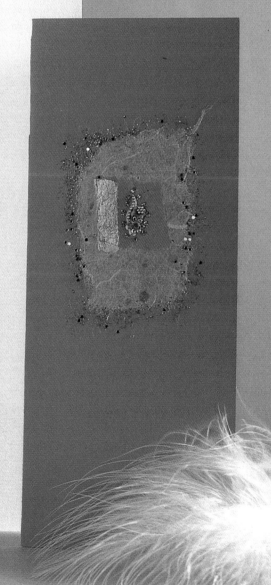

Wedding wonders
The cute image of love birds and a traditional "good luck" horseshoe embellished with pearls, raffia and ribbon combine to make a delightful congratulation!
Tracey Anne Turner

WEDDING CAKE

Whether you are a beginner or an expert with the needle, this is the card for you! A beautiful and elegant card, it is perfect for sending on the wedding day itself or for an anniversary. You could cut the cake from gold or silver paper instead. If you prefer to use your sewing machine, try the variation on page 32.

ARTIST: DAWN IRELAND

1 On the reverse of the handmade petal paper, measure and mark lightly with a pencil a rectangle measuring approximately 6 x 8 cm (2¼ x 3⅛ in), then tear along the marked lines. This will form the background for the wedding cake design.

YOU WILL NEED

Handmade petal paper, A4
Pencil
Steel ruler
Lilac plain paper, A4
Template (page 72)
Craft knife
Cutting mat
Glue stick
Small piece of gold paper
Needle
Metallic gold embroidery thread
White card, 230 gsm, A5, folded in half
Metallic gold envelope, C6

TIP

You can also achieve the sewing effect by drawing dotted lines with gold or silver pen.

VARIATIONS

Cut out a house shape or a pram in similar craft papers and you have another perfect greetings card.

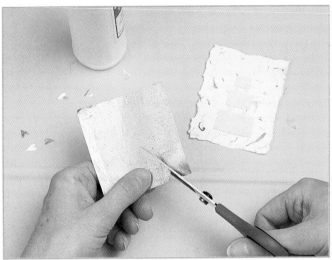

2 Using the template from page 72, draw out the wedding cake on a piece of the lilac paper. Carefully cut out the cake using the craft knife and cutting mat.

3 Glue the cake slightly lower than central onto the handmade petal paper. With the scissors, cut out a small heart from the gold paper. Glue in position on the petal paper at the top of the cake.

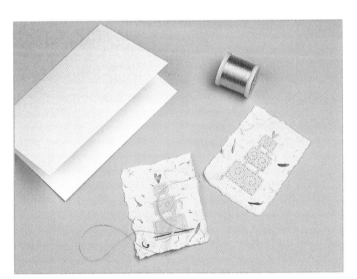

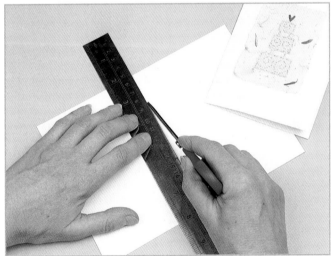

4 Faintly pencil the design from the template onto the cake shape, outlining each layer of the cake and adding swirls inside, then make evenly spaced holes with the needle before sewing. Using the needle, threaded with gold embroidery thread, work along the swirls and edges of the cake in running stitch.

5 Score and fold the card in half. Position the collage neatly on the front of the card and glue in place.

SILK PAINTED HOUSE

Silk painting is a traditional craft used on scarves and wall hangings. These miniature adaptations for the card format work perfectly for many different occasions. Flowers for birthdays, hearts for Valentine's Day, champagne glasses for celebrations – the list is endless. We've featured the house for a lovely, welcoming New Home card.

ARTIST: ROWENA BURTON

1 Stretch the plain white silk over the wooden frame, securing it on all sides with masking tape, so that it is smooth and taut.

YOU WILL NEED

A piece of white silk approx.
15 x 15 cm (6 x 6 in)

A frame (you can use a wooden picture frame), approx. 12 x 12 cm (4¾ x 4¾ in)

Masking tape

20ml tube of Marabu Konturmittel (gold contour liner) 084

Template (page 76)

Brush

Silk paints in Marabu karminrot (red) 032, Marabu mittelgelb (yellow) 021, Marabu violett dunkel (purple) 051, Marabu maigrun (green) 064, Marabu mittelblau (blue) 052,

Wide double sided tape

Scissors

White, textured greetings card blank, 250 gsm, A5, folded in half

Envelope, C6

--- TIP ---

You could use drawing pins to secure the silk on the frame. Alternatively, use an embroidery hoop to stretch the silk.

2 Using the tube of gold contour liner, draw a rectangle 4 x 4.5 cm (1½ x 1¾ in) in the middle of the silk.

3 Still using the gold contour liner, draw the house design in gold inside the gold rectangle. Alternatively, copy the template on page 76, place it underneath the silk when stretching it over the frame and trace the design.

4 Using the silk dyes, paint a red door, yellow front, purple roof, green hill and blue sky within the outlines. Leave to dry after applying each colour.

5 Apply double-sided tape to cover the back of the design. Carefully peel the silk off the frame and gently remove the masking tape. Cut out the design close to the gold outline. Peel the paper backing from the tape and stick the design in place on the front of the white card.

6 You can enlarge the design on a photocopier for a bigger card, or reduce it to make a smaller design suitable for a gift tag.

NEW HOME POP-UP

This card is easier to make than it appears. The perfect card for the momentous occasion of moving house, this 3-D card can be personalized or left stylishly simple for maximum effect.

ARTIST: ANKE UEBERBERG

1 Photocopy or trace the base and roof of the house from the templates on page 73 and cut out using the ruler and craft knife. Cut out the window openings. Place the house base template onto the dark green card and mark the fold lines, then draw around the whole template and pencil in the windows. Do the same with the roof template on the lime green card.

YOU WILL NEED

Template (page 73)
White paper, A4
Felt-tip pen
Ruler
Pencil
Craft knife
Dark green cartridge paper, A4
Lime green cartridge paper, A4
PVA glue
White card, 250 gsm, 12.5 x 12.5 cm (4⅞ x 4⅞ in)
Dark green ribbon, approx. 100 cm (39½ in) long

TIP

Create a decoupage or stencilled garden around the house, or simply use pencils to draw in trees and flowers. You can also stick translucent paper behind the windows for added interest.

2 First, gently score the fold lines using the ruler and knitting needle. Cut out the house base using the ruler and craft knife. Cut out the windows and the door opening and fold the door and the flaps along the scored lines. Do the same with the roof. Write your message onto the side of the roof parallel to the flap.

3 Glue the roof flap onto the inside of the house base as shown, with the message on the outside. Measure and lightly mark 6 cm (2¼ in) from either side of the fold of the white card, both in the middle and at the bottom, and glue down the flaps of the house base, lining it up with the bottom of the card.

4 Check immediately that the house and roof fold down flat and straight. Make sure the roof does not stick out when the card is closed. Trim, if necessary, using ruler and craft knife. Leave to dry.

5 With the card closed, make a small cut close to the fold of the card and thread through the dark green ribbon (or whichever colour you prefer). Cross the ribbon at the back and tie a bow at the front.

ACETATE DAISY WINDOW

Simple graphics on clear material such as acetate create a subtle, contemporary look, suitable for any occasion. Pick your favourite image and simply photocopy it to make this stylish card, or choose an image appropriate for a specific occasion.

FUNKY ECLECTICA

1 Photocopy the daisy onto plain paper first to check the copy picks out as much detail as you would like. Photocopy the daisy onto the sheet of acetate.

2 Using the steel ruler and pencil, mark out the frame shape on the reverse of the shiny silver card. Measure and mark a square of approximately 8 cm (3⅛ in) square on the outside. Measure 1 cm (⅜ in) in from each side and mark with the pencil. This will give you the thickness of the frame.

3 Cut out the frame using the craft knife and ruler. Take care not to cut into the corners. You can avoid this by cutting the corners first with the point of the craft knife.

4 Score the blue chromolux card on the inside and fold in half to make the card. Glue the frame, silver side up, onto the front of the card just above the centre. Using the steel ruler and craft knife, cut out the chromolux card inside the frame to produce a window.

5 Cut out a square of at least 9 cm (3½ in) around the daisy print on the acetate sheet. Stick the acetate square to the the inside of the card using the white self-adhesive labels, making sure that the daisy is centered within the window.

GREETINGS GALLERY

Country cowslip
Clever use of pressed flowers on a gentle coloured paper are ideal to make this charming card. *Nadia Moncrieff*

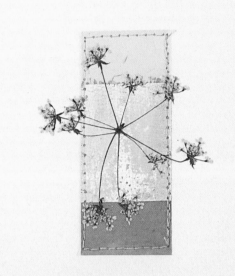

Holiday inspiration
All those favourite shells collected over time on special days can be made into a collage backed simply with sandpaper and netting for that beach effect!
Funky Eclectica

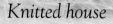

Fluffy cat
A wonderful idea and one of this artist's signature designs, the cat's fur tail flows over the mantelpiece – the bigger, longer and fluffier the better! *Kate Twelvetrees*

Knitted house
A new home with a quirk! Knitted and embroidered, this house is simple but effective on a plain background.
Mandy Jane

Ahoy!

Left: Rope, boats and painted balsa wood create a maritime moment for a special bon voyage card. *RaRa*

Little ladybird

This delightful, deep red card is gold-foil embossed and embellished with a fabric paint pen spot detail. *Kathryn Ferrier*

Celebrations

Champagne and ribbon on delicious hand-crafted paper with delicate inclusions is ideal for any celebration. *Funky Eclectica*

Wrapped baby

This sweet new baby card is made from fabric shaped into a blanket with a toy and dummy found in a junk shop! *Bizara*

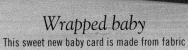

STORK MOBILE

The movement created by dangling the stork and its baby bundle from a gold thread is simple but very effective. The cut-out shape could be simplified to a rectangle if preferred.

ARTIST: TRACEY ANNE TURNER

1 Using the template on page 74, draw a cloud shape onto the front of the card blank and cut out with a craft knife.

TIP

We have used blue card but you many want to use pink for a baby girl. The stork could be cut from metallic card, so that it will catch the light as it swings about.

2 Using the templates from page 74, draw the stork and its wing onto the square of white card. Draw on the eye. Colour the stork legs orange, then cut out the stork and the wing using the craft knife.

3 Using the craft knife, cut out a beak shape from the gold crepe paper and glue in place on the cut-out stork. Cut out a wing tip shape from the gold crepe paper. Glue onto the wing, then glue the wing into place on the stork's body.

4 Fold the square of blue handmade paper in half. From the folded edge draw a bag shape using the template on page 74 and cut out with scissors. Make a tiny hole at the top of the bag with the needle, then thread a 15 cm (6 in) length of gold thread through and tie in a bow.

5 Glue the "handle" of the bag to the back of the stork's beak. Make a tiny hole in the stork's back. Thread a 15 cm (6 in) length of gold thread through it and tie in a knot. Dangle the stork by glueing the knotted end of the thread to the inside top of the card and secure it by glueing a tiny strip of card on top.

6 Draw three simple flower shapes onto the leftover handmade paper, using the template on page 74, and cut out with the craft knife. Glue to the bag, back of the card and the envelope flap. Cut three tiny circles from white scrap paper and glue to the middle of the flowers. Finish with a gold wire bow, twisted into shape with pliers and glued above the cloud shape.

AQUARIUM SHAKER

Will the cat catch the fish or only get the bones? Shake this exciting card designed for cat (or fish) lovers and see the holographic fish sparkle in the light. A great card for children, too, it can be adapted for special occasions using anything from stars to Easter bunnies.

FUNKY ECLECTICA

1 Ink the frame stamp and stamp firmly onto a sheet of white paper. Leave to dry, then apply spray adhesive and stick onto a piece of polyboard. Using the steel ruler and the craft knife, trim the polyboard close to the outside of the stamped design and cut out the centre to produce a window.

YOU WILL NEED

Stamp ink pad
Stamp for frame design, approx. 10 x 14.5 cm (4 x 5 ¾ in)
White paper, A4
Spray adhesive
Poly board, A4 or trimmed to fit the stamp size
Steel ruler
Craft knife
Cutting mat
Fish confetti or fish stickers
Coloured card, A4
Scissors
White greetings card blank, 250 gsm, A5, folded in half
Pencil
Sheet of acetate, A4 (or two small sheets window card acetate)
Aqua-coloured tracing paper or greeny-blue, slightly translucent paper, approx. A5
Template (page 77)
All-purpose glue
Cat stamp for inside of card

2 If you are using small fish stickers, peel them off the backing sheet and stick them onto coloured card. Cut them out with the scissors. You could also use nail scissors for this.

3 Position the frame on the greetings card blank along the fold line and mark the outline and the inside window with a pencil. Trim the card to size and cut out the window from the front of the card using ruler and craft knife. Put to one side.

4 Apply spray adhesive to the front of the frame and firmly press onto one piece of acetate. Trim off the excess around the edge of the frame. Place the frame face down onto a surface and position the fish, picture side down, inside the frame. Using the template on page 77, cut out some seaweed shapes from the coloured tracing paper, spray one side with glue and stick them onto the second piece of acetate.

5 Apply all-purpose glue to the back of the frame and position onto the seaweed-decorated acetate, creating a clear pocket with the fish inside. Trim off any excess around the frame. Glue the frame in position exactly over the window of the greetings card blank. Stamp the cat inside the card, so that it appears to look through the fish tank.

CARDS AS GIFTS GALLERY

Sweet cone
Bright colourful papers
and sweeties – who would
not enjoy such a gift!
Funky Eclectica

Crazy daisies
These flower hairgrips, handmade from
painted buttons and stuck into lime-
coloured funky foam, are a fantastic,
original idea by this artist. *Emma Angel*

Bunny girl
Part of a commercially available set,
this is an innovative idea, threading a
handmade bracelet through rivets
in the card. *Emma Angel*

Golden bookmark
An elongated shape cut out with pattern edge scissors,
this metal bookmark is embossed on gold paper and
finished with a bow. *Funky Eclectica*

Spangly tree

A Christmas card doubling as a decoration, easily made with shiny stars, silver snowflake stickers and layers of stiff, coloured mirror paper. Complete with a ribbon at the top.
Funky Eclectica

Heart necklace

A seductive idea: the heart necklace echoes the heart background and adorns a glamorous woman's neck. A perfect gift card! *Emma Angel*

A cute purse – for cute things

An iconic image, sweet buttons and mirrors form a lovely girly card with this Chinese fabric purse.
Emma Angel

Groovy key ring

This sewn key ring can have your favourite actress, popstar of friends inside.
Emma Angel

FINGER PUPPET CLOWN

Is it a card or is it a toy? A fun idea to send to the little ones in the family, this card can be made using whatever colours and materials you can conjure up from your box of collected bits and pieces.

FUNKY ECLECTICA

1 Using the template on page 75, draw the shape of the clown onto the white card. Use a biro or felt-tip pen to get a good strong outline.

YOU WILL NEED

White card, A4
Biro or felt-tip pen
Template (page 75)
Scissors
Pink or flesh-coloured plain chromolux card, 300 gsm, A4
Funky foam in red, purple and white
All-purpose glue
Black permanent ink pen
Orange felt-tip pen
Scrap of fake fur, matching the colour of funky foam (optional)

TIP

Instead of a circle of bright funky foam, you may wish to add a pom-pom or a bell to the top of the clown's hat. You could use glitter pen to decorate his hat and belt. Finally, red fingernails make fabulous clown shoes!

2 Cut out the template and draw around it onto the back of the flesh-coloured card. Cut out the shape.

3 On the template, mark out the hat, the clown's top and shorts with the fingerholes, the ruffle, belt, cuffs and hatband. Cut these into sections and use them as templates for the clown's clothes.

4 Using the templates, draw around each one on the desired coloured sheet of funky foam and cut out the sections. We have used purple for hat and top, white for hatband, mouth, ruffle, cuffs and belt and red for the trousers, but you can use any other colour combination you have available. Make sure you have each template the right way up.

5 Now, using the flesh-coloured clown shape as a base, start glueing the pieces of funky foam in the relevant places. Once all sections are glued in place, you can draw around each section with the black permanent pen to give the clown a more cartoon-like character.

6 Cut out the holes for the fingers into the shorts. If you want to add fun fur, make the holes slightly bigger than your fingers. Spread a line of glue around each of the holes, stick down the strips of fun fur and trim as necessary.

7 Cut out four small circles from the red funky foam and a mouth shape from the white. Glue these in position, using two of the red circles for buttons, one for the hat and one for the nose. Draw around the edges of the buttons with black permanent ink pen. Colour the ears orange with the felt-tip pen. Write your message on the back.

EMBOSSED METAL HEARTS

Embossed metal gives an artistic and charming effect. This romantic cherub and heart card lends itself to this medium, but you can use any other suitable line drawing to adapt the card to your own requirements. Have a go – its easier than it looks!

FUNKY ECLECTICA

1 Place the folded greetings card blank on the aluminium sheet and draw around it with the point of a wooden skewer to make a rectangle of 15 cm (6 in) long and 10.5 cm (4¼ in) high. Press firmly to score a clear line into the foil.

YOU WILL NEED

Medium gauge aluminium foil, approx. 11 x 15.5 cm (4⅜ x 6⅛)

Template (page 76)

Greetings card blank, 250 gsm, A5, folded in half

Wooden skewer

Scissors

Tracing paper

PVA glue

TIPS

You can include a message on the card, but remember that the scoring is done from the reverse of the card, so any words will have to be written in mirror writing.

Spray the foil with gold paint for a Golden Wedding Anniversary card (see gallery pages 32-33).

2 Using the scissors, trim off the excess foil just outside the scored outline. Take care not to cut yourself on the sharp edges of the foil.

3 Inside the first rectangle, score another one measuring 10 x 6.5 cm (4 x 2½ in) on the same (reverse) side of the foil, to create an equal border all around the card. Score a zigzag pattern within the border and add small circles inside each triangle.

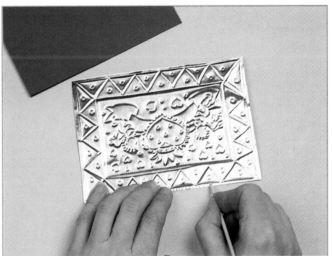

4 Trace the design from page 76. Lay the tracing paper over the reverse of the foil and, using the border to position the template, score the design onto the aluminium sheet in a fluid movement. Add hearts and small circles as desired.

5 Now turn the foil over, and, still using the skewer, draw along either side of any key lines of the picture again to highlight them. Score a series of short vertical lines all along the very edge of the foil to create a border decoration. Glue the foil to the front of the card blank.

CONCERTINA STARS

Sparkly, glittery silver – we love this idea! This unusual card is not as complex as it appears, and the matt silver and gun metal card combined with the glitter glue finish all add to the seasonal effect. It also has lots of space for greetings and messages.

Funky Eclectica

YOU WILL NEED

3 matt silver card squares, 13 x 13 cm (5⅛ x 5⅛ in)
Long piece of cream card, 280 gsm, 70 x 13 cm (28 x 5⅛ in)
Pencil
Steel ruler
Craft knife
Template (page 77)
White card
Paper glue stick/all-purpose glue
Shiny gun metal/dark silver card, A4
Scissors
Silver glitter glue pen

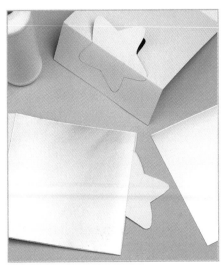

1 Using one of the matt silver squares as a guide, mark 13 cm (5⅛ in) squares along the cream card strip. Score along these lines gently using the steel ruler and the back of a craft knife or scissor blade. Fold along the scored lines to create a concertina effect. You will be left with a small fold at the righthand end.

2 Using the template on page 77, cut out a star shape from the spare card. Rule a line down the centre of the star shape. Align the pencil line with the fold line of the short fold, centered between top and bottom, and draw around the star shape with a pencil.

3 Cut out the righthand half of the star on the short fold and open out, then glue down the short fold on the front. Glue the first of the matt silver squares on top. This will be the front of the card. Next, glue down the remaining two matt silver squares on alternate squares along the concertina.

4 Using the star template, cut out three stars from the shiny gun metal card. Outline the stars with the silver glitter glue pen and add extra decoration. Leave to dry overnight.

5 Glue the first star in position exactly on top of the fold-out star shape on the top leaf. Then position the remaining two stars exactly behind the first on the other two folds, mark lightly with a pencil where they will go, apply glue and stick them down. Finally decorate the front of the card with extra glitter swirls. Send in a stiff-backed or padded envelope.

SEAHORSE STAMPS

Stamps can be purchased through all good craft stores and by mail order. They are easy and fun to use, and you can make the design as basic or as complicated as you choose. This is an ideal card to make with children. Simple repeating patterns on bright backgrounds often work best.

FUNKY ECLECTICA

1 Using the stamp and ink pad, stamp seahorses on a piece of orange card, leaving a gap between them. Put to one side to dry.

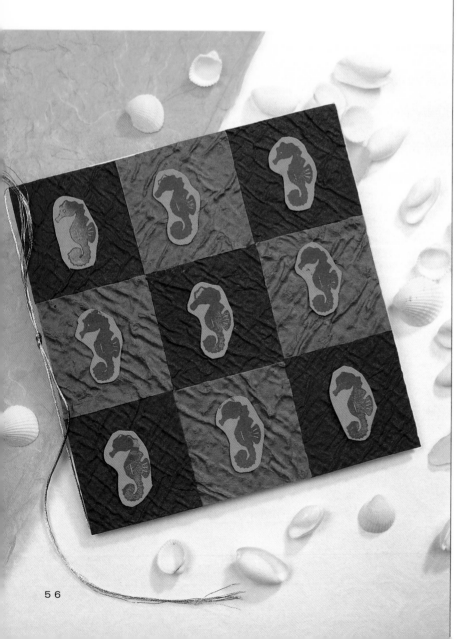

YOU WILL NEED

Seahorse stamp

Turquoise ink pad

Orange card, approx. A5

Purple and turquoise handmade paper or textured card, approx. A5

Steel ruler

Craft knife

Glue stick

Scissors

Greetings card blank, 250 gsm, 13.5 x 13.5 cm (5¼ x 5¼ in)

Turquoise tracing paper, 26.5 x 13 cm (10⅜ x 5⅛ in), folded in half

Silver cord

— TIP —

Try using different kinds of handmade paper, such as petal or rice paper in varying colours, for unusual effects.

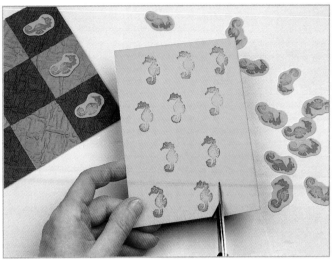

2 Cut nine 4½ cm (1¾ in) squares from the handmade paper – five of one colour and four of the other. Glue them onto the greetings card blank, starting in one corner with the colour of which there are more squares, continuing using alternating colours to achieve a chequerboard effect. Textured card is easier to use than flat card as it covers up any gaps between the squares.

3 The stamped seahorses should now be dry. Cut each one out with the scissors, following the shape of the seahorse and leaving a small orange border. Glue the seahorse shapes onto the card, one in each square.

4 Insert the turquoise tracing paper into the card and tie a coloured cord around the spine to hold it in place. Trim off the ends of the cord at the bottom of the card or tie it in a bow to sit centrally on the spine.

5 This technique can be adapted to suit special occasions or themes, using many combinations of coloured card and stamp designs. The stamp should be small enough to fit the paper squares. Contrasting colours make an eye-catching design.

BIRTHDAY GALLERY

Funky fishes
Holographic fish stickers and squares of funky foam create a seaside flavour. *Funky Eclectica*

A taste of the country
This collage of hand-picked, pressed flowers and a wonderful combination of purple papers will be a joy to receive. *Chiu Mei Au-Yeung*

Space odyssey
Silk painting at its best! This great rocket image is a perfect birthday surprise for all ages. *Rowena Burton*

Fimo fun
Various textured, layered papers, torn edges and a varnished fimo square make a bright background for a fimo detail. *Jana Pana*

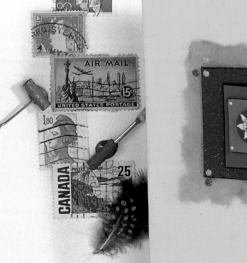

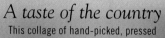

Unusual stamp collection
This male-oriented card with bird feathers, foreign stamps and toy garden tools is ideal for Father's Day as well as Grandad's birthday! *Funky Eclectica*

Birthday parcel

This 3-D dangly parcel was made in the same way as the stork mobile on page 44. *Tracey Anne Turner*

Sweet honesty

Honesty and black-and-white graphic details say "good luck" feng shui-style to those fashion-conscious friends! *Lucinda Beatty*

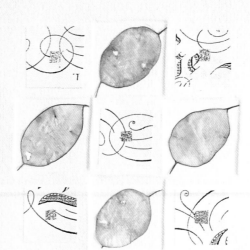

Pandamonium

Press me and I squeak! The cuddly felt panda on this fun card is hand-sewn, and the number is embossed on metal. *Funky Eclectica*

No 4

Balloon stickers and carefully dotted ink from an acrylic pen in subtle combinations of colours make a stunning child age card. *Julie By Design*

Dreamy daisies

Three daisies in a row on coloured tissue paper are ideal for a cute card or a special gift tag. *Funky Eclectica*

QUILLED FLOWER

This intricate quilled flower card makes a lovely "thank you". The traditional craft of paper lace can be used to create stunning, delicate patterns and motifs. This project is perfect for nimble fingers.

ARTIST: ANKE UEBERBERG

1 Score and fold the yellow card. Cut out a square 2 cm (¾ in) in from the edges all round to make a frame. Score and fold the blue card and trim 3 mm (⅛ in) off all open sides. Apply a thin line of glue along the fold line of the blue card and stick down just to the right of the fold line inside the yellow card.

YOU WILL NEED

Yellow card, 250 gsm, 9 x 18 cm (3½ x 7 in)
Steel ruler
Craft knife
Pencil
Eraser
Blue card, 250 gsm, 9 x 18 cm (3½ x 7 in)
PVA glue
Quilling tool or round pencil
White, orange and yellow quilling paper
Toothpick
Tweezers

TIP

If you want to send the card in the post, use a padded envelope or cushion the flower design with a piece of bubble wrap. If you present the card in person, you might want to embellish the envelope with a tiny quilled flower on the flap.

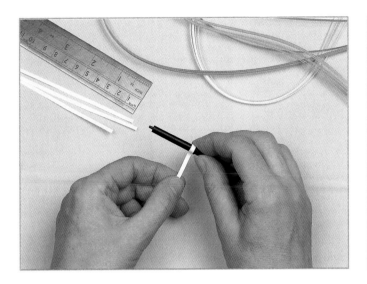

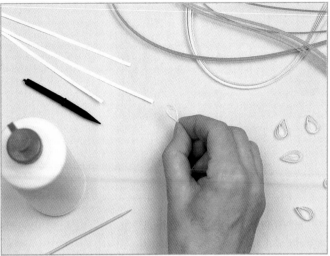

2 To make the petals, tightly wind a 15 cm (6 in) strip of white quilling paper around the middle of the quilling tool. Ease off and leave to unwind to the desired size.

3 Pinch one end of the loose coil to make a teardrop-shaped petal. Fix down the loose end of the strip with a dab of glue – use a toothpick or matchstick for this. Make another five petals in this way.

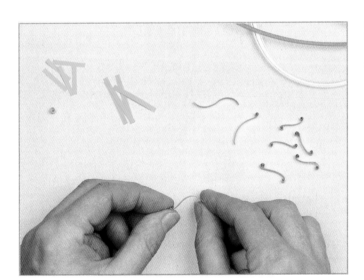

4 Make the orange curls by bending the ends of a 3 cm (1 in) strip of quilling paper in opposite directions using you fingernail, then roll tiny curls between thumb and forefinger. Finally, make the centre of the flower out of a 1 cm (⅜ in) strip of yellow quilling paper, rolled tightly between thumb and forefinger. Stick down the loose end with a dab of glue.

5 Starting with the centre coil, pick up each quilled element with the tweezers, dab spots of glue on the underside using the toothpick and position on the blue background within the yellow frame. Next, position the orange curls at even intervals, radiating out from the centre. Finally, stick down the white petals.

FELT CHRISTMAS TREE

*Christmas time is not complete
without a tree! This three-dimensional
felt cut-out appeals to children and
adults alike, and you can personalize
the tree with the materials you have
to hand. Instead of bells, you could
use gold buttons or gold-coloured
confetti, hole-punched from gold
foil or paper.*

FUNKY ECLECTICA

YOU WILL NEED

White card for template
Template (page 77)
Craft knife
Dark green felt, 18 x 9 cm (7 x 3½ in)
Biro
Scissors
Needle and light coloured thread
Wadding or foam
Pencil
Small piece brown felt, 2 x 1.5 cm (¾ x ½ in)
Gold bells
All-purpose glue
Small piece red shiny card
Green greetings card blank, 280 gsm, A5, folded in half
Gold star

1 Using the template on page 77, draw a Christmas tree on a piece of white card. Cut out using a craft knife.

2 Fold the green felt in half to make two layers, place the template on top and draw around it with the biro. Cut out the double-layer tree shape using the scissors.

3 Sew the two halves of the tree together with a simple running stitch along the edges. Stop sewing at the base of the tree, leaving a large gap.

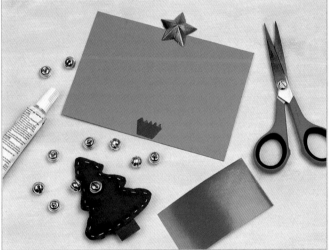

4 Fill the tree with wadding or foam, using a pencil to push the stuffing right into the corners. Next, tuck the small rectangle of brown felt in at the base to make the tree trunk. Finish sewing round the tree shape to enclose the wadding and secure the tree trunk.

5 Glue the bells onto the tree. Cut a pot shape from shiny red card. Glue the star at the top of the card, sticking out over the top as shown, and glue the pot down at the bottom. Position the tree between pot and star and glue down.

SEASONAL GALLERY

Shiny foils
Save all those sweet foil wrappers to create a bright, shiny collage egg, seen through an oval window with a tidy border.
Funky Eclectica

Happy Easter
A hand painted egg and felt borders mounted on material make this a lovely representation of Easter.
Alison Orr

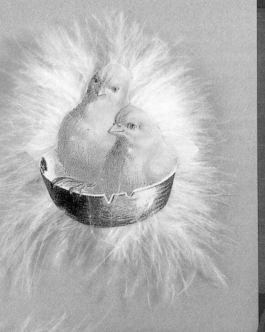

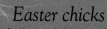

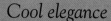

Easter chicks
Fluffy feathers and chirping chicks are perfect for Easter. *Amanda Caine*

Cool elegance
Cream-coloured, clean and fresh, this embossed watercolour paper is beautifully decorated with delicate gold lines and a simple, corrugated beige paper detail. *Lucinda Beatty*

Crowning glory

This 3-D crown made from high quality craft paper and dangled on gold thread with wire details on top and bottom makes this card a special addition to the mantelpiece. *Tracey Anne Turner*

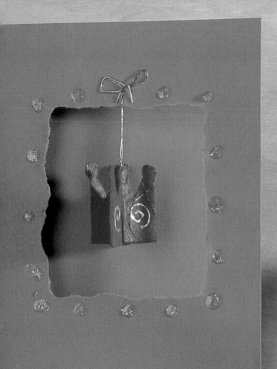

Pudding fun

Alternating orange and green, textured, handmade paper squares and an unusual pudding stamp made by the artist create this simple yet effective design. *Funky Eclectica*

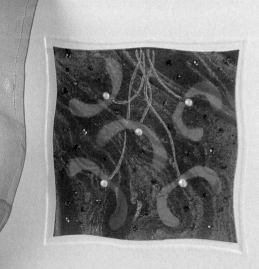

Sweet mistletoe

Lovely mistletoe adds a romantic flavour to this seasonal greeting. A clean-cut use of fabric pen works wonders! *Kathryn Ferrier*

Shimmering Christmas

Use crazy holographics for a crazy Christmas card with great colour combinations for a startling effect. *Funky Eclectica*

CHRISTMAS CRACKER TOKEN HOLDER

Christmas conjures up images of bright and sparkly textures. This cracker card, made with shiny red foil and gold glitter, is both fun and festive. Simply put your greeting inside or use it to present a cheque or gift voucher.

FUNKY ECLECTICA

1 Cut a piece of red shiny card to measure 26 x 25 cm (10¼ x 9¾ in). Using the scissors and steel ruler, gently score the card at 10.5 cm (4⅛ in) and 21 cm (8¼ in) from the lefthand long edge. Take care not to actually cut the card.

YOU WILL NEED

Red or green shiny card, 250 gsm, A4
Pencil
Scissors
Steel ruler
All-purpose glue
Craft knife
White card, 300 gsm, A4
Gold or silver glitter glue pen
Plastic jewels/stars/decorations

2 Fold the card along the scored lines, apply glue to the small overlap and stick down the large overlap on top. Leave to dry, then using the craft knife, cut a V-shape about one fifth of the way from the end of the tube. Do the same at the other end of the tube. Turn the tube over and repeat to make the cracker shape.

3 Cut a zigzag line down the middle of the cracker so it is now in two parts. Cut a strip of white card measuring 3 x 25 cm (1½ x 10 in) and score at 10.3 cm (4¹⁄₁₆ in) and 20.6 cm (8¼ in). Glue as before to make a smaller sleeve.

4 Glue the white sleeve in place inside one half of the cracker, halfway in. This will ensure the two halves of the cracker will stay in place.

5 Decorate the edges with the glitter glue pen for gold piping and glue on the stars and jewels. The glitter pen should disguise any marks made by the scissors or the craft knife. Leave to dry overnight. All that remains is to pop the token or voucher inside.

DRIVING TEST COLLAGE

Little toy cars are ideal for congratulations cards like this one. Of course it could also be a birthday card for the car enthusiast amongst your friends. Get into the habit of picking up small 3-D toys from jumble sales and junk shops – they might come in handy one day.

FUNKY ECLECTICA

1 Cut out a rectangle of red glittery paper 8 x 4 cm (3 x 1½ in). It should be just a little bigger than the toy car. Peel off the backing and stick at the top of the card at an angle.

YOU WILL NEED

Glittery red paper (self adhesive)
Scissors
Ruler
Black greetings card blank, 250 gsm, A5, folded in half
White piece of card or thick writing paper
All-purpose glue
Small piece silver card
Hole punch
Miniature keys
Piece of string
Small toy car
Round, red, yellow and green stickers

2 Cut out six small strips of white card about 3 cm long and 0.5 cm wide (1½ x ¼ in) and glue them in a curve just below the red glittery rectangle. Leave equal gaps between the strips to create a "pedestrian crossing", and leave a bigger gap in the middle.

3 Cut out a rectangle of silver card just bigger than the miniature keys. Using the hole-punch, make two holes at the top. Thread the string through the keys, then through the card, and tie a knot at the top of the string, leaving enough slack for the keys to dangle.

4 Glue the knot of the string onto the middle of the red glittery paper. Glue the silver card in place overlapping the bottom of the red paper at a slight angle.

5 Glue the car in place on top of the knot. Add the traffic lights.

6 Instead of a toy car, you could use a car-shaped eraser and spray it silver or any other appropriate colour.

OCCASIONS GALLERY

Shining angel
A decoupage cherub makes an angelic centre for this clever tag-type card. Glitter on metal creates a spangly effect, finished with a colourful orange bow. *Amanda Caines*

Lily-white
Silver corrugated card is used as a background for a lily fashioned from craft foam. Ideal for a birthday or a sympathy card. *Jan and Di*

Spiritual patterns
Top: A gorgeous ethnic effect is created here with ingenious use of glitter and a sewing machine in a spiritual combination of colour swirls: a little piece of art! *Amanda Hallam*

Paper parcels
This handmade collage of tiny parcels tied with cotton on pretty paper, cleverly juxtaposed with a lovely typographic surround, requires a lot of patience! *Susan Coomer*

Ethnic mix

Etched metal, glitter, sari material and braid combine beautifully to make a special card with an ethnic vibe. *Taro Taranton*

Precious jewel

Shiny silver mirror board, fabric pen swirls and dots, glitter glue and a clear glass bead on shimmery material form a strikingly modern collage. *Lucy Thomas*

Daisy fun

Fun fur in bright orange combined with a paper daisy is a perennial favourite and very simple to make. *Funky Eclectica*

Petals and paper

Hand-painted tissue paper, gold paint and a beautiful pressed flower from the English country side create a delicate, natural effect. *Claire Lucas*

TEMPLATES

The templates shown here are actual size.
All can easily be reduced or enlarged on a
photocopier, but remember to adapt the
size of the card to the size of the item
you plan to use on it. Dotted lines indicate
fold lines.

Embossed heart
(see page 20)

Stencilled cupid
(see page 22)

Wedding cake
(see page 34)

Bouquet of tulips
(see page 28)

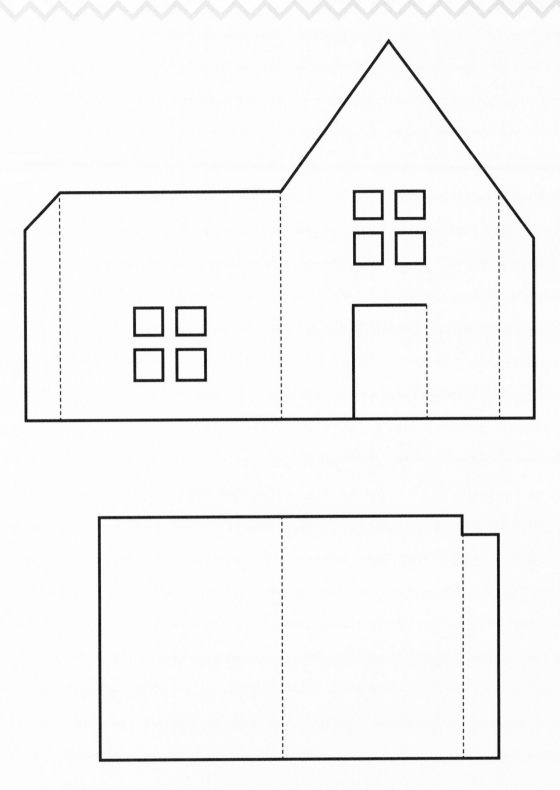

New home pop-up
(see page 38)

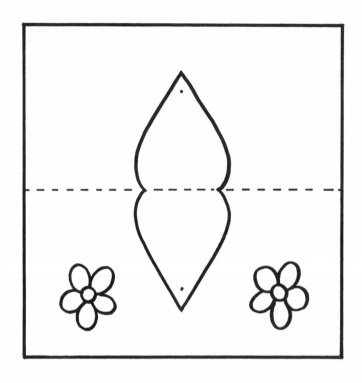

Stork mobile

Stork's bundle, flowers, cloud cut-out,
stork and wing (see page 44)

Finger puppet clown
(see page 50)

Embossed metal heart
(see page 52)

Silk painted house
(see page 36)

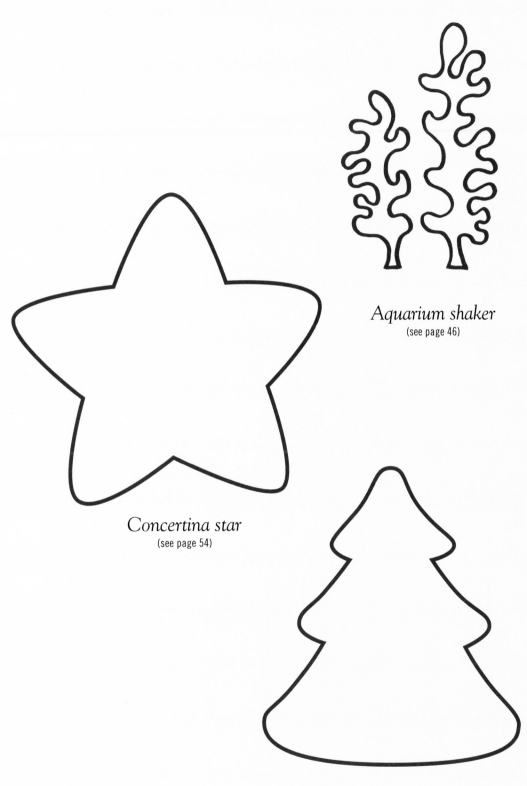

Aquarium shaker
(see page 46)

Concertina star
(see page 54)

Felt Christmas tree
(see page 62)

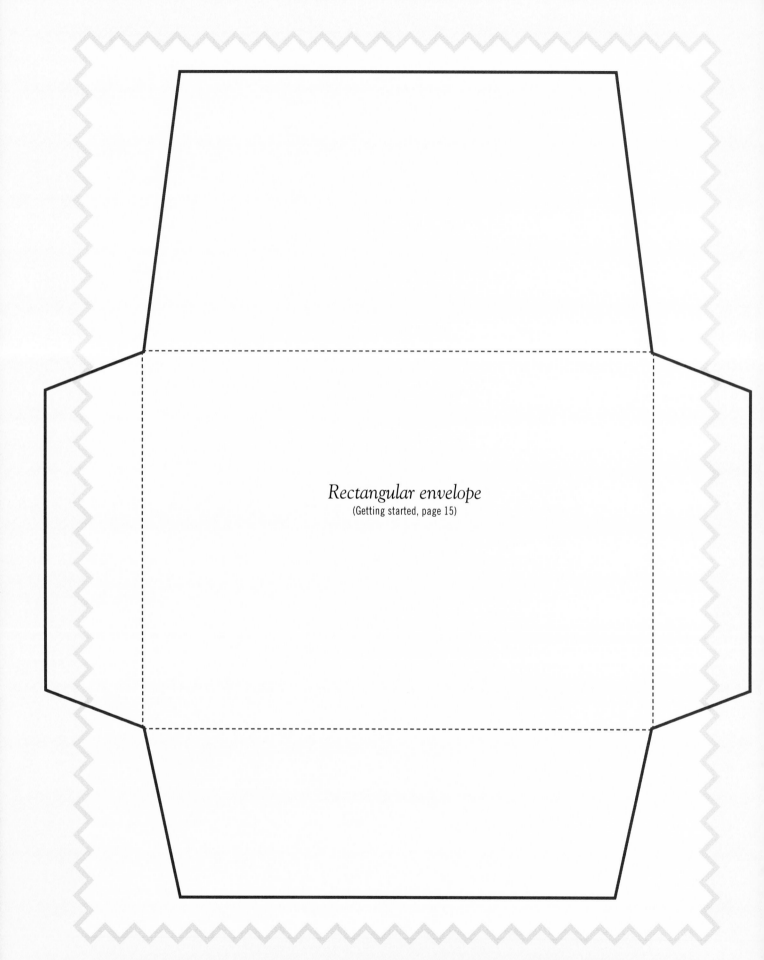

Rectangular envelope
(Getting started, page 15)

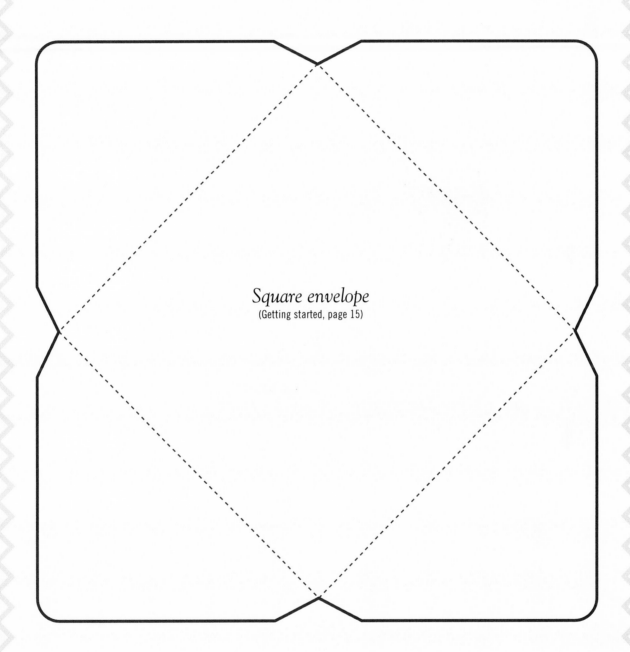

Square envelope
(Getting started, page 15)

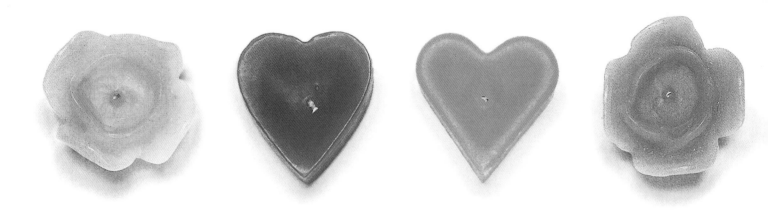

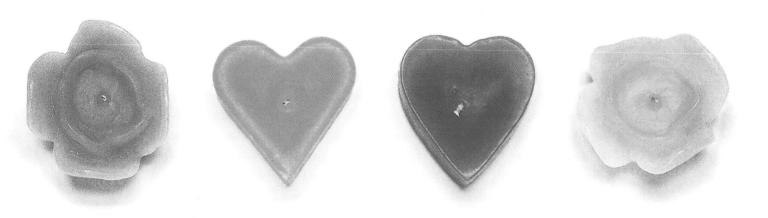

CANDLE MAKING

Sue Spear

INTRODUCTION

I have been making candles since 1968 when a friend came to dinner and brought me a hand-made candle rather than a bottle of wine as a gift. In those days candles that were not of the straight-forward, single colour, tall and slim variety were not to be seen. Even thicker candles were only used in churches. I was so intrigued with the possibilities of wax that I started to research the subject and to begin making my own candles.

I soon discovered that wax is a marvellous substance to work with. You can dye it wonderful colours, pour it into unusually shaped moulds, perfume it and model with it. The art of making a candle that will burn the way you want it to and also have the colours and effects that you design is very absorbing.

Dining or spending an evening in the warm glow of candlelight is now very much a part of our everyday lives, and the use of aromatherapy oils and other perfumes in wax adds to the charm of candles.

Candles also make wonderful presents. Making your own is far more satisfying than buying something ready-made from a shop, and it is easy to personalize them – either simply by using colours and shapes you know your friends will love, or by decorating them with names, numbers or special messages. In the same way, you can change a basic candle to make something special for occasions such as Christmas, Thanksgiving, Halloween or Valentine's Day.

Candle making is an extremely satisfying hobby. The basic techniques are very simple, and you will probably be able to produce professional-looking candles at your first attempt. It is also relatively inexpensive, and you can recycle both your more unsuccessful efforts and any candle ends. Many people progress from candle making as a hobby to selling candles professionally. Never be afraid to experiment – some of the more thriving candle companies in the world today have based their success on a very simple but innovative candle making idea.

Sue Spear

A BRIEF HISTORY

Before the eighteenth century and the Industrial Revolution, most candles for domestic use were made in the home. They were usually made from tallow, a substance obtained from beef fat. Everyday candles were nothing like the clean burning, smell-free, controlled fires we so enjoy today – they smoked, dripped and smelt revolting. The only quality candles were made from beeswax for the sole use of the churches and the royal family. But even these quality candles would smoke and drip.

With the onset of the Industrial Revolution, longer working hours meant that more sources of light were required and the production of commercial candles began. Fairly sophisticated dipping machines were devised where many wicks were dipped at once and lifted out of the vats of hot wax by a counterweight.

In the early part of the nineteenth century, Michael Chevreul, a French chemist, discovered that tallow contained an important chemical ingredient – stearic acid. Through experiments, he learnt how to separate the stearic acid from the other fatty acids and glycerine also present in the tallow. The result was stearin. The next advance was the extraction of paraffin wax from coal or peat. These two basic ingredients – stearin and paraffin wax – transformed the burning quality of candles. They remain the materials that are still used today, with paraffin wax now obtained as a by-product of refining petrol, and stearin extracted from palm nuts.

The other major improvement in candle making that occurred at the same time was the introduction of plaited cotton wicks. Many different yet inferior materials had been used in the past, including reeds, cloth, thread and string. The idea of plaiting wicks was visionary and a candle made with braided wick burned far more brightly. In fact, Queen Victoria used the new plaited wicks in the candles made for her wedding.

However, the ash produced by the braided cotton was still a problem, causing the candle to smoke excessively. This was resolved in the late eighteenth century when it was discovered that if wicks were first soaked in boric acid, they became self-consuming. If you look closely at a burning candle today you will notice that the wick bends over and the end of the wick is continuously consumed by the flame. This means that no carbon is left on the end of the wick, and the candle burns cleanly.

The mass production of candles began with dipping small batches of candles on frames. This technique is still used, particularly in Scandinavia, and is a development of the technique described in the project on page 108. Other technical advances include compresing powdered wax into shape under great pressure and also extruding wax into long cylindrical poles which are then cut to size. Needless to say, these methods are not suitable for use in the home!

It is rather ironic that it was not until the advent of the use of electricity for lighting that the basic art of candle making was finally perfected. Since then manufacturing techniques have continued to developed – to the joy of those of us who love sitting in the warm glow of a candle flame.

GETTING STARTED

This book clearly describes all the basic techniques you will need for candle making, and also lets you in on the tricks of the trade. Each project in the section that follows not only has a creative idea for you to learn, but also teaches you a basic candle making or decoration technique. If you complete all the projects, you will become an extremely proficient candle maker. Simply start by reading through this chapter thoroughly as it describes all the materials and equipment you will need and explains the basic techniques.

EQUIPMENT

You will need the following basic equipment. You may already have some of it in your kitchen cupboards.

A double saucepan or metal bowl placed over a saucepan of water. If you heat wax directly over the gas or electric ring on your stove, there is a chance it may overheat. This can happen surprising quickly and the wax will then catch fire

---

A wax thermometer (you can also use a sugar thermometer)

A lipped pouring jug

A metal ladle

Kitchen scales – if you are using powdered wax and stearin you can judge the proportion by volume. However, if you are using slab wax you will need to calculate the proportion of wax to stearin by weight

---

A wicking needle – a huge darning needle that enables you to thread fairly thick wick through small holes in the end of moulds

---

Wick supports – cocktail or kebab sticks make excellent wick supports

---

Mould seal – used to seal the base of moulds so the wax does not seep through. You can also use Plasticine

---

Moulds or containers – see pages 89-91 for more details

The following equipment is not required for all the projects that follow, but will probably come in useful.

Baking trays – several of the projects use baking trays. Using a deep baking tray to place your prepared mould on ensures that if it leaks the wax will not go everywhere

---

Oven gloves – although wax at 82°C (180°F) is not hot enough to hurt you, it can be more comfortable to use gloves when pouring wax

---

Craft knife or scalpel – used in several of the projects which follow

---

Right: A selection of waxes. Clockwise from top left: slab wax, micro soft and micro hard, powder wax, stearin.

MATERIALS

PARAFFIN WAX

Most candles are made from paraffin wax with an additional 10 per cent stearin. Paraffin wax is a by-product of petrol – not as horrid as it sounds when you consider that petrol comes from very old trees!

The wax you buy from suppliers of candle making equipment will already be blended for candle making, and you can buy the stearin either already mixed with the wax or separate.

This type of wax usually melts at about 71°C (160°F). It comes in a variety of forms, either in large 5 kg (11 lb) slabs, or in pellets or powder. The pellets or powder are simpler to use as they are easier to weigh accurately. Buying slabs of wax is generally cheaper, but they have to be broken up first. The easiest way to break a slab of wax is to put it into a large plastic rubbish bag and drop it onto a hard floor.

It is possible to make candles just from paraffin wax. Hand-dipped candles, moulded candles or candles made in rubber moulds do not require

stearin. However, do not use paraffin wax on its own with any type of rigid mould (i.e. moulds made of plastic, metal or glass) as they will be very difficult to get out of the mould. Candles made with paraffin wax without stearin burn slightly quicker, but they also have a translucent appearance and glow very brightly.

ADDITIVES FOR PARAFFIN WAX

STEARIN
Now made from palm nuts, stearin or stearic acid was once obtained from whales, but thankfully animals are no longer used in its production. It has four basic uses and qualities:
• It makes candles easier to get out of the mould – candles contract more when they cool when stearin has been added to the wax.
• Most dyes dissolve more thoroughly in stearin.
• It makes the candle burn longer.
• It makes the candle more opaque, and white candles much whiter.

MICRO SOFT
This is a very soft wax that makes the wax stay soft long enough to mould it. You usually add 10-20 per cent to a quantity of paraffin wax. It is used when you need to keep the wax pliable whilst you mould it (see the floating flower project on page 142).

MICRO HARD
Micro hard wax has a higher melting point than paraffin wax. It can be used in chip candles, so ensure that the coloured chips you put into the mould do not melt when the wax is poured over them. It can also be used when embedding wax shapes into the sides of a mould (see the landscape candle in the layered candle project on page 104).

CRYSTAL WAX
This is an over-dipping wax which crystallizes as it cools. See the text on achieving different results on page 94 for more details.

OTHER CANDLE MAKING WAXES

BEESWAX
A wonderful wax which is expensive – but well worth the money. It is available either in blocks or sheets. Blocks are used for melting down. The natural colour of block beeswax is a rich honey brown, but it is also available in bleached form which is better for dyeing ①.

The beeswax sheets can be rolled up to form candles. Beeswax, although long burning, has a very soft consistency and this makes it ideal for rolling. Beeswax sheets are available in a wonderful range of colours.

BAYBERRY WAX
Made from bayberries as its name suggests, this wax is almost impossible to obtain in Europe, but it is available in America where it is traditionally used for Christmas candles.

DIP AND CARVE WAX
This is a specially prepared blend of wax for making dip and carve candles (see page 148). It is much more malleable than paraffin wax and will not crack or splinter when carved.

APPLIQUE WAXES
This soft wax is formed into flat sheets which can be pressed onto a candle's surface, adhering firmly without glue. It is also available in different colours, shapes and numbers ②.

WICKS

Wicks are the most important part of any candle because it is the size of the wick which determines how the candle will burn. Wicks are made from plaited cotton which has been treated with boric acid.

It took hundreds of years to perfect wick making and ironically the final improvements came at about the same

with a pool of wax reaching just to the outside of the candle. Similarly, a candle with a diameter of 2.5 cm (1 in) will need a 2.5 cm (1 in) wick ①.

Professional candle makers classify a wick by the number of strands it contains, for instance a 3/24 wick contains three strands, each made up of 24 smaller strands. It is useful to know this so that you can also count the number of strands if you should lose the wick labels.

• For **dinner candles**, use a wick that approximates as closely as possible the diameter of the candle you are making – usually 1.25 cm (½ in) or 2.5 cm (1 in).

• For **church and block candles**, the wick should be suitable for the diameter of the candle.

• For **cone or pyramid shaped candles**, it is best to opt for a wick size which is suitable for a diameter of about half the width of the candle base. These shaped candles cannot burn perfectly all the way down, but using a wick of this size ensures the candle will burn correctly at first and then leave a shell as it reaches the bottom.

• For **floating candles**, use the correct wick for the diameter of the candle, or use a wick attached to a wick sustainer (see right). Make sure the wick is primed so that it will not draw up water from the base while floating.

• For **refillable candles**, choose a wick much smaller than the diameter of the candle so that it burns down in the middle. You can then refill the candle with a nightlight or powdered wax. A 2.5 cm (1 in) wick is usually adequate for a refillable candle.

• For **container candles**, use a smaller wick than you would use for a free-standing candle. You can buy wax-covered wicks already attached to small metal sustainers which are easy to use.

time as the introduction of electricity. Modern wicks are designed so that they curl over slightly at their tip at the candle burns. This means that the carbon burns off and cannot build up. Before this improvement, carbon would build up, creating smoke, or would fall off, which could be dangerous and a fire risk. Never use string or any other kind of twine for your candles – it really is essential only to use candle wick.

CHOOSING THE RIGHT SIZE OF CANDLE WICK

Candle wick is made from three braided strands. Each strand contains several smaller strands of cotton. Wick sold to amateur candle makers is generally classified by the diameter of the wax the flame will melt as it burns. Therefore, a 5 cm (2 in) candle requires a 5 cm (2 in) diameter wick which will burn

WICK SUSTAINERS

These are small, round metal disks about 1 cm (½ in) in diameter, which hold the wick. You can either buy these on their own or already attached to primed wick for container candles.

PRIMED WICK

This is wick that has been put into molten wax, taken out immediately and then straightened. This stiffens it and is useful for some candle-making methods. It is also good to prime the wick that will protrude from the finished candle as it make the candle easier to light. Wicks for floating candles should always be primed so they do not draw up water ②.

TROUBLESHOOTING

If the wick is just slightly too small, the candle will drip. When making wider candles, if the wick is much too small it will burn down the middle of the candle. If this happens, save the candle and refill it.

    If the wick is too large, the candle will burn with a large flame and will smoke. Even one faulty candle can produce a large amount of smoke which can ruin a room's decoration. This can be avoided by cutting off surplus wick as it burns.

    Having chosen the correct wick, it is very important to position the wick securely in the centre of the candle. If the wick leans to one side, the candle will drip and burn very quickly and could be dangerous. If making candles in glass containers, the glass will crack if the flame touches the side.

CANDLE MOULDS

It is now possible to buy a large variety of ready-made candle moulds ③. These come in a variety of forms:

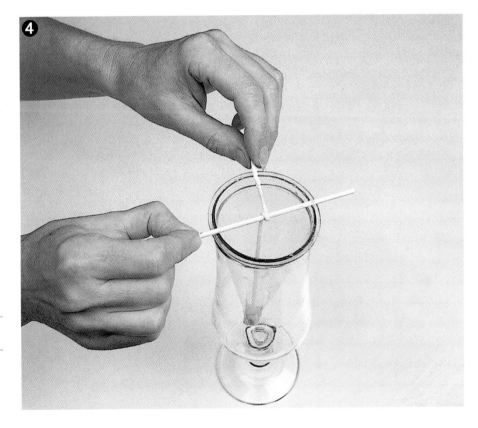

PLASTIC MOULDS

These are available in both clear plastic (which is useful when you need to see what you are doing) and opaque plastic. They are easy to use and will last for a great many candles if handled with care. They produce professional results, but temperature control is essential as

the moulds may melt if pouring in wax that has been heated above 82°C (180°F) ④. A plastic mould has been used in the shell project on page 122.

METAL MOULDS

Metal moulds are similar to plastic, but they last forever. They have the added

advantage in that they will not buckle if extremely hot wax is poured in.

LATEX MOULDS

Latex moulds are used when you want to make a candle in a particular shape. To use them, thread the wick in through the tip of the mould using a wicking

❺

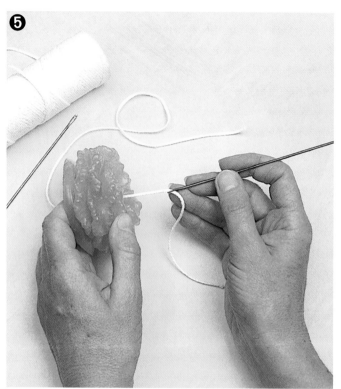

❻

needle ❺. Then coat the inside of the mould with mould release, pour in the wax and support the mould in a suitable container while the wax cools ❻.

You can make you own latex moulds of a chosen object using liquid latex and a non-porous master. Here we have used an orange ❼.

First wash the orange or chosen object in hot soapy water to remove any grease. Place the orange on a surface such as an old plate. Following the manufacturer's instructions, mix the latex with a little thickener. Using a brush, paint the latex over the object. You will need to apply several layers in order to build the latex up to a thickness of 3 mm (⅛ in). Allow the latex to dry until it is just sticky between coats. The mould should be left to dry overnight before peeling off the master.

All kinds of household objects make very satisfactory candle moulds. Try using milk or yoghurt cartons for block candles, bun tins or chocolate moulds for small floating candles, or large cake tins for multi-wicked candles. Take a look around your kitchen and you will be surprised at how many kitchen objects can be adapted. If using old plastic containers take care not to pour in wax over 82°C (180°F) ❽.

CARDBOARD MOULDS

A cardboard mould is used for the project on page 110. Cardboard is ideal for making candles when the wax is poured in at a very cold temperature, producing a white, scaly effect. If you try to make candles like this in an ordinary mould, you may not be able to remove them from the mould as they may not have contracted enough.

OPEN ENDED MOULDS

It is possible to make candles in a mould which does not have a base. The floating candles on page 144 made with cake cutters show one method. Alternatively, you can surround the base of the mould with mould seal and then pour in the wax.

To position the wick when using open ended moulds, either stick it to

❼

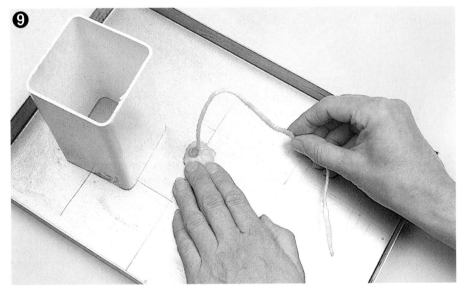

expensive and are only sold in large quantities. Dyes come in two forms.

DYE DISCS

These are dyes that have already been dissolved in some stearin. Even so, you will ensure that you get the most out of your dye disc by dissolving some of it yourself in stearin first. These dyes are very concentrated – one dye disc will usually dye about 2 kg (4½ lb) of wax. It is easy to cut pieces off with a sharp knife, so you do not have to use the whole disc at once.

POWDERED DYES

Powdered dyes are extremely strong. A portion the size of a match-head will colour about 1 kg (2¼ lb) of wax. All powdered dyes must be dissolved in heated stearin first or you will be left with dark spots in the candle and waste the dye. Powdered dyes can also be messy and have to be used with great care, as the powder can get everywhere if spilt. The dye will stain even if it is spilt when dry and some colours are very difficult to remove.

CALCULATING HOW MUCH DYE TO USE

Obviously this is very much to do with your personal taste. However, remember it is always possible to make a colour darker or brighter by gradually adding more dye. Making a candle lighter is much more problematic as you have to add more wax – sometimes

your worksurface with mould seal, or make a hole in a piece of wood or stiff card, thread the wick through and seal it underneath with mould seal in the usual way ⑨.

DYES

Always use dyes which are prepared especially for candle making ①. They come in a wonderful variety of colours which can be mixed. Dyes will fade if they are exposed to sunlight – especially the pink and red shades – so be sure to keep your finished candles away from direct sunlight. You can buy pigments which do not fade, but they are more

very much more than you want. So always add to a pale colour until you get used to the potency of the dye you are using.

PREPARING DYED WAX FOR OVER-DIPPING

When a candle is dipped in a different colour once it has been made, the proportion of dye to wax will have to be much larger. Because you are relying on a very thin layer of wax to change the colour, the dyed wax has to be very strong. Experiment by gradually adding more dye until you have the over-dip colour you need.

MIXING CANDLE DYE COLOURS

Candle dyes mix very easily but not always predictably. Experiment with small quantities first, and don't be afraid to use strange combinations. The usual rules of colour combinations do not always apply. For example, orange and pink mixed together make a bright Christmassy red.

PERFUMES

One of the wonderful qualities of wax is how well it absorbs perfume. A burning candle functions just like an atomiser. The molten pool of warm wax at the top of the candle gently heats the perfume which rises and permeates the atmosphere. The larger the pool of molten wax, the more effective the scent will be. This is why container candles which create a comparatively large pool of molten wax are ideal for perfume candles, and dinner candles, which have a very small diameter, the least effective.

As with other candle ingredients, it is essential that you use only scents which have been especially designed for candles. It can be dangerous to use other perfumes as the perfume must be oil-based and mixed with a 'carrier' only suitable for candle use. Other perfumes may, at worst, flare up or leave the wick clogged with carbon.

HOW MUCH TO USE

This depends on how strong you want the scent to be, and of course some perfumes are more pervasive than others. However, most reasonably strongly scented candles contain about 6 per cent of perfume to wax. The easiest way to judge this is by weight. You can put as much as 10 per cent in but this makes a very strongly perfumed candle which may be overpowering.

HOW PERFUMES AFFECT COLOUR

Only make up small batches of perfumed wax to begin with as they can affect the candles' colour. Some perfumes already have a slight colour of their own and their use can, for instance, change a white candle to ivory.

DIFFERENT SCENTS AND THEIR USES

You can use different scents to for different functions. All aromatherapy scents are available in candle perfumes, as is citronella (for repelling insects). Other special uses include smoke-repelling scents (usually a sweet smelling perfume like rose – all candles help to absorb cigarette smoke).

MAKING A BASIC CANDLE

PREPARE THE MOULD

Take a length of wick twice the length of the mould. Prime the tip by dipping it into hot wax. Using a wicking needle, thread the wick through the hole at the top of the mould and seal it with mould seal. Press it down well. (This is not necessary if you are using rubber moulds as they seal themselves). Thread a cocktail stick through the wick at the base so that it is centred in the middle of the mould.

SUPPORT THE MOULD

Use a roll of cardboard, cup, jug or anything else you can find to do the job.

WEIGH THE WAX AND STEARIN

With practice you will be able to judge how much wax you will need for your finished candle. A good rough guide is to weigh a ready-made candle of approximately the same size as the mould you are going to use. When you have decided the total weight needed,

subtract 10 per cent. Weigh out this amount (i.e. 10 per cent) of stearin. Weigh out 90 per cent of the total weight in wax.

HEAT THE STEARIN IN A DOUBLE SAUCEPAN

You could also use a bowl placed over a saucepan of hot water. The stearin has completely melted when it has turned into a clear liquid.

ADD THE DYE TO THE MELTED STEARIN

Judging the right amount of dye to use is also easier with experience. However, don't worry if the colour is not strong enough. You can always heat up a little more stearin and add more dye later. It will not matter if the candle contains more than 10 per cent stearin.

ADD THE WAX

Add the wax to the stearin and dye mixture and heat in the double saucepan until it is all melted.

ADD THE PERFUME

Add perfume to the wax (if you are making a scented candle), and then gently stir.

TEST THE TEMPERATURE OF THE WAX

Heat the wax to 82°C (180°F). Make sure that you stir the wax gently before taking its final temperature. Leave the thermometer in the wax until it has stopped rising. It is very important that you do not overheat the wax as there is a possibility that it could catch fire.

FILLING A PREPARED MOULD

Warm the dipping jug with hot water – if it is too cold it will alter the temperature of the wax. Then ladle the wax into the jug and pour gently into the mould creating as little turbulence as possible. Leave some wax in the saucepan for 'topping up'.

TOPPING UP

While the wax cools, it contracts and the wax sinks. Wait until a thick skin has formed on the top of the wax and then pierce it with a pencil or wicking needle. Make sure you prod the surface properly or you may be left with holes in the finished candle! Then pour in some more wax also heated to 82°C (180°F), being very careful that the wax is not too hot (it may crack the candle), too cold (it will not adhere to candle) or that you do not fill it over the original level of the candle (making it difficult to get out of the mould). You may have to top up more than once before the final surface is flat.

It is always surprising how much a candle contracts and less experienced makers often underestimate how much extra wax they will need for this stage. As you usually make candles upside down (you are 'topping up' what will become the bottom of the candle), you can top up with a different coloured wax if necessary.

REMOVE THE CANDLE FROM THE MOULD

The candle must be left until it is completely cold before removing it from the mould. This can vary from a few hours to overnight, depending on the size of the candle and the wax used. When properly set, the candle should come out easily from the mould when you pull it.

OTHER CANDLE MAKING TECHNIQUES

As well as moulding candles, there are two other techniques that can be used. The first, and most traditional, is hand-dipping. This is fully explained in the project on page 108.

The second, and more unusual, is rolling. This is illustrated in the project on page 118, using beeswax sheets. However, the same basic method can

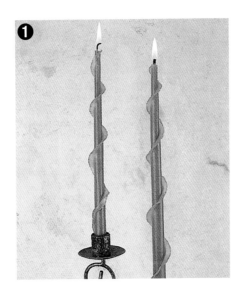

be used with paraffin wax mixed with 20 per cent micro soft which has been poured into a tray and left to just set. The wax is then lifted out of the tray and rolled. The rolled wax candle shown here has been made with a triangular piece of wax rolled around a wick ①. The pretty foliating edges have been made simply by squeezing the edges and turning them outwards.

MAKING CANDLES IN CONTAINERS

You do not have to make candles in moulds. It is really easy to make candles in containers and many of the most un-likely objects can make really attractive candles. The method is demonstrated in the project on page 114.

The photograph here shows some ideas, but almost any container made of ceramic, metal or glass can be used ②. Use terracotta pots of varying sizes for garden candles. Shells, coconut shells, household tins, glasses, vases and even egg shells can all be used. Although it can only be used once, hollowed out fruit is also a possibility.

ACHIEVING DIFFERENT EFFECTS AFTER THE CANDLE HAS SET

OVER-DIPPING IN CLEAR WAX

If you have made a candle and you do not like its final finish, for instance if you have used an open ended mould and the top looks a bit rugged, you can over-dip the candle for a different effect. Dip the candle in clear wax heated to about 88°C (190°F) and then into water. This will smooth out any deficiencies and make the candle shiny.

OVER-DIPPING IN DIFFERENT COLOURED WAX

Using very strongly dyed wax, a candle can be dipped into a can of wax and its colour changed completely. The same principle can be used to make pretty designs on candles. Different colours can be poured over the candle to completely change its appearance. The candle illustrated has had blue wax poured over it, followed by a complete over-dip in green. The over-dipping wax should be kept at a temperature of about 77°C (170°F) ①.

OVER-DIPPING OR SPLASHING WITH CRYSTALLINE WAX

Crystalline wax forms little crystals as it cools. It looks extremely effective if carefully splashed or poured over a coloured candle ②.

❶

❷

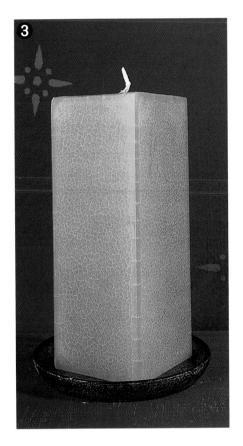

OVER-DIPPING IN ICE COLD WATER

If you dip the candle in uncoloured wax heated to 88°C (190°F) and then plunge it immediately into a bucket of ice cold water, a square crystal formation will decorate the outside of the candle ③.

HAMMERING

Using a round headed hammer you can build up a pattern of white edged craters around the candle ⑤.

SANDPAPERING

Gently rub the candle, either using a very fine sandpaper, which gives an almost silken finish, or a coarser sandpaper, which gives the candle a more rustic appearance ④.

EMBEDDING OBJECTS

There are two basic methods for embedding objects into the sides of candles. The first, and simplest, is to use wax glue. This is shown in the project on page 112. The second method is to soften the outside of the candle by immersing it in a bath of warm wax until it is soft, then take it out and press the objects into the soft exterior ⑥.

You can also dip the finished candle into clear wax, just to fix the items, such as appliquéd numbers or letters, a little more firmly. If this final dip covers up the objects too much, carefully scrape away the excess from the surface of the decorations.

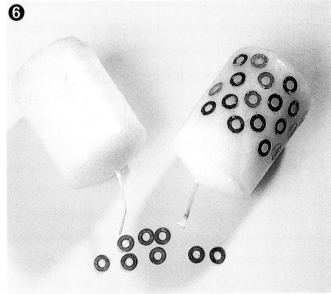

CANDLE VARNISH
This is a special varnish that will give the candle a hard surface and a brilliant shine. It should be painted onto the candle using a soft brush. Varnish has been used in the project on page 148.

GOLD AND SILVER WAX
This rub-on coloured wax is easy to use and produces very satisfying results.

POSTER PAINTS
These paints can be used to decorate candles. Dilute them slightly with washing-up liquid to make them easier to apply. You can also experiment with other types of paint – the general rule is that water-based paint will adhere to wax successfully.

FELT-TIPPED PENS
It is well worth experimenting with felt-tipped and metallic pens. Some brands can be used on candles very successfully, whilst others do not produce good results.

HEART-PATTERNED CANDLE
This candle has been decorated by dipping a candle twice into a can of wax that has been dyed red. While the wax is still warm, use a cake cutter to remove the heart shape from the red wax, leaving a white heart exposed ⑦.

HOW TO BURN CANDLES SAFELY AND CLEANLY

POSITIONING CANDLES
Ensure candles are placed safely in your room. They should be put well away from other objects. Be especially careful not to put them on shelving where they might light the shelf above. Do not place candles where dripping wax could cause damage. Candle wax is very difficult to remove from the inside of televisions!

CHOOSING CANDLE HOLDERS
It is important that any candle holder you use should sit steadily and that it is not made from inflammable materials.

NEVER LEAVE A CANDLE UNATTENDED
It is extremely dangerous to leave burning candles unattended. Always make sure that all candles are extinguished if you leave the room and take extra care if there are young children present.

KEEP THE WICK TRIMMED
Sometimes the wick on a candle becomes too long and the candle begins to smoke. If the flame is not rounded but flares out at the top, the wick needs trimming. You can trim the wick with a pair of scissors whilst it is still burning.

KEEP THE WICK CENTRED
In larger diameter candles the wick does not always go straight down the middle. Keep an eye on it and if it appears to be on one side, push it into the centre again using a small stick or match stick.

POSITION OUT OF A DRAUGHT
No candle will burn well when it is placed in a draught. Always place your candles in sheltered positions.

GET THE MOST OUT OF THE CANDLE FLAME
If you want the most light from your candles, place them in front of mirrors so the light is reflected ①.

• If you do have a fire, do not use water to put it out. Wax fires should be treated the same way as an oil fire. You should switch off the heat source and then smother the flames with a saucepan lid, damp cloth or with a special fire blanket.

WORKING CLEANLY

Always wear an apron when candle making. If you do get any wax on your clothes, place some tissue or newspaper over the wax and run a hot iron over it. Keep doing this until no more wax appears on the paper.

Try and work in such a way that the potential problem of wax spillage is minimised. It is a good idea to cover your kitchen surface with newspaper before you start. Also, for added security, place your prepared candle moulds in a deep baking tray to catch the wax in case the mould leaks. Holding a tray under the jug as you pour minimises the drips.

If you do spill wax, it will usually come off a kitchen surface quite easily when it has cooled. A paint scraper or spatula is the easiest implement for this.

Be very careful never to pour wax down the kitchen sink as it will harden and block the drain. If this happens, try pouring boiling water down the sink. If that fails, call a plumber. If you are making candles near the sink, it is safer simply to put the plug in.

Keep your moulds and equipment clean. In most cases the wax will come out of its container easily when it contracts. If you are left with a wax residue, wash the container in very hot soapy water, making sure that you keep the hot tap running and that only a little wax goes down the plug hole.

White spirit is an excellent cleaner and will dissolve small drops of wax. One word of caution – some of the dyes, particularly pink and purple, are very powerful and if they come into contact with plastic it is almost impossible to get them out.

Foil containers and bowls are excellent for keeping pieces of leftover wax. You can also use them for topping up and for chip candles.

CANDLE HINTS AND TIPS

REFILLING A REFILLABLE CANDLE

When using a candle that is designed to burn down the middle and then be refilled with a nightlight or wax when a well has formed, it is important that you burn it correctly to create the well. Light the candle and burn until the wax has melted to a diameter of about 4.5 cm (1¾ in). When the pool of wax is about 3 mm (⅛ in) deep, extinguish the candle and pour out the molten wax. Re-light the candle and trim the wick. Repeat these steps until the candle has burnt down far enough to refill with a nightlight or wax ①.

PLACING A CANDLE ON A METAL SPIKED HOLDER

If you push a candle down directly onto a spiked holder it may split. To avoid this, heat the spike with a match or cigarette lighter flame before you push the candle onto it.

PUTTING CANDLES IN THE FRIDGE

Leave your candles in the fridge for several hours before you burn them. This will harden the wax and they will burn longer. This is particularly useful if you live in a very warm climate.

HOW TO PUT CANDLES OUT

When extinguishing a container candle, a refillable candle or any candle where a large well of wax has melted in the middle, never simply blow the candle out. The wick may well sink into the molten well and be impossible to retrieve when you want to re-light the candle. Instead, using a match stick or pencil, push the wick down into the wax, and then lift it up again so it is ready for re-lighting.

WORKING SAFELY

Candle making is a safe and enjoyable hobby, but wax will ignite when it is overheated so it is essential that you follow these guidelines.

If wax is heated above 100°C (212°F) it will ignite, so:
• Never leave heating wax unattended.
• Always heat the wax over indirect heat. Use either a double saucepan with the bottom half filled with water and wax in the top half or a bowl over a saucepan of hot water.
• Make sure the water does not boil dry.

PROJECTS AND GALLERIES
FOR MAKING CANDLES

MARBLED CANDLE

This easy project shows how a simple, plain candle can be dipped several times in coloured wax and transformed into a jewel-like object using a creative marbling technique.

1 Dip the prepared candle once into the heated pink wax. Set aside and allow the wax to cool – this should only take 2-3 minutes. Repeat the dipping process while the wax is hot if you are making more than one candle.

YOU WILL NEED

7.5 cm (3 in) round ball candle

Container of pink wax, heated to 85°C (185°F) ready for dipping

Container of chalky white wax, heated to 85°C (185°F) ready for dipping

Container of blue wax, heated to 85°C (185°F) ready for dipping

Container of clear wax, heated to 85°C (185°F) ready for dipping

Sharp knife

Potato peeler

Bowl of cold water

--- TIP ---

REFILLING THE CANDLE
Burn the candle for an hour or until the wax has burnt to a diameter of 3 cm (1¼ in). Blow out the candle and pour in more molten wax. Repeat until you have a hole in the candle about 2 cm (¾ in) deep. Either refill this with a nightlight or some powdered wax and a wick.

2 Now dip the candle three times in white wax, three times in blue wax, then a further three dips in white wax and one last dip in pink wax. Allow the candle to cool slightly between each dipping.

3 Using a sharp knife, cut a section off the bottom of the candle so that it will stand safely. You may need to scrape some wax off to ensure the base is flat and even.

4 Using both your thumbs, press firmly down all around the circumference of the candle to create little craters or indentations.

5 Using a sharp potato peeler, gently begin to shave pieces off the surface of the candle. Work horizontally at first, almost as if you are peeling an orange, then work evenly up and down the surface of the candle.

6 Continue carving the candle's surface until you have created a pleasing effect by exposing enough of the underlying colours. You may have to shave off quite a lot of wax to achieve this.

7 Check that the temperature of the clear wax is at 85°C (185°F). Suspend the candle in the hot wax. The rough edges will melt off, and slightly more layers will become exposed. Remove the candle from the wax as soon as you have achieved the desired effect. Finally, dip the candle in cold water to give it a good shine.

DRIPPED WAX CANDLE

Any candle made with a wick that is too small will drip. This 'defect' can be used to your advantage with this project, where the candle is deliberately designed to drip wax in a variety of colours. The wax cascades down the sides of the candle, producing this pretty effect.

1 Holding the candle by the wick, dip it into the red wax and then into water. Repeat this three times.

YOU WILL NEED

A ready-made 25 cm (10 in) candle

A dipping can filled with red paraffin wax, heated to 79°C (175°F)

A dipping can filled with blue paraffin wax, heated to 79°C (175°F)

A dipping can filled with green paraffin wax, heated to 79°C (175°F)

A dipping can filled with yellow paraffin wax, heated to 79°C (175°F)

A dipping can filled with ivory paraffin wax, heated to 79°C (175°F)

Container of water

Scalpel or craft knife

— VARIATIONS —

You can also make this candle by pouring the wax over the candle. This means that you will have to prepare far less wax.

2 Dip the candle into the can of blue wax and then into the can of cold water. Repeat three times.

3 Dip the candle into the green wax and then into water. Repeat three times. Then continue in the same way with four dips in yellow wax and finally four dips in ivory wax.

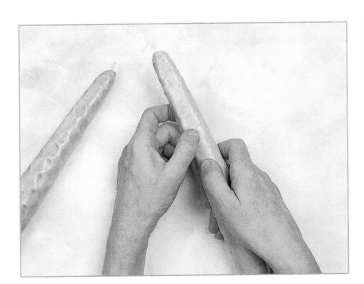

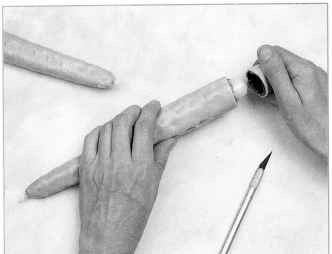

4 Using your fingers, press firmly against the candle to make small indentations all the way around the candle. Place the candle in cold water to cool.

5 Using a craft knife, score a circle around the base of the candle and gently pull off the coloured layers of wax so that the candle will fit into the neck of the bottle.

LAYERED CANDLE

The colours of this candle blend into each other to produce a simple yet effective finish. This basic technique can take a while to master as each layer must be poured in at the right time and at the right temperature.

1 Set up the mould. Heat all four waxes separately until they are molten. Heat the turquoise wax to 82°C (180°F) and pour gently into the mould to a depth of 1 cm (½ in). Try to avoid splashing the sides. Make a hole in the centre and position the wick. Twist the top of the wick around a stick to support it.

TIP

Make sure that the temperature has been accurately read before you pour. If it is too hot, the colours will mix; too cold and you will get a white ridge around the join.
If the candle is not perfect enough to polish, don't despair. A final dip in wax at 88°C (190°F) will cover up a multitude of sins.

2 Wait until the turquoise wax is completely set around the edge, but still very soft to the touch in the middle. Heat the lilac wax to 82°C (180°F) and pour in another layer 1 cm (½ in) deep.

3 Continue in the same manner with the blue and then the pink wax. Then repeat steps one and two and finally add a thin layer of blue wax. Give the candle a final top up.

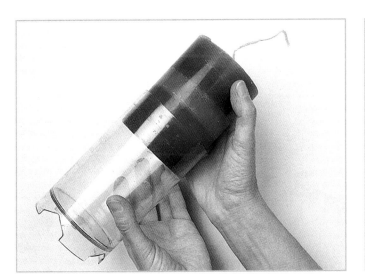

4 Leave the candle until completely cold and then carefully remove from the mould.

5 To finish off, polish the layered candle with a soft cloth or duster.

VARIATIONS

Tipping the mould at different angles when you pour in the wax also produces some interesting effects when the colours set at varying angles.

MULTI-WICKED CANDLES GALLERY

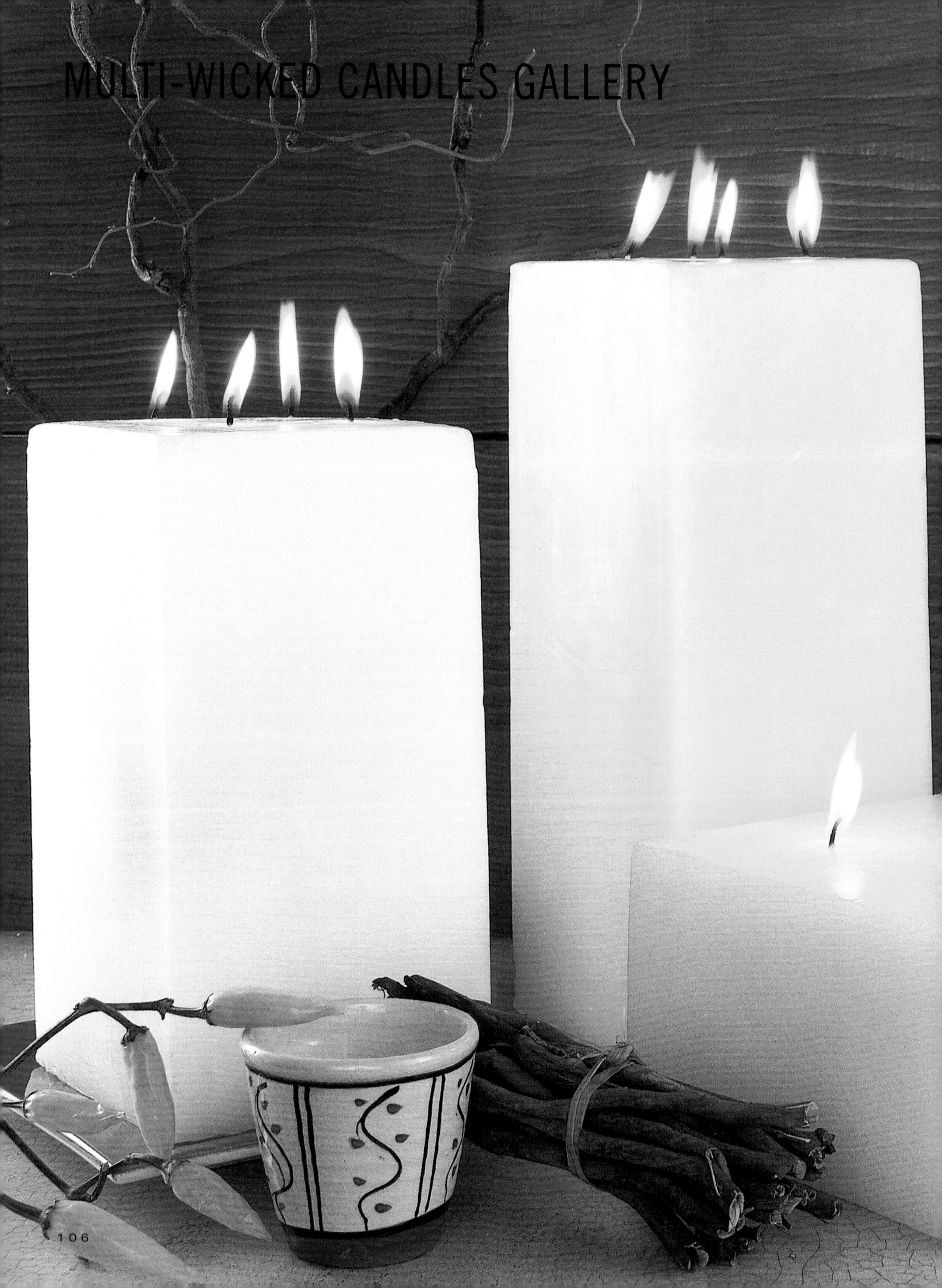

PURE BEESWAX DIPPED CANDLE

This project explains the earliest form of candlemaking – hand-dipping. Although time-consuming, hand-dipped candles burn beautifully and no wax is better suited to this technique than pure beeswax.

1 Heat the wax until it has all melted. Measure out a length of wick and hold it in the middle. Dip both ends of the wick into the beeswax, and then remove. Repeat the dipping three times.

─────── **TIP** ───────

If possible, it may help to make these candles in a dipping can placed in a saucepan on the stove. Because so many dips are involved, the wax may form a skin several times and have to be re-heated before the candles are finished.

2 Continue dipping the ends of the wick until the coating of wax becomes thicker. This hand-dipping means you will end up with candles that are much thicker than those produced commercially.

3 After approximately 30 dips you will have an ordinary sized pair of candles, similar to the standard ones available in shops.

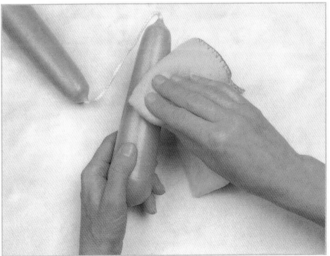

4 Continue dipping, reheating the wax as necessary. Stop when the candles have reach a diameter of 4 cm (1½ in) at the base.

5 Dip the candles immediately into cold water to produce a final shine. When dry, you can also buff them with a soft cloth.

PYRAMID CANDLE

This project illustrates how easy it is to make candles in cardboard moulds. This candle uses a pyramid shape, but is it just as simple to make squares and cylinders. The mould is thrown away after use, so it can simply be torn off the candle. The coldness of the wax gives it its scaly appearance.

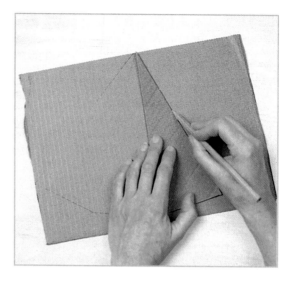

1 Using the smaller piece of cardboard, cut out a triangular template 9.5 cm (3¾ in) across the base and 21 cm (8½ in) along the sides. Cut out the template. On the large piece of cardboard, draw around the template four times to make a fan shape as shown. Alternatively copy the template on page 150.

YOU WILL NEED

A sheet of cardboard 15 x 23 cm (6 x 9 in)
A sheet of cardboard 30 x 23 cm (12 x 9 in)
Pencil
Scalpel or craft knife
Metal ruler
Brown tape
Scissors
20 cm (8 in) of 4 cm (1½ in) primed wick
Wicking needle
Stick, to support the wick
Tall container (see step 5)
250 g (9 oz) orange wax
25 g (1 oz) stearin
Double saucepan

TIP

Pouring in cold wax is possible when using a cardboard mould as the mould can be torn off the set candle and it does not matter if the candle sticks to the sides.

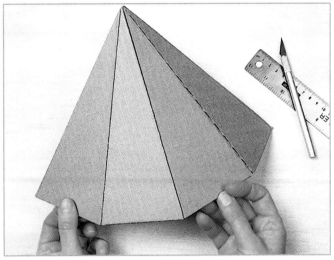

2 Cut out around the outside of the fan shape using the craft knife and metal ruler and discard the trimmings.

3 Score down the lines of the diagonals using the ruler and craft knife. Score just deep enough to bend the board, taking care not to cut right through the board.

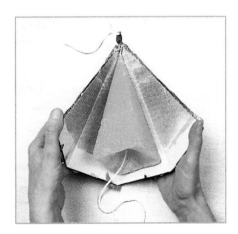

4 Fold the shape into a pyramid shape and tape the two edges together with a strip of brown tape.

5 Using a wicking needle, thread the wick through the centre of the mould and out through the taped, pointed end. Turn the mould upside down, place a stick across the base and bend the wick over. Place the cardboard mould into a tall container for support. Heat the prepared orange wax and stearin mix to just 71°C (160°F) and pour into the mould. Pierce the surface and top up in the usual way.

6 When the candle is completely cold, peel off the cardboard to reveal your candle. Remember that the top of the wick is secured by the brown tape, so take care not to break off the top of the candle.

CANDLE WITH BARK SURROUND

Natural bark is used to wonderful effect in this unusual woodland candle. Wax glue is used to fix the bark to the candle and because a small wick is used, the candle can be re-filled several times.

1 Using the hacksaw and protecting the work surface if necessary, cut the bark into lengths of approximately 5 cm (2 in).

TIP

Because this candle uses a wick size which is so much smaller than the diameter of the candle it is quite safe. You can also refill it with a nightlight or powdered wax and primed wick when it has burnt down about 2.5 cm (1 in).

2 Heat the wax and stearin mixture until it reaches a temperature of 82°C (180°F) and pour into the solid-based cake tin.

3 Wait until the wax has nearly cooled and then insert a length of primed wick. Push it down until it reaches the bottom. Then lift it up 3 mm (⅛ in) so that it will not burn right down to the bottom when alight.

4 Support the wick with a wick support resting across the cake tin. Then top up the candle with more wax. Leave to cool.

5 When completely cold, remove the candle from the cake tin. Apply a liberal amount of wax glue to the bark strips and press them against the side of the candle.

AROMATIC REFILL CANDLE

Candle perfumes can be used for many purposes, from soothing aromatherapy to practical smoke repelling. Burning them in a glass makes sure there is a pool of molten wax. This is essential if the perfume is to become atomised and permeate the surroundings.

1 Prepare wax, dye and perfume mix (see pages 91-92). Heat the wax to a temperature of 82°C (180°F). Pour into the base of the tumbler to a depth of about 4 mm (¼ in). Wait until it has almost set and then push the wick and sustainer down into the soft wax. Use a skewer or wicking needle to help push the sustainer down.

YOU WILL NEED

100 g (4 oz) paraffin wax
Dye in a colour of your choice
6-8 g (⅛-¼ oz) candle perfume
Double saucepan
Wax thermometer
Glass tumbler
Length of 10 cm (4 in) primed wick
Wick sustainer
Stick, to support the wick
Skewer or wicking needle
Cocktail stick

TIP

Make sure the wick is properly centred. If the flame touches the sides, it will break the glass.

2 Place a cocktail stick across the top of the tumbler and twist the wick around it. Pour in the wax and perfume mix to within 1 cm (½ in) of the top of the tumbler.

3 When the candle is half set, pierce the top of the wax in several places using the skewer or needle.

4 Leave until the candle is almost cold then top up with the remaining wax. Try not to top up over the original level of wax – this will make it easier for the candle to drop out of the glass.

5 Turn the glass upside down and remove the candle from the glass. You now have the glass free to make more refills.

ROLLED BEESWAX CANDLE

These square candles are made from the textured sheets of beeswax. They are fairly easy to make, with very little mess as only a small amount of melted wax is used.

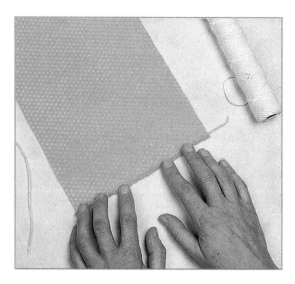

1 Lay the primed wick across the beeswax sheet and gently fold over the short edge of the beeswax to enclose it, pressing it firmly into place. Roll up the entire sheet around the wick.

YOU WILL NEED

7 sheets of beeswax, each 23 x 30 cm
(9 x 12 in)

25 cm (10 in) length of 2.5 cm (1 in)
primed wick

Scalpel or craft knife

Metal ruler

50 g (2 oz) melted beeswax

Spoon

TIP

Making a really neat rolled beeswax candle takes practice. Always make sure that you are rolling as tightly as possible.

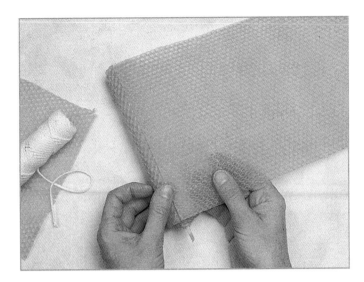

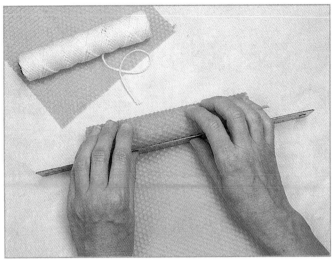

2 Place a second sheet of beeswax next to the edge of the first, and roll up tightly as in the previous step. Make sure you roll the candle evenly, so that all the edges remain at the same height.

3 Take the third sheet of beeswax. Press the metal ruler against the roll to make a sharp 90° angle and begin pressing the roll into a square shape, turning it over each time rather than rolling it.

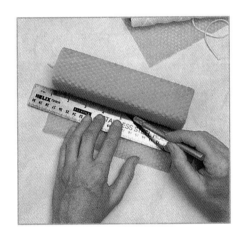

4 Continue adding sheets, using the ruler at each turn to form the sides. Once the edges are defined, score the sheet against the ruler before you roll it. This will help to make sharp corners, but take care not to cut all the way through the wax sheet.

5 When all the sheets have been used, press the end of the last sheet very firmly into the candle to make sure it does not unravel.

6 Spoon a little molten beeswax on to the base of the candle to seal all the layers.

STACKED CANDLE

This striking spiral-stacked candle makes an unusual gift. It is very quick and easy to make and no mould is required. The brilliant white texture is produced by adding a large amount of stearin to the wax mixture.

1 Cut the paper to the same width as the shortest side of the baking tray. Fold it into three lengthwise. Heat the wax and stearin together to 82°C (180°F), pour into the baking tray and leave it to cool to a soft, pliable consistency. Using the folded paper as a guide, mark the edge of the wax at the folds. Repeat at the other end. Using the same piece of paper as a guide, mark the longer sides at the same evenly spaced intervals.

YOU WILL NEED

A square-sided baking tray
Sheet of paper slightly larger than the baking tray
Scalpel or craft knife
150 g (5 oz) wax
150 g (5 oz) stearin
Wax thermometer
Metal ruler
Sharp object, such as a skewer or wicking needle
Wick sustainer
30 cm (12 in) length of 5 cm (2 in) primed wick
Wicking needle
Pliers

TIP

The addition of stearin not only whitens the wax but also ensures that the candle will be very long-burning.

2 Place the ruler across your marks and, using a craft knife, cut the soft wax into even squares.

3 Using a sharp object, make a hole in the centre of each square. Wait until the wax is completely cold and then remove the squares from the baking tray.

4 Using a wicking needle, thread the wick sustainer with the length of primed wick. Gently use a pair of pliers to pinch the wick sustainer to secure the wick firmly in place.

5 Thread the wick through the holes in the centre of the squares, setting the squares on top of each other at a slight angle.

NEPTUNE CANDLE

Conjure up the natural beauty of the sea by combining shells and undyed natural paraffin wax in this simple but effective candle. If you are making it as a gift, wrap the finished candle in clear cellophane and tie with a raffia bow. Other flammable objects, for example fresh or dried flowers and herbs, could also be used for a different effect.

1 Have the prepared mould ready. Fix the wick but leave it hanging free over the side of the mould. Put the paraffin wax and stearin together in a double saucepan and heat to 82°C (180°F). Pour the wax mix into the mould.

YOU WILL NEED

Candle mould, approximately 15 x 7.5 cm (6 x 3 in)
Length of 5 cm (2 in) primed wick
Stick, to support the wick
Mould seal
450 g (1 lb) paraffin wax
50 g (2 oz) stearin
Double saucepan
Thermometer
Sharp knife
Sea shells
Wicking needle
Wax thermometer

SAFETY TIP

For extra safety when decorating with flammable materials such as dried flowers or herbs, put the wick in so that it reaches only halfway down the mould so that the candle will not burn below the point where the embedded decoration starts.

TIP

When adding the wax in step 5, it must be cooler than the wax already in the mould or it will melt it and the shells will fall off.

2 Wait for about 3-5 minutes until the wax has formed a skin about 1 cm (½ in) thick. Starting about 1 cm (½ in) from the edge and working quickly, cut off a 'lid' of skin from the top of the mould.

3 Pour the wax mixture back into the double saucepan with the wax disk. Clean the rim of the mould, if necessary.

4 Gently press shells into the thin layer of wax on the sides of the mould. Make sure they are embedded deeply enough to be seen from outside, taking care not to let them break through the outer surface of the wax.

5 Fix the wick in position in the usual way. Check the temperature of the hot wax and wait until it has cooled to about 73°C (165°F). Cool rapidly, if necessary by adding unmelted wax. Pour the hot wax into the mould up to the original level. Top up, allow to cool for 3-4 hours, then remove from the mould in the usual way.

LANTERN CANDLE WITH DRIED FRUITS

A wonderful, everlasting gift, this unique wax lantern would make a welcome decoration in any home. The warm colours of the dried fruit embedded in the sides glow warmly when a candle is placed inside the lantern and lit.

1 Cut the fruit into slices and place on a baking tray in a very low oven for about 1½ hours. Remove and lay out on a plate ready for use.

TIP

The same method can be used for embedding other objects. Experiment with small shells or dried herbs, or study the gallery on pages 124-125 for inspiration.

2 Heat the wax to a temperature of 82°C (180°F) and carefully pour it into the container.

3 Wait until it has cooled sufficiently for a layer of wax about 5 mm (¼ in) to have formed on the surface. Using a craft knife, cut a square about 1 cm (¾ in) from the edge of the candle and then remove the cut out square from the wax using a kitchen spatula.

4 Pour out the excess molten wax from the container into a bowl and set aside for use in step 6.

5 Take a piece of fruit and press it firmly into the wax. Repeat with all the fruit and the parsley leaves. You will have to work quite quickly. You will probably have about seven minutes before the wax is too hard.

6 Pour in wax again to just below the edge of the candle. Wait until a layer about 3 mm (⅛ in) has set, and then cut out the top and pour away the wax as you did in step 3.

7 Place a nightlight or a small scented candle in a glass container into the base of the candle and light.

APPLIQUED CANDLE

This intricately designed candle shows the versatility and ease of appliqué wax. A base colour is first wrapped around the candle, then a delicate pattern is cut out of the sheet wax and pressed down. The final touch of thin gold strips produces a sophisticated candle.

1 Wrap a piece of paper around the candle and mark where it meets with a pencil. Open out the paper and measure from the edge of the paper to the pencil mark. This is the size of the candle's circumference.

TIP

Appliqué wax is very easy to use. It is very effective when you want to make personalised candles or candles for special occasions.

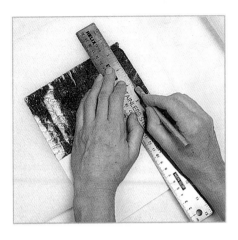

2 Place the sheets of silver appliqué wax on the cutting board and cut out two pieces of wax exactly the length of the candle's circumference. (You need to use two sheets of wax as a single sheet will not be large enough to wrap around a candle of this size.)

3 Wrap the two lengths of appliqué wax firmly around the candle. If they do not quite fill the length of the candle, use the offcut around the base.

4 Divide a piece of graph paper up into 2.5 cm (1 in) squares. Draw a diagonal across each square. Then draw a petal shape on each diagonal. Using a soft pencil draw around the petal shapes again. This template is shown in detail on page 151.

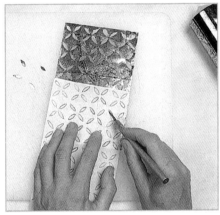

5 Turn the graph paper upside down and place on top of the tracing paper. Pressing hard, use a biro to transfer the petal shapes on to the tracing paper.

6 Using the template, cut out two sheets of multi-coloured appliqué wax. Place the sheets on the cutting board and lay the tracing paper over the sheets. Cut out the petal shapes using a craft knife.

7 Next, carefully place these cut multi-coloured sheets around the candle, as you did in step 3.

8 Cut the sheet of gold appliqué wax into very thin strips. Lay them vertically down the candle between the petal patterns. Then repeat to lay the strips horizontally around the candle, forming squares.

DECORATED CANDLES GALLERY

STENCILLED CANDLE

Stencilling is one of the easiest ways of decorating a simple candle and giving it an added finish. This project shows how to produce an attractive design using paper as a stencil.

1 Holding the candle by the wick, dip it into a dipping can of mint green wax.

TIP

Use this method for making personalised candles for special occasions, such as gold hearts on red candles for Valentines' Day or personalised wedding candles with gold paint on white wax.

VARIATIONS

If you wish, you could use a pre-cut paper doily wrapped around a candle for a pretty paint effect.

2 Fold the sheet of paper in half and make three long triangular cuts along the folded edge.

3 Fold over another 1 cm (½ in) of the paper lengthways. Make three triangular cuts just below the thickest part of each of the first cuts.

4 Then cut three small slithers off the gaps in between the triangles and open out the paper. If you find this cutting difficult, use the template on page 151 and simply trace the design on to a flat piece of paper.

5 Place the paper around the candle and hold tightly in place. Using your finger, rub the silver paste over the holes in the paper, making sure that you get the paste right into the edges. Leaving time for the paste to dry between each application, repeat four times until the candle is complete.

SNOWBALL CANDLE

Whipped wax is used here to create the realistic snow-like surface on this Christmas candle. Whip the wax just as you would an egg white. The resulting consistency resembles the texture of snow.

1 Set up a round candle mould, leaving about 5 cm (2 in) of extra wick at the base. Pour in the wax and stearin mix. Top up and allow to cool, then remove from the mould.

YOU WILL NEED

500 g (1 lb 1½ oz) white wax with 20 per cent stearin added, heated to 82°C (180°F)
Round candle mould
20 cm (8 in) length of 4 cm (1½ in) primed wick
Fork
Baking tray

TIP

If you allow the whipped wax to cool until it is almost set, you can mould whipped wax with your hands. Children love hand-moulding their own snowball candles just as they would real snow.

2 Heat the remainder of the wax to 18°C (65°F) or until it has melted, then wait until it has cooled so that skin 5 mm (¼ in) thick has formed over the surface. Using a fork, beat the wax until it has reached a soft, snow-like consistency.

3 Hold the candle in one hand and, using the fork, begin to smear the whipped wax over the candle.

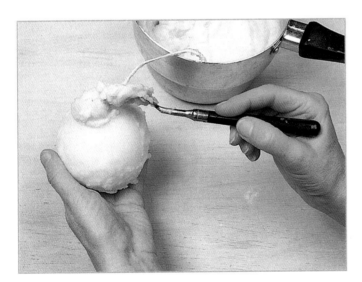

4 Continue forking over the wax until a thick layer has been built up all over the candle.

5 Place the candle in a baking tray and, using a fork, make sure the wax has been applied as evenly as possible all round. Leave the candle on the tray to cool.

GOLD CHRISTMAS CANDLE

This is a simple and elegant candle ideal for a traditional Christmas centrepiece. Using micro soft makes it easier to serrate the surface of the candle, and the application of rub-on gold enhances the pattern inscribed by the zest peeler.

1 Heat the ivory wax to 79°C (175°F) and add the micro soft. Pour the ivory wax and the micro soft into a dipping can. Holding the candle by the wick, dip it three times.

YOU WILL NEED

A ready-made candle
2 kg (4½ lb) ivory paraffin wax
20 g (¾ oz) micro soft
Dipping can
Zest peeler
Rub-on gold wax paint

—————— TIP ——————

If you wish, you could use a lino cutting tool to create different patterns on the side on the candle.

2 Pour the remaining wax into a container for future use. Fill the dipping can with cold water and dip the candle once again.

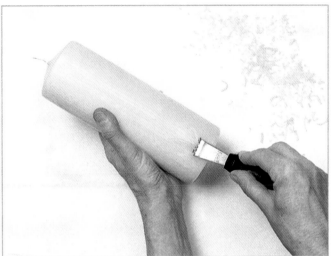

3 Wait until the wax has cooled so it is just slightly warm to the touch. Press the zest peeler firmly against the side of the candle and score a line down the side of the candle. Repeat until you have gone right around the candle.

4 Smear a little gold wax paint on your finger. Gently rub the raised surface of the candle with the gold. Continue until you are half-way around the candle.

5 Leave the candle to dry for at least two hours, and then continue around the undecorated side of the candle until all the raised surface is covered with gold. Leave to dry.

GARDEN FLARE

These pretty garden flares will brighten any barbecue. The lily design adds interest and makes these flares exciting as well as functional. Always stick the flare securely into the ground, well away from any inflammable surroundings, such as leaves or wooden fences.

1 Wrap the bandage tightly around the top 20 cm (8 in) of the bamboo stick, pulling it out at the top so that the top 2 cm (¾ in) protrudes beyond the bamboo.

YOU WILL NEED

1 m (3 ft) length of bamboo
A bandage or length of rag
10cm (4 in) length of 5 cm (2 in) primed wick
200 g (7 oz) purple wax with 20 g (¾ oz) micro soft
100 g (4 oz) shocking pink wax and stearin mix
100 g (4 oz) green wax and stearin mix
Wax thermometer
Sheet of paper
Template (see page 150)
Baking tray
Scalpel or craft knife

TIP

It is essential to use rag or bandage for making garden flares as they act as a wick. If you do not wish to use the petal shape, simply pour more wax over the bandage. The thicker the wax layer, the longer the flare will burn.

2 Heat the green wax to 73°C (165°F). Hold the covered bamboo stick over the saucepan and ladle wax over the first 15 cm (6 in) of the bandaged end. Keep pouring over the wax until the bandage is completely covered.

3 Push the length of wick into the top of the bandage. Heat the pink wax to 73°C (165°F). Hold the bamboo stick over the saucepan and ladle wax over the remaining exposed bandage.

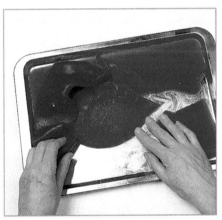

4 Using the template on page 150, cut out a piece of paper to the correct size. Heat the purple wax and micro soft mix to 82°C (180°F) and pour into the baking tray. Wait until the wax has set to a soft 'fudge' consistency. Place the petal-shaped paper on it and cut around it with a craft knife.

5 Remove the paper template. Peel away the unwanted wax around the petal on the baking tray.

6 Lift the petal shape from the baking tray and carefully fold it around the top of the bamboo stick. Place the flare in a bucket of water to cool and set the wax.

FLOATING LILY

Floating candles are always pretty and this vibrantly coloured and unusually large candle will grace any candle bowl. The shaped outer layer is made possible by the use of micro soft which keeps the wax soft for long enough for it to be shaped.

1 Pour the lime green wax into a baking tray and wait until it is almost set (i.e. warm but still soft to the touch). Using a bowl or plate as a template, cut out a circle in the middle of the wax with a craft knife.

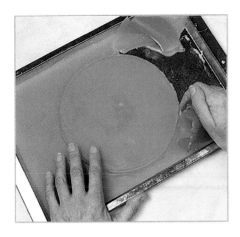

2 Gently pull away the wax from around the circle. Carefully lift the remaining circle on to a cutting board.

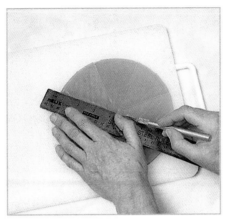

3 Using the craft knife, divide the circle into eight portions. Do not cut into the middle of the circle – leave an uncut circle with a diameter of approximately 2 cm (¾ in) in the centre.

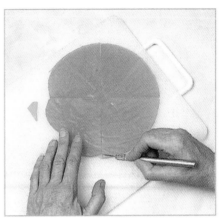

4 Using the craft knife, neatly shape the top of each of the eight segments into a scallop shape.

5 Lift up the wax from the cutting board and place into a small bowl. Place each segment so that it slightly overlaps the neighbouring segment.

6 Using a spoon, smear some green wax around the inside of the wax bowl to hold the segments in place, making sure that any holes are sealed.

7 Pour in the pink wax to within 2 mm (⅛ in) of the top.

8 Wait until the wax is almost set and press in the primed wick.

9 Resting the wick on a stick for support, carefully top up the lily with orange wax.

FLOATING HEARTS

We have used three sizes of biscuit cutter to form the shape of these delicate, yet easy-to-make candles. Sitting in a shallow glass bowl filled with water, they make a lovely centrepiece for a dinner table.

1 Pour the hot purple wax into baking tray to a depth of about 6 mm (¼ in). Press the heart-shaped biscuit moulds into the wax and leave them there.

YOU WILL NEED

Shallow baking tray
Set of 3 heart-shaped biscuit cutters
50 g (2 oz) purple wax, heated to 82°C (180°F)
150 g (6 oz) pink wax, heated to 82°C (180°F)
Length of 2.5 cm (1 in) primed wick
Skewer or wicking needle

—— TIP ——

There is now a wide range of biscuit cutters available in cooks' shops and department stores, so experiment with different shapes.

2 Carefully pour the hot pink wax into the three heart moulds, filling them up to their rims.

3 Make a hole in the centre of each heart, using a skewer or wicking needle. Push a short length of primed wick into each hole.

4 Top up each mould with more hot pink wax. Make sure the wicks are still positioned in the centre of each candle. Leave to cool.

5 When the wax is completely cold, push the pink hearts out of the moulds. The purple wax can be re-used for other candles.

CARVED TAPER CANDLES

These unusual candles have been carved into eye-catching designs. They are made using special dip-and-carve wax which will not crack or splinter during carving.

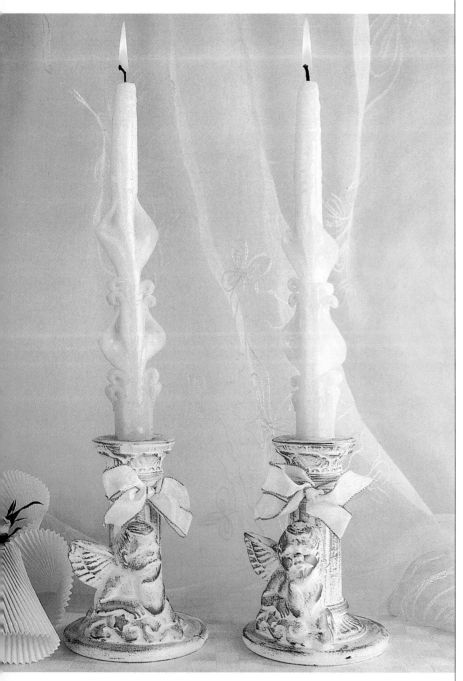

1 Heat both dipping cans to 77°C (170°F). Hold the candle in the white wax for about three minutes, or until it is slightly soft.

── TIP ──

It is much easier to make dip and carve candles in warm conditions. Whilst learning this technique, fix a light close to your work surface. The warmth from the light will give you precious extra seconds before the candle cools.

2 Next, dip the candle three times into ivory wax dipping can.

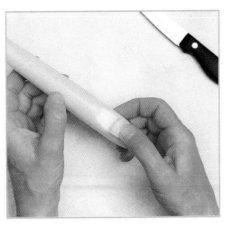

3 Using a sharp knife, make a cut 3 mm (⅛ in) deep 4 cm (1½ in) above the base of the candle. Pinch with your fingers, and gently fold back.

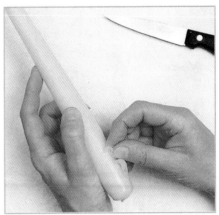

4 Make a second cut immediately above the one you have just made and roll it up above the first cut.

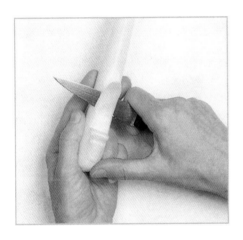

5 Make a cut 5 cm (2 in) long, finishing just below the wax you have just rolled.

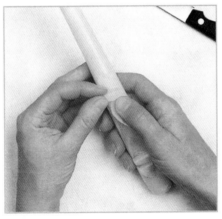

6 Carefully twist the flap around and push it firmly against the side of the candle.

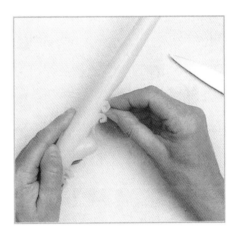

7 Next, make a further cut and roll it up as before. Then make one more cut just above it.

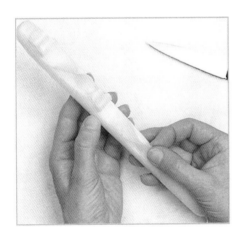

8 Cut another 5 cm (2 in) flap (as in step 5), twist it and place it gently back onto the candle.

9 Repeat the design on the opposite side of the candle, then cut across the bottom of the candle to give it an even base.

10 Sit the candle in an old candlestick or fashion a support out of thick card, then give the candle a coat of varnish.

TEMPLATES

The templates shown here are smaller than required for the projects. They may be easily enlarged to the correct size on a photocopier set at 111%.

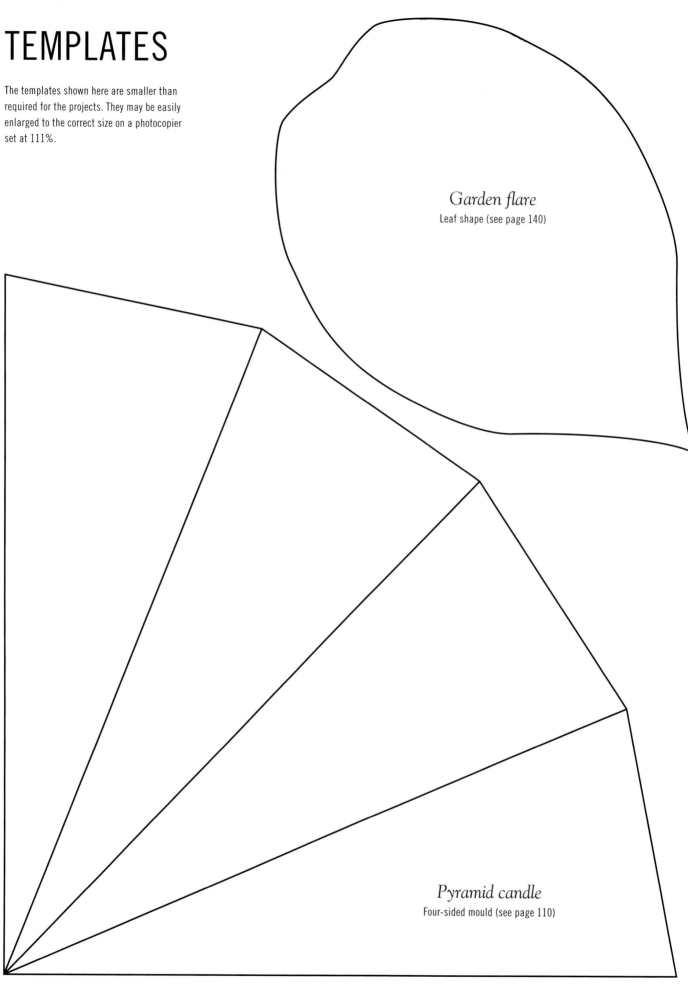

Garden flare
Leaf shape (see page 140)

Pyramid candle
Four-sided mould (see page 110)

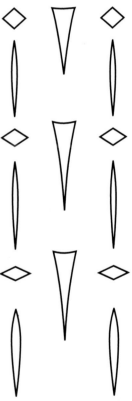

Appliquéd candle
Repeat pattern (see page 128)

Stencilled candle
Repeat pattern (see page 132)

MAKING MOSAICS

Martin Cheek

INTRODUCTION

Surprisingly, the word 'mosaic' has no literal translation. Some scholars have suggested that it means 'crazy', which even if not absolutely accurate, seems to be entirely appropriate at times.

Mosaic is certainly enjoying something of a renaissance at the moment. I have been running three-day mosaic courses for many years now and their popularity has grown as the public have slowly realized that they, too, can make beautiful mosaics for themselves. It never fails to amaze me that what appears at first glance to be such an inflexible material, can produce results that are so stylistically different and individual.

The Italian master mosaicists had to train for many years before being allowed to tackle big public works. Understandably, they were (and still are) very secretive about their techniques. What they would think of a three-day mosaic course (or this book, which for some projects works on the principle that just completing the mosaicing can take a 'long weekend' – three days) is not worth repeating. But the fact remains that wonderful things can be, and are, achieved in this short space of time. So let's let the mosaics speak for themselves.

ABOUT THE PROJECTS IN THIS BOOK

The projects have been chosen to show the wide range of styles, materials and techniques available to the modern mosaicist. Choose the ones that suit your temperament – it is unlikely that someone who feels drawn to the Gaudiesque style of using great big chunks of broken pottery is also going to enjoy the painstaking work involved in nibbling fine detail for an intricate design.

I strongly recommend that you read the chosen project through carefully before you start. There is nothing more maddening than to have to stop work because you have forgotten a vital piece of equipment. You will also notice that there are times when you will need to wait, say, for glue to dry. It is important to realize this before you begin a project, so that you don't get disappointed when you find you have to wait, for example, a whole week for cement to set.

I have tried to choose projects that range from simple ones that can be achieved in a morning (for example, the Trivet on pages 174-175 and the Shell Door Number on pages 180-181), although the grouting will have to be left to set for the next two to three days. Others are more advanced (for example, the Roman Paving Slab on pages 198-199), and it may take up to three days to complete the mosaic work and then there will be additional waiting time while the concrete sets. There are plenty of mosaics for internal and external settings. Mosaic has the added advantage of being able to be wiped clean, so you can hang it in your kitchen or bathroom. Other projects have been chosen simply because they make perfect gifts.

MATERIALS AND QUANTITIES

The tile quantities listed at the beginning of each project are meant as a guide only, and in the lists of quantities required, I have always allowed an additional 25 per cent for wastage. If you don't have, or have run out of, a certain colour, feel free to substitute a different one of your own choice – if you choose a colour that has the same tone (imagine it in a black and white reproduction – is your choice tonally similar?), then the tonal range of the piece, and more importantly, the contrast between the subject and background, will remain.

You won't be able to buy the mosaic tiles in the small quantities listed in each project, so please don't try. Instead, I suggest that you buy a 25-kg (50 lb) box of vitreous mix, which is basically scrap, but it is soon sorted into jars. This also has the benefit of containing some colours that are not available in the standard range and you can make up any particular colour you need separately once you know what you have got.

You may also find, when buying specific colours, that they can vary in shade from batch to batch. Because of this, if you want consistency in a certain colour, make sure that you buy a sufficient quantity before you start. I actually like the fact that the mixed box gives you subtle differences of the same colour and for this reason always keep a box or two handy in my mosaic studio. You will find that in the mixed boxes you get a predominance of blues, greens and whites. This is because 95 per cent of all 'vitmos' is bought for cladding swimming pools – and who wants a flaming red swimming pool?

Your mosaic room will soon resemble a sweet shop with jars full of beautifully coloured tiles inspiring you to get started – so off you go!

Martin Cheek

GETTING STARTED

The list of tools, equipment and materials, given at the beginning of each project certainly looks daunting, but you will soon realize that apart from the mosaic tiles, many of the tools are standard and can be used around the house for other jobs. You are likely to have many of them already.

EQUIPMENT AND MATERIALS

MOSAIC TILE NIPPERS

The first thing that you will notice about the mosaic nippers, compared with, say, a pair of scissors, is that the pivot point is extremely high. The handles curve in towards the bottom and this is where you are meant to hold them. The combination of these two factors gives the nippers maximum leverage so that you do not have to work hard when you are cutting the tiles. The handles are sprung so that you do not have to pull them apart each time you cut a tile. The jaws of the nippers are made of tungsten carbide for strength. They don't meet up when you close them, this is correct.

Also in contrast to a pair of scissors, they cut at right angles to the handles. One side juts out and this is the side that you use to cut the tiles in straight lines. If you practice at using the jaws the 'wrong' way round you will soon learn how to cut curved lines.

TWEEZERS, TONGS AND DENTAL TOOLS

From time to time you may find it helpful to use a pair of tweezers to finely 'tweak' the tesserae. Some people prefer a simple cocktail stick.

Miniature tongs can also be obtained. At first these might be mistaken for tweezers, but in fact the prongs open, not close when you squeeze your fingers. A pair of these are excellent for picking up small fiddly tesserae, too small for your fingers. (Or too close to your recently completed area to risk picking up with the naked hand.)

Dentist's tools can be bought from surgical or sculptural suppliers and are excellent for 'poking' and 'prodding'. Being made of metal, you can remove the glue with a scalpel once it has dried. They are expensive though, so try asking your dentist if he has any old ones he no longer needs, you may be lucky.

BUILDER'S FLOAT

A builder's float is a square piece of wood about 30 x 30 cm (12 x 12 in). It has a handle on one side and is used to smooth or flatten sand, cement or concrete.

LEVELLING TOOL

A levelling tool is needed to flatten out the surface of a sand bed prior to making an indirect pebble mosaic (see page 194). You can make a levelling tool quite easily. For example, for the Pebble Mosaic, which measures 66 x 48 cm (26 x 19 in), cut two lengths of 10 x 2.5 cm (4 x 1 in) batten. Cut one to 48 cm (19 in) and the second to 74 cm (29 in). Then glue and nail them together with 13 cm (5 in) sticking out at either end. This levelling tool sits on the adjacent sides of the mould, and by running the tool across the top of the mould you can level out the sand.

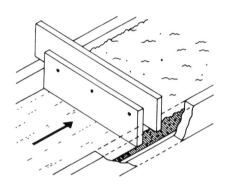

GLUES

• **PVA (POLYVINYL ACETATE)** is the standard glue used for gluing down the tesserae when making a direct mosaic. Although you can buy 'waterproof' PVA (EVA), it is still not recommended that you put a direct mosaic made using PVA out of doors. In winter, moisture can seep in through the grout and freeze into frost. As it freezes, it will expand and force the tesserae off the board.

For indoor use, though, PVA is perfect and has the added advantage of being very user-friendly – no harmful smells and it washes off your hands easily with soap and water. When wet it is white, but as it sets it turns clear. Once set, the bond is actually very strong, as anyone who has tried to correct mistakes by ripping up glued-down tesserae can testify.

• **WALLPAPER PASTE AND WATER-SOLUBLE GUM.** The basic principle of indirect mosaic is to glue the tesserae, flat side down, to craft paper, cement it to your rendered wall or floor and then soak off the paper with warm water.

Thus the glue required needs to be water-soluble. I find wallpaper paste ideal for this. It is cheap, it lasts a long time and you can mix it to the consistency that you like. Children's paper paste that comes in little pots with a rubber nozzle dispenser is also fine. Basically, any water-soluble glue will do the job.

• **EPOXY RESIN.** For outdoor purposes and when occasionally a stronger glue than PVA is required, two-part epoxy resin is the answer. It is available from ironmongers and department stores and comes in 'tube' or 'syringe' form. I recommend the syringe type as this ensures equal dispensing of the two parts. In a well-ventilated room, mix the two parts together thoroughly with a metal modelling tool or lollipop stick. It is advisable to use a metal modelling tool to do this as it is stronger and more controllable and you have the advantage of being able to clean it with the scalpel once the glue has hardened. If you use a lollipop stick, you will need to change it from time to time. The quick-setting epoxy resin has a 'working time' of about five minutes and a 'setting time' of about 15 minutes. The slow-setting epoxy resin has a 'working time' of about an hour and a 'setting time' of about 16 hours.

MOSAIC MATERIALS

• **VITREOUS GLASS.** 'Vitreous' simply means non-porous. This is the material which is used to line swimming pools and is therefore familiar to all of us. The colour range is good, the standard range consists of 50 colours and extra ones become available from time to time. (Snap these up whenever you see them!) Naturally, because the majority of the market for these tiles is swimming pools there is a much better choice of blues, greens and whites than of any other colour.

Vitreous glass tiles come mounted on paper in sheets of 15 x 15 tiles, each square measuring 2 x 2 cm (¾ x ¾ in). Each coloured sheet has a 'series number' rather like oil paints. Not surprisingly, the very pale colours are the cheapest (Series 1) and the brightest colours with metallic 'veining' are the most expensive

A selection of vitreous tiles

(Series 4). For chemical reasons, Candy Pink makes it to Series 5 all on its own.

To soak off the backing paper, place the sheet of tiles in a basin of warm water. After a few minutes, the paper will float off. Remove the paper and rinse the tiles in more warm water. Put them into a colander to drain and finally spread them out onto old dry towels, separating the colours as you go. Each colour can then be given its own jar and the end result is a studio which looks more like a sweet shop than an artist's studio.

A selection of ceramic tiles

Alternatively, vitreous can be purchased in large 25 kg (55 lb) boxes, sold as mixed 'scrap' for about one third the price of the tiled sheets. There is nothing wrong with these tiles and they are soon sorted out into their jars. In fact it is a good idea to always have a mixed box around as they often contain colours that are not widely available or are from a different 'batch' to the one you have bought – the same colour sometimes being a slightly different hue.

• **CERAMIC.** All types of ceramic can, of course, be broken up and incorporated into a mosaic. It is very useful, though, to be able to buy sheets of ceramic tiles in various consistent colours and to know that you won't run out of any particular colour. Cinca is the brand name of one such type of unglazed ceramic tile made in Portugal but exported around the world. It comes in sheets of 14 x 14 tiles, each square measuring 23 x 23 mm (1 x 1 in). Because Cinca is so much heavier than vitreous glass, the glue binding it to the backing paper is stronger and takes longer to soak off. Even then, the tiles tend to stick together while drying, so it is advisable to spread them out on the towel so that they don't touch each other.

The range of ceramic tiles is good and there are usually 25 different colours to choose from. The main difference between vitreous and Cinca is that vitreous is made of glass and is therefore shiny and reflective, whereas Cinca is an un-glazed (non-reflective) ceramic. This can be used to good effect by placing an area of one next to the other; the vitreous will appear to come forward while the Cinca will appear to recede, thus a Cinca-mosaiced background will allow a vitreous or smalti subject to stand out.

Cinca tiles don't have a 'right' and 'wrong' side which means that you have the added advantage of being able to flip them over if you wish. As you work, you will appreciate how advantageous this is.

If the mosaic is made entirely of Cinca then the effect will be a calm one, reminiscent of Indian mosaics (see Gallery piece 'Resting Plaice').

Cinca is excellent for floor mosaics as the tiles are completely flat, and if set into a solid floor, can withstand the weight of a person walking across it.

• **SMALTI** is the Roman word for 'melt'. Smalti tesserae are hand-made in Venice and until recently there were only three families still making it. The recipes and techniques have been kept secret and handed down from father to son through the generations. Glass is melted in a cauldron and then poured out onto a metal sheet where it is pressed down like a pizza. This is then sawn up into little briquettes about 2 x 1 cm (¾ x ½ in). It is supposed to be used with the sides uppermost, emphasizing its rippled surface. Tiny air bubbles are sometimes visible, which is not a mistake but moreover part of its intrinsic quality. It can be bought loose by weight in an 'irregular mix' 25 kg (55 lb) box in much the same way as vitreous. In amongst the mixed assortment you will find tesserae that have a curved edge – these are the edges of the 'pizza'. Although purists would argue that these should not be used, I find them invaluable where rounded edges are a great help.

Roman mosaics, though made mainly of natural stones, do sometimes contain the odd bit of smalti – usually bright colours like orange or blue, but it was really the Byzantines that made the material their own, creating entire wall mosaics out of it. Needless to say, being hand-made, smalti is very expensive. Despite the price, it makes a lovely addition to any mosaic and can be incorporated in small quantities.

Because of its uneven surface you do not need to grout smalti when working direct. The theory is that it self-grouts. As you push the smalti into the tile adhesive, so it is forced up between the gaps in the smalti.

Using smalti indirect is no problem. Although it has a different thickness to vitreous glass tiles, in the case of indirect mosaic, this does not matter because the final face of the mosaic will be flat.

• **GOLD AND SILVER LEAF TILES** Gold and silver smalti have real gold or silver leaf in the glass tile. 'Ripple gold' and 'ripple silver', where the top surface of glass is undulated to create a rippled effect, are also available. Not surprisingly, these are the most expensive tiles of all. Both can be used upside down – the gold is a shiny green underneath, and the silver a shiny blue. Despite the cost, even when used sparingly, they can lift an otherwise lacklustre mosaic.

Assorted pebbles

• **FOUND OBJECTS** Roman mosaics were made of natural stone cut up into small cubes. Natural stone and marble are still used extensively in mosaics throughout the world. It is also possible to use found objects such as beads, buttons and shells; in fact, anything that can be combined with anything to make a cohesive whole.

Anyone who has ever played with pebbles on the beach (and who hasn't?) will immediately recognize the attraction of pebble mosaics. The Alhambra in Granada, Spain, is one of the most impressive places to see pebble mosaics, where they line the Moorish gardens of the Generalife.

What surprises most people is the fact that the amount of pebble visible above the cement is only the tip of the iceberg. The pebbles can be inserted straight into a bed of wet sand and cement, but if you intend to walk on your finished pebble mosaic it is worth making a simple mould and laying the pebbles indirect into a bed of sand (see the Pebble Mosaic Paving Slab on pages 194-197).

It is horrifying to see broken bottles on the beach. However, glass worn down by the motion of the sea is very pleasing and a treasure to any self-respecting mosaic artist. Likewise, broken crockery is a wonderful material to use for mosaics (see pages 204-205 and 215-217). Indeed, some mosaic artists have made this medium their own.

SAND
Some of the projects in this book include sand in the list of materials. I usually use plain builder's sand or, occasionally, sharp sand. Never use sand straight off the beach because it contains salt, which is corrosive.

Assorted smalti

CUTTING TECHNIQUES

Before you begin cutting vitreous glass, consider the mosaic tiles. Each tile is 2 cm (¾ in) square with a flat face and an uneven 'ribbed' face. The ribbed surface acts as a key to take the glue while the flat surface always goes uppermost when working direct and will become the final surface of your mosaic. Each tile will cut into four basic mosaic pieces or tesserae, whose average size will be 1 cm (⅜ in) square, i.e. 10,000 per square metre.

A single piece of mosaic is called a tessera which comes from the Roman word meaning a cube. Traditionally, Roman tesserae were small 1 cm (⅜ in) cubes of natural stone cut down from large pieces of stone using a hammer and hardie. The hammer used (see below) is a small, thin, pointed one, rather like a jeweller's or geologist's hammer. A hardie (see below also) is a chisel embedded in wood or cast into a lump of concrete with its cutting edge uppermost. Although our mosaic pieces are not always cubic, the word tessera has been adopted through the ages.

Hammer and hardie

CUTTING A TILE INTO HALVES

① The nippers only have to crack the tile, so you need only place the tile about 4 mm (¼ in) into the jaws, halfway down the edge of the tile.

Apply a small amount of pressure to the handles and you will find that the tile will crack in two.

CUTTING A TILE INTO QUARTERS

② Pick up one of the halves and make a bridge with it across your index and middle finger, securing the tile with your thumb. Place the nippers halfway down and 4 mm (¼ in) in and apply a small amount of pressure to the handles again – the rectangle will crack into two small squares. Repeat.

You have now made four basic 1 cm (⅜ in) square tesserae out of one tile. (Even if one is bigger or smaller than the other three, they will still average 1 cm [⅜ in] square.)

CUTTING LONG, THIN LINES

③ Place the nippers further into the tile, say, about halfway in. Three or four thin lengths can be made out of each tile. The tiles sometimes have a tendency to shatter when you do this, so don't blame yourself if it takes a few attempts and some wastage before you achieve what you want.

CUTTING WEDGES

While laying a line of square tesserae next to each other will give you a straight line, to achieve a curved line, the tesserae should be cut at a slight angle into wedges. The closer the angle of each wedge is to 90 degrees, the softer the resulting curve will be when they are laid together.

In the course of cutting a pool of tesserae, you will naturally end up with a large percentage of wedges, anyway. If you are mosaicing a curved line, you can select these from your pool. ④ To cut wedges on purpose, halve the tiles as described above, but when you come to dividing them into quarters, place the nippers at a slight angle to the vertical before applying the pressure to the handles.

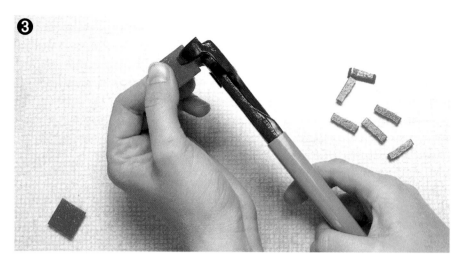

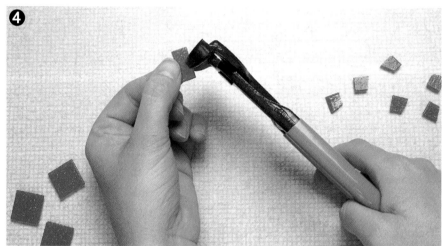

HEALTH AND SAFETY INSTRUCTIONS WHEN CUTTING VITREOUS GLASS

- Work in a well-ventilated room.
- Always wear safety spectacles and a face mask.
- When you are cutting the tiles, don't allow anyone to come near you, unless they are also wearing mask and eye protection.
- Use a dust pan and brush to sweep up all the little glass shards. Never use your hands as you may cut yourself on a glass splinter.
- Keep your work surfaces clean at all times. Sweep up or vacuum after each session.
- Keep glass particles away from food and drink, children, pets and wild animals.
- To keep all the glass waste under control when cutting tiles, you may like to work with your hands, nippers and tiles inside a clear plastic bag.

NIBBLING

⑤ 'Nibbling', or shaping, an individual tessera to a definite shape such as two small triangles from one square tessera, is achieved by placing the jaws of the nippers all the way along the diagonal.

Always try and keep hold of both halves of the tile as you cut it.

❻

❼

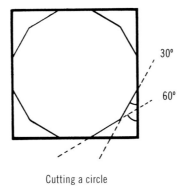

CUTTING A CIRCLE

⑥,⑦ A circle can be achieved by cutting each corner twice at 30 degrees and 60 degrees to the side edge. Place the jaws of the nippers right across the tile when you make these cuts. Don't worry if your circle is not perfectly circular, what we are creating here is a man-made piece of work; if you want perfect circles, buy them! (They are called beads!)

If you cut a 1 cm (⅜ in) square tessera in half you will notice that one half will stand up and the other one won't. This is because the unstable one has come from the edge of the tile and so only has a small base. Despite this fact, you may well find that in

some cases this is the only piece that will do. If that is the case, simply glue it down and prop it up with an unglued tessera until the glue dries.

Cutting a circle

CUTTING A MOSAIC 'EYE'

⑧ To make the iris, first cut a blue (or brown or green) tile into a circle. Then cut it in half and in half again, laying the quarter circles down on the table so that they still fit together. If any of the quarters shatter, start again. Next, nibble the centre out of each quarter circle. Glue the four pieces back down in their rightful place. Now cut a black tessera for the pupil. Make it small enough to fit inside the iris and glue it in place. To make the white of the eye, use the nippers the 'wrong' way round and cut a curved line (this may take several attempts!), and then cut around the curve to create crescent moon shapes. Repeat four times and glue in place around the iris. This completes the eye.

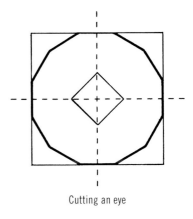

Cutting an eye

❽

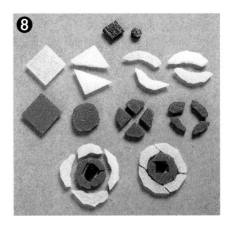

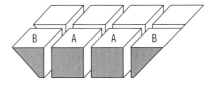

Cross-section of a tessera cut into eighths. The inner eighths (A) are more stable than the outer eighths (B) owing to their wider base.

MOSAIC TECHNIQUES

DIRECT MOSAIC

There are two basic methods of making a mosaic – direct and indirect. A direct mosaic is one where the tesserae are glued directly onto the surface that you are mosaicing. The tesserae are glued the right way up, the uppermost surface becoming the final surface of the finished mosaic. The advantage of working direct is that you can see what you are getting at all stages of the creative process. The resultant mosaic can be transported and exhibited and if you move house, you can take it with you. The disadvantage of direct mosaic is that the final surface is not completely flat and is therefore not suitable for floors or other circumstances where a flat surface is required, such as a table top or work surface.

A direct mosaic panel on medium density fibreboard (MDF) is only suitable for indoor use. If an external mosaic is required, then it is recommended that you work indirect (see opposite).

• **PREPARATION.** Before starting to lay tesserae, it is a good idea to cut up a handful of tiles and build up a small pool to choose from. If you place each colour on a separate, small piece of paper, then not only will you be able to work in each colour when you need it, but clearing away will also be made easier by simply inverting the paper, pouring the tesserae back into its jar.

It is often said that making a mosaic is like doing a jigsaw puzzle. This is a remark that is guaranteed to infuriate any self-respecting mosaic artist. Is painting someone's portrait in oils like painting by numbers? The fact is, that a jigsaw is a puzzle, with a pre-determined solution. No matter how good or bad you are at solving the puzzle, the end result will always be the same. This is certainly not true in mosaic where the result would never be the same, and making a mosaic definitely involves the creative process. That said, it is true that when you select a tessera from your pool of tesserae, you have to look for the correct shape which has the right angle to the line that you are trying to make. To help yourself, make the distance between the pool of tesserae on the paper and the mosaic as short as possible. I often place the paper on the mosaic, but you may feel that you need to see the entire piece at all times.

• **GLUING DOWN TESSERAE.** The glue dispenser is designed to release a small quantity of glue at a time, so only cut off the very tip of the nozzle.

If you are new to mosaic, it helps if you 'butter' each tessera individually until you become more experienced. As you become more confident, you can run a 'bead' of glue along the line that you are about to mosaic.

Be generous with the glue, but not to the extent that it squidges out over the top of the tesserae. The PVA is meant to hold the tesserae in position until you grout the finished mosaic, so

you need to ensure that there is still sufficient room for the grout to do its job, too. If the glue dispenser empties, you can top it up by decanting from a larger pot of glue.

Spaces between the tesserae are a necessary part of the mosaic. The spaces, or interstices, that they create when grouted create the flow or *andamento* of the finished mosaic. The grout when set, is very strong and will hold the tesserae in place, preventing any side to side movement. The size of the gap you leave between tesserae really depends on your personal style of working. I work very 'tight' and find it difficult to leave a decent gap. Sylvia's work is much more precise with neat spaces between each tesserae.

• **MOSAICING A STRAIGHT LINE OF TESSERAE.** Draw a straight line with a pencil and try and mosaic a line of tesserae along it. You will soon see that it is a bit like steering a car – if you are slightly out at the beginning you don't notice, but 100 yards further down the road and you are driving on the wrong side! ① Try and 'steer' along the line by choosing each successive tessera so that the angle between the line and the previous tessera is the same. If your attempt at a straight line was a success, it was due to the fact that the angles were correct. Indeed, if all the angles were 90 degrees, then you will not have experienced any difficulty; only when the angle varies, do you have to choose a tessera with the same angle in order to compensate and steer back on course.

It will soon become apparent that as well as the line you are working to, it is equally important to leave yourself a straight line for the next row of tesserae. Thus, like ploughing a field, you need to keep on track and try and think ahead. ② If a tessera looks good next to its neighbours but juts out below the bottom line, simply nibble it down to the same length. If you don't do this, you can correct things on the next row by placing a thinner tessera next to it, putting yourself back on course. If you don't compensate, you may well find matters getting progressively worse with each subsequent row.

• **MOSAICING A CURVED LINE OF TESSERAE.** The same is true when mosaicing a curved line – if you try to leave a right angle to the curve each time, then it all becomes much easier. Not surprisingly, what you end up with are a series of wedges that steer themselves around the curve ③.

INDIRECT MOSAIC

When you buy a sheet of mosaic tiles, you will see that the tiles are spaced apart on the backing paper, the gap allowing for the finished grouting when being used for swimming pools. The reverse of the tiles (the face not attached to the paper) are 'ribbed' to allow cement to be buttered to them to 'key' them so that they can be applied to the rendered wall. When dry, the backing paper can be soaked off and the tiles grouted. This is the basic principle of an indirect mosaic.

When a flat surface is required, such as a floor, a tabletop, a swimming pool or a work surface, the mosaic needs to be made indirect. An indirect mosaic is one where the tesserae (vitreous, smalti, or whatever material you are using) have been laid face down onto paper using a water-soluble adhesive. Because the surface of the paper is flat, the resultant surface of the mosaic will also be flat. Working indirect also means that if working on, say, a swimming pool, the mosaic artist can work in their studio instead of having to travel to be 'on site'. If you wish, you can cement the papered mosaic to a board and then stick it to a wall (see the Frog Splashback on pages 206-209).

When set into cement or concrete, an indirect mosaic is suitable for external use and will last not only a lifetime, but if the Roman mosaics are anything to go by, for centuries to come.

Incidentally, there is much debate as to whether the Romans worked indirect or direct. In my opinion, the very reason why Roman mosaics were designed around 'emblemata' (circular pictures in the centre of a larger area containing a background and border) is precisely so that the master mosaicist could work comfortably in a studio on the indirect insertion, whilst the poor apprentices battled it out on their hands and knees working in the direct method on site.

• **WAXING A BOARD FOR AN INDIRECT MOSAIC.** I once had the embarrassing experience of delivering

a series of mosaics half way across the country only to find that I couldn't remove the paper from the board! Because I had worked on them slowly over a period of time, the wallpaper paste had soaked through the stretched paper and adhered to the board. There was no alternative but to return home and spend the following week transferring the mosaic, piece-by-

---

HELPFUL HINTS WHEN WORKING DIRECT

• Use 12 mm (½ in) plywood for boards up to 60 cm (2 ft) square, 2 cm (¾ in) if larger. Better still, use Medite MDF which is the most expensive brand because it contains the highest percentage of resin and therefore doesn't warp in normal conditions. I use 16 mm (⅝ in) MDF because it allows one to frame the mosaic with 2 cm (¾ in) long vitreous tiles.

• Make sure that the tesserae are placed with their flat side uppermost, particularly when nibbled to less than 1 cm (⅜ in) square. If you are using ceramic Cinca tesserae then this is not a problem as both sides are flat. You can use this fact to your advantage and flip over the shapes, if necessary, in order to fit them in.

HELPFUL HINTS WHEN WORKING INDIRECT

• If the mosaic is a large one and will need to be cut into pieces, draw a series of horizontal and vertical wavy lines on the back of the paper. These will later act as registration marks.

• Always use a water-soluble glue; wallpaper paste is ideal.

• Remember to place the tesserae flat side down, if using a mirror this means silver side up. When placing the tesserae, allow slightly larger interstices between them to allow for paper shrinkage. If you need to cut the mosaic into sections, remember to allow a big enough gap to drive a scalpel through the paper between the tesserae.

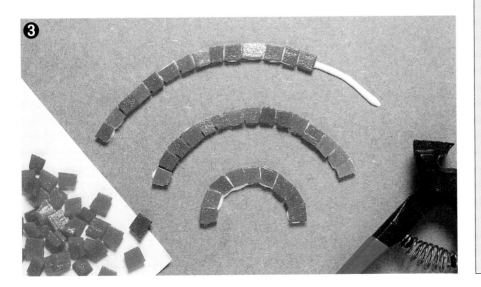

❸

piece, to a board which had had beeswax rubbed into the area where the mosaic was to go. Needless to say, I now only use waxed boards.

To wax a board, draw a line 5 cm (2 in) all around from the edge of the board. Rub beeswax into this internal area (you can make do with rubbing a candle over it if you wish). Only wax the 'mosaic image' area; the surround needs to be kept wax-free so that the gummed paper tape will stick to it. You are now ready to stretch your paper.

• **STRETCHING A SHEET OF PAPER**
The sort of paper that is ideal for stretching is the thick brown craft paper sold in stationer's shops. The paper has a smooth side and a ribbed side. Although it is largely a matter of choice, I prefer to lay the ribbed side of the wrapping paper uppermost so that the tesserae 'key' to the paper better.

Cut the paper 2.5 cm (1 in) larger all around than the waxed mosaic area that you are about to work (see Roman Paving Slab on pages 198-201). Then tear off four lengths of 5 cm (2 in) wide gummed paper strips from a roll that can also be purchased from your local stationery supplier.

Wet the wrapping paper by running it through a bath of cold water. Then lay it down on the waxed board and hold in place while it dries out with the gummed paper strips that have also been wetted. As the paper dries, it will shrink and the end result will be that the paper is stretched taught and held down on the waxed mosaic board which can then be reused indefinitely.

• **GLUING DOWN TESSERAE FOR AN INDIRECT MOSAIC.** Any water-soluble glue or gum can be used (see page 156).
I recommend wallpaper paste as it is cheap and you can mix it to the quantity and viscosity that you prefer. Use the glue sparingly as it only needs to act as a temporary fixing. Too much glue will make the brown paper buckle, but if you have stretched it properly then the buckling will not be too great. In any case, it will shrink back again, but make sure that your tesserae have not been laid too close together otherwise they will get 'scrunched up' when the glue dries and

HINTS ABOUT DESIGN AND CHOOSING COLOURS

• Keep your design simple and uncluttered. Make sure that you have a strong tonal contrast between the subject and its background so that the subject stands out visually, even from a distance. Be kind to your mistakes. If you get it wrong, you will get it right next time.

• Remember that tonal contrast between the subject and the background is of vital importance. If the two are tonally similar, then from a distance the subject will disappear.

• It is a good idea to limit the colour palette, at least until you are an experienced mosaicist. One or two carefully chosen colours are usually more effective than a whole spectrum.

• Don't be frightened of having plain areas of mosaic. For example, look at the Frog Splashback on pages 206-209. The plain area is necessary to stress the fact that the frog is swimming. On your initial design, plain areas look boring, but when mosaiced they become a necessary part of the overall piece, emphasizing that this is a mosaic that we are looking at. If the entire picture surface is busy, this effect is lessened somewhat.

• If in doubt, simplify. Consider the silhouette of your subject, say, a gecko. If it works as a silhouette, then it will certainly work when it is 'filled in'. If the silhouette is messy and incongruous, the finished piece may not look good either. This is why creatures such as fish, geckoes or butterflies, which have clear outlines, are so popular with mosaic artists.

• Think in terms of whether your colours need to be 'warm' or 'cool'. Basically, a warm colour is one that contains red, while a cool colour is one that contains blue. Thus purple, which is a mixture of red and blue, can be warm or cool depending on whether there is a predominance of red or blue. I find that this can help enormously when I am having trouble choosing a colour, say for a background. If I want the overall effect to be warm I can choose, say, a caramel or a soft pink. If cool, then a pastel blue or green may be more appropriate.

the paper re-stretches.
GROUTING
Anyone who has ever had the pleasure of mixing cement will have no trouble grouting.

Buy the finest grout available. Powdered grout is available in grey, white, ivory and brown. It is also available in a variety of colours 'ready mixed' which is fine, but has a shorter shelf life. This can be greatly improved by cutting out a circular piece of paper and laying it on the surface of the grout that is left in the pot to prevent the air from getting to it and drying out.

Always follow the health and safety instructions on the packet. If you are using powdered grout, you can colour it at the 'dry' stage by adding coloured powder paints and/or up to 50 per cent fine sand. I recommend that you stick to plain grey grout nine times out of ten. The grout delineates the tesserae and if it is brightly coloured, it can distract or even overpower the effect of the mosaic. I occasionally use brown grout if the overall colour of the mosaic is 'warm' and brown seems to be the harmonious choice. Although I don't often use brightly coloured grouts, I have seen them used to excellent dramatic effect, especially in jazzy, abstract mosaics.

To mix the grout, wear rubber gloves and make a 'volcano' by pouring out the grout onto a flat piece of scrap wood (hardboard is ideal) and make a 'well' in the centre. Gradually add water to the well and mix thoroughly with a small hand trowel. The mixed grout should be of a 'mud pie' consistency – if it is too stiff, it won't flow into the gaps, if it is too wet it will wash out of the gaps when you clean it off.

Starting on the vertical edges, spread the grout with a 'squeegee' or tile grout spreader. Then grout the top surface of the mosaic, running the grout spreader across the surface in all directions in order to fill the gaps thoroughly.

Wipe off the excess grout from the sides and top surface using a damp cloth. Sometimes in a direct mosaic, a few of the tesserae are set lower than the rest and so become submerged by grout. Once grouted, reveal any such tesserae using a penknife or other suitable tool. Take some trouble at this stage; it is much harder to remove grout once it has set.

The drying of the grout is a chemical process and takes about 24 hours. There is nothing to be gained by placing the mosaic in the hot sun to speed up the drying time.

You will notice that the finished mosaic lacks some of the shine it had before it was grouted. This is partially due to an unavoidable scum of grout remaining on the surface. In a couple of days, when the grout has set, give the mosaic a scrub with a liquid floor cleaner using an abrasive sponge pad.

If you are making a direct mosaic plaque, screw in 'D' rings or mirror plates, available from your local ironmongers, and hang it in a suitable place – somewhere that allows the light to play on the surface.

WHERE TO BEGIN

To transfer a design from an existing template or illustration, place carbon paper, ink-side down onto the surface you are about to mosaic. Trace off your chosen design onto tracing paper and place it on the carbon paper. Firmly trace over the design with a sharp pencil to transfer it (see also page 218).

If you are a beginner working on a project to, say, mosaic a straightforward plaque such as the Gecko on pages 184-187, the temptation is to start on the Gecko's face. In fact, there are three good reasons why it is best to start on the border first.

First of all, you will get useful practice at cutting the tiles into tesserae. If a tile accidentally cuts at an angle that is not straight, you can compensate by cutting another to match this angle.

Mosaicing straight lines. Compensate for ill-cut tesserae by cutting other tesserae with angles to match.

Secondly, when the time comes to grout the finished piece, it is the edge tesserae that take the biggest knocks with the grout spreader. If any tesserae are going to fall off, it is invariably these ones. Those in the middle have their neighbours to support them, the edge ones don't. So if you have mosaiced the edge first, you will be certain that the glue has well and truly set and that these tesserae are firmly in place.

And lastly, before mosaicing the edge tiles, the work surface has to be completely clean. If there are any glass shards under the board from where you have been cutting, the board will not rest flat. If you begin to mosaic the edge first, before you have done any cutting at all, there is no need to clear and clean the work surface, it is ready to make a start. Remember to place a sheet of paper or newspaper underneath the MDF panel to prevent it from sticking to the work surface.

MOSAICING THE IMAGE

Having mosaiced the border, you are now ready to start on the image itself. You will soon find that it is a lot easier to mosaic next to tesserae that have already set. So, if you are mosaicing, say, an eye, it is a good idea to initially place the pupil in position and let it set for half an hour or so (if you are using PVA). When you later add the iris, there is no possibility of the pupil being disturbed. This is only necessary on very precise areas such as facial features, where you want to capture a specific expression and the exact placing of a single tessera can be vital.

Always mosaic the object that is closest to you in visual terms. This is because, however hard you try, the mosaiced line will never precisely follow your pencil line. Imagine you are mosaicing a fish swimming through water. If you worked the *opus vermiculatum* (see right) of the background first, this would dictate the outline of the fish, which is obviously more important. Thus, if a fish is swimming through seaweed, for example, the seaweed needs to be worked on first, then the fish, and finally the watery background.

GLOSSARY OF MOSAIC TERMS

Andamento The generic word to describe the general 'flow' of the mosaic.
Interstices The spaces between the *tesserae*.
Opus musivum See below.
Opus regulatum A Roman mosaic technique whereby regular, square tesserae are applied in straight rows. The result is like a 'brick wall' pattern and was frequently used to fill expanses of background.
Opus sectile When a part of the mosaic, such as a head, consists of only one part then this part is known as *opus sectile*. If the whole area of the mosaic is covered in this way the resulting effect is more akin to stained glass or marquetry.
Opus tessellatum A Roman mosaic technique whereby regular, square *tesserae* are applied in a rectilinear arrangement. The resulting uniform 'grid' design was most frequently used to fill expanses of background. You would reasonably expect this to be the most common *opus* for background work, but in fact, because the tesserae are irregular, the rows rarely meet up on two axis. Thus *Opus regulatum* is the most common *opus* used for background work.
Opus vermiculatum A Roman mosaic technique whereby regular, square *tesserae* are applied in a row around the main mosaic motif to create a halo effect and emphasize the setting lines of the design. *Vermis* is the Latin word for worm (as in vermicelli!), so you can think of this as the 'worm' of *tesserae* that outline the main figure(s) (see 'White Flamingo' mosaic on page 168).

If the *opus vermiculatum* is continued outwards to fill a larger area then this area becomes **Opus musivum**, such as in the background of the Gecko Plaque on page 184. This is the most rhythmic and lyrical of all the *opus* and literally it means 'pertaining to the Muses'.
Tesserae 'Tessera' is a Roman word meaning cube (pl. *tesserae*). These cubes are the basic building blocks of mosaic. The term embraces diverse materials, including marble, ceramic, glass and pebbles.

GALLERY

The King's Head

This was Kim's first attempt at mosaic, made when she came on one of my courses. The human face, though so familiar to us all, is surely one of the most challenging subjects to achieve successfully in mosaic. Skin tones are particularly difficult, given that the limited range of colours means that one's palette is so restricted. The fact that Kim succeeded first time, and so perfectly, is a testament to her great artistic ability. The gold smalti, though used sparingly, lifts the whole piece and leaves us in no doubt that it is a king that we are looking at. The wonderful stylization owes much to the Byzantine mosaics which Kim saw in the church of St Sophia in Salonika, northern Greece.

Designer and maker: Kim Williams
Size: 23 cm (9 in) square
Method: Direct
Medium: Vitreous glass and gold smalti

Roman Paving Slab

This simple but effective paving slab is derived from a Roman design. The diamond in the middle, with its *opus regulatum* flowing at 45 degrees to the rest of the mosaic, draws one's attention to the centre of the slab. This is an ideal design to repeat and make up as a chequerboard, reversing the black and white areas for each alternate square. Or if you wanted to make a herb garden, you could leave each alternate square for earth, and plant with a different herb. Sometimes on Roman floors, different chequerboard designs are themselves arranged in a chequerboard pattern.

Designer and maker: Martin Cheek
Size: 25 cm (10 in) square
Method: Indirect
Medium: Vitreous glass

Chess Board

I am a keen chess player. I also collect and enjoy making my own chess sets and boards. The subtlety of marble is such that even a very basic design like this has its own natural beauty. In fact, as any chess player will tell you, a busy design is far too distracting if the grey matter is to do its work properly.

In this case, it is essential to make the mosaic indirect if you want to play on it, otherwise the pieces won't be able to stand up. Incidentally, the way to calculate if you have the right size pieces for the board is to lay the king on its side across the squares. The king's height should measure exactly two squares long.

Designer and maker: Martin Cheek
Size: 26.5 cm (10⅜ in) square
Method: Indirect
Medium: Marble

Abstract Mirror

This mirror is terribly simple in design but very cheerful. It would liven up any bathroom. The soft pastel greys are visually pushed back, allowing the red, orange and blue tesserae to stand out. White grout was used in this case, to keep the overall effect light.

Designer and maker: Kim Williams
Size: 26.5 cm (10⅜ in) square
Method: Direct
Medium: Vitreous glass

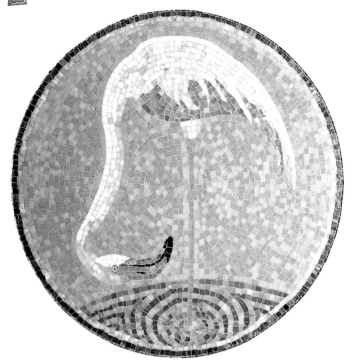

White Flamingo

The design for this mosaic was inspired by a visit to the zoo. On seeing the flamingo, my son remarked, 'Daddy – look at that bird sitting on a stick!'. Back home, I immediately drew the flamingo more or less as he appears here in the mosaic. The concentric circles of mosaic echo the ripples we saw on the surface of his pool.

Designer and maker: Martin Cheek
Size: 66 cm (26 in) diameter
Method: Direct   Medium: Vitreous glass

Pink Flamingo

This plaque was commissioned as a companion piece to the White Flamingo and they now hang in coy, flirtatious splendour on the wall of a formal dining room in a city townhouse. I felt that the original flamingo was a male and so tried to make this one female and sufficiently different while at the same time obviously part of a pair.
This pair of flamingoes is a good example of how the *opus vermiculatum* 'cleans up' the edge of a subject (in this case, the flamingo), making a clean line and allowing the *opus* of the background (here, the water) to 'crash' into it rather than into the bird.

Designer and maker: Martin Cheek
Size: 66 cm (26 in) diameter
Method: Direct   Medium: Vitreous glass

Tumbling Clown

This entire design is based on the shape of a cross – from the blue and gold border to the shape of the subject's spread limbs. The clown was drawn from life, inspired by a visit I made to the Moscow State Circus, which had a rather old-fashioned, 1950s' feel to it. The central X of the figure dictated the line of action of the background which radiates out from it, while the zig-zag border is very much part of the design and helps to emphasize the overall joviality of the piece.

Designer and maker: Martin Cheek
Size: 42.5 cm (17 in) square
Method: Direct
Medium: Vitreous glass, gold smalti
and natural Jasper stones

Carrion Crow

This crow is one of a pair of marble paving slabs. I chose this particular bird as a subject because I wanted to use a large area of black granite which contains tiny flecks of sparkling mineral. They catch the light in much the same way as the sheen on the feathers of the real bird sometimes does. I like the way such a simple design with its large, 'plain' areas allows the subtle changes in the natural stone to give the work its intrinsic beauty.

Designer and maker: Martin Cheek
Size: 46 cm (18 in) square
Method: Indirect
Medium: Marble and granite

Fire Salamander

The design for this paving slab is based on a live creature which Thomas found in a sewerage tank while on holiday in the Ardèche in southern France. Its jet black body had flaming 'Van Gogh yellow' patches and the pose shown here is one he kept for hours on end as he basked in the sun. I left the background deliberately plain and muted to show off the creature's bold colouring.

Designer and maker: Martin Cheek
Size: 46 cm (18 in) square
Method: Indirect   Medium: Marble

Winged Horse

This design has a charming, deliberately naive and slightly airy quality about it, which is not surprising, as it was inspired by a child's drawing. The purple and gold border lend a rich quality to the piece and the positioning of the gold smalti 'dots' was crucial to that overall effect.

I like the challenge of taking a simple drawing, executed in about a minute, and trying to keep that immediacy and spontaneity, even though it takes three days to make as a mosaic.

Designer and maker: Martin Cheek
Size: 42.5 cm (17 in) square
Method: Direct
Medium: Vitreous glass and gold smalti

169

Palm Tree Pot

This colourful pot proves the point of how, when viewed from a distance, the different coloured tesserae fuse together and the mosaic can appear to come alive – or is it just a mirage?!

Designer and maker: Liz Sims
Size: 12.5 cm (5 in) high
Method: Direct
Medium: Vitreous glass

Button Box

This piece is a lively alternative to the Bead Box (see pages 182-183). Once again, the essential beauty of the buttons have been allowed to dominate the design. As with the bead box, if the entire box had been covered in buttons the finished effect would be overwhelming. So often it proves to be the case that 'less is more', particularly in the case of a mosaic, where the very nature of making an image from many small parts creates a rich, busy result. Limiting the palette, or in this case, the number of buttons, helps to combat this.

Designer and maker: Paul Hazelton
Size: 14.5 x 14.5 x 12.5 cm (5¾ x 5¾ x 5 in)
Method: Direct
Medium: Buttons and vitreous glass

Crocodile and Sausages

This mixed-media mosaic was made to amuse my son, Thomas. Even as a small baby he loved to watch our friend Martin Bridle perform his Punch and Judy show. The idea of sculpting and Raku-firing a string of sausages as a border struck me as amusing. To make the sausages sing out, I chose the dark purple background you can see, but in doing so I lost the definition of the croc's back because it is the same tone as the purple background. If I were to re-make this piece I would choose a soft, pastel green for the background.

Designer and maker: Martin Cheek
Size: 44.5 x 61.5 cm (17½ x 24 in)
Method: Direct
Medium: Vitreous glass and
sculpted Raku tile sausages

Resting Plaice

I don't often use the ceramic Cinca tiles in my mosaics, but I wanted to include one in the book, because I do like them in other people's work. Originally, I started with a blue ceramic background, but I remembered that flat fish are usually to be found lying on the sea bed as opposed to swimming through the water. The natural patina on the background tiles is a gift as it adds a sandy quality to the piece. I chose a plaice because I love the way that their orange spots sing out, so I used the shiny orange vitreous glass tiles to achieve this effect. The caramel glass tesserae peppering the background were added to echo the orange spots of the plaice itself.

Designer and maker: Martin Cheek
Size: 30.5 x 21.5 cm (12 x 8½ in)
Method: Direct
Medium: Ceramic Cinca and vitreous glass

Cat Firescreen

Kim Williams is a mosaic artist with a very strong sense of colour and design. Placing a cat on a mat in front of a roaring fire is a very witty idea for this firescreen. The colourful vitreous flames shine out because they are glass, in contrast to the non-reflective surface of the ceramic Cinca tiles which were used for the tabby.

Designer and maker: Kim Williams   Size: 51 x 71 cm (20 x 28 in)
Method: Direct   Medium: Ceramic Cinca and vitreous glass

Whiting Table

The starting point for this design was the way that, as part of their window displays, traditional fishmongers used to place the tail of whole round fish in their mouths, ready for the pot.

It was important to mosaic the dark line of the whiting's back neatly, as this line gives the piece its circular *andamento*. Long, thin tesserae were used to mosaic the delicate fins. Pieces of broken mirror juxtaposed with silver smalti, placed both right (silver) side and wrong (blue) side uppermost, were used to 'pepper' the background and give it sparkle.

Designer and maker: Martin Cheek
Size: 50.5 cm (20 in) diameter
Method: Direct
Medium: Vitreous glass, silver smalti and
broken mirror with Raku tile eye

Peacock Butterfly

Whenever we need inspiration for good colour combinations, we can do no better than to turn to Nature and there are few more beautiful sights than the colours of butterflies. As its name suggests, the Peacock is the most multi-coloured of all butterflies and it was therefore a challenge to try to create it in mosaic. Even though my butterfly is many times bigger than an actual one, it was still very difficult to get the smalti intricate enough. If you try to paint a Peacock butterfly from life, you will notice that the colours seem to be different each time you look at them (it is remarkable to think that it is powder that makes up this wonderful effect) – purples transform to blues and then to greens, and, of course, the same is true when you try to mosaic one. Although I am still unhappy with the result, I believe that unless we strive to achieve perfection we will never even approach it.

Designer and maker: Martin Cheek
Size: 47 x 37 cm (18½ x 14½ in)
Method: Direct
Medium: Vitreous glass, smalti and broken mirror

Indian Elephant

Sylvia was already a very accomplished mosaic artist before she came on one of my courses. I like to fire my own tiles and incorporate them into my mosaics. This idea appealed to Sylvia very much so she fired the intricate pattern of the elephant's blanket onto a pre-shaped tile. The colours in interior designer Jane Churchill's fabric 'Indian Summer' inspired those of this piece.

Designer and maker: Sylvia Bell
Size:50.5 cm (20 in) square
Method: Direct
Medium: Ceramic Cinca with a Raku tile

Dancing Octopus

'I marvel at thee, Octopus, if I were thou, I'd call me us'. OGDEN NASH

This short poem by Ogden Nash was the inspiration for this early work. I think that this piece shows that prior to being a mosaic artist, I was a puppet animator and even now, character and movement play a very important part in my work. In this piece I wanted to try to capture the way that the octopus seems to dance elegantly through the water. The design is also tipping a knowing wink to the Minoans and Mycaenaens, who loved to show similarly jolly octopuses on their ceramic pots.

Designer and maker: Martin Cheek
Size: 46 x 58 cm (35½ x 16 in)
Method: Direct   Medium: Vitreous glass

Masticating Goat

Sylvia's goat is inspired by a Roman mosaic which she saw in the Bardo Museum in Tunis. The long ringlets of hair were especially appealing to Sylvia's sense of mosaic design. The few fronds of grass serve to echo the hairy quality of the goat's fleece.

Designer and maker: Sylvia Bell
Size: 61 x 51 cm (24 x 20 in)
Method: Direct
Medium: Ceramic Cinca and vitreous glass

TRIVET

Liz Sims is a young mosaic artist with a strong sense for simple pattern and colour. Geometric designs such as this lend themselves very well to mosaic. The strong contrast between black and white set off by the mid-tone brown make this a very striking mosaic. Although simple, it is very important to be as neat as possible when making this sort of geometric mosaic. For this reason this trivet is an ideal practice piece.

Our trivet had a recessed top meant to hold a tile 5 mm (¼ in) thick. This means that the depth is 2 mm (¹⁄₁₆ in) deeper than the 3 mm (⅛ in) thick Cinca ceramic tiles. To overcome this we cut out a piece of 2 mm (¹⁄₁₆ in) thick skim ply the size of the top and glued it in position with fast setting two-part epoxy resin to make up the difference. The finished mosaic will now be flush with the edges of the trivet.

SIZE: 15 CM (6 IN) SQUARE
DESIGNER AND MAKER: LIZ SIMS

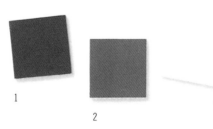

1 black (40 tiles)
2 brown (32 tiles)
3 white (180 tiles)

1 Transfer the design onto the skim ply as described on page 218. Cut a brown tile into quarters and glue one of the four tesserae in the centre of the design on the skim ply. Cut up some black tiles into square tesserae and mosaic the square border around the centre. Try to keep the tesserae the same size, as this will make the finished mosaic look neater. Allow small gaps of about 1 mm (¹⁄₁₆ in) between the tesserae; these will be filled when the mosaic is grouted and make the whole mosaic stronger.

2 Fill in the area between the brown and black tesserae with white ones. Continue to work outwards by mosaicing the next brown border, filling in the triangular corner gaps with white tesserae nibbled diagonally in half to form small triangles. The nibbling process may take a number of attempts before you get neat triangles. Don't worry, this is perfectly normal.

3 Continue working outwards, revolving the trivet as you work. Mosaic each border in turn. Try to achieve straight lines as you work. Although this design is simple, the lines need to be neat and straight.

4 Finally, fill in the four remaining triangles with white tesserae. Wait for three hours for the glue to dry, then grout and clean in the normal way. Allow to dry for at least two days before cleaning off the surface scum with the liquid floor cleaner and abrasive pad.

FINGERPLATES

To have mosaics around the home is a real treat, but owing to their richness, too many can easily overpower a room. This does not necessarily have to be the case. The understated design for this project is more suggestive than descriptive and the subtle colour scheme makes for an harmonious, quietly pleasing result and makes an ideal gift. We have mosaiced the second fingerplate in a slightly different colour scheme, so that you can see what a difference a subtle change makes.

If you wish, you can ignore the screws and simply glue the fingerplate to the door with quick-setting epoxy resin. Use masking tape to keep it in place while the glue sets.

SIZE 30 x 7.5 CM (12 x 3 IN)
DESIGNER AND MAKER:
REBECCA DRISCOLL

YOU WILL NEED

Sheet of skim ply 30 cm (12 in) square x 2 mm (1/16 in) thick	Sheets of newspaper
	Safety spectacles
Sheets of A4 carbon paper	Face mask
Template (page 218)	Rubber gloves
Sharp pencil	450 g (1 lb) of powdered grout
Tracing paper	
Jeweller's saw	Bowl of water
Craft knife	Mixing board for the grout
Metal ruler	Trowel
Drill	Plastic grout spreader
3 mm (1/8 in) drill bit	Cleaning cloth
Vitreous glass tiles as shown right	Liquid floor cleaner
	Abrasive cleaning pad
Mosaic nippers	Eight 2 cm (3/4 in) screws
125 ml (4 fl oz) wood glue in a dispenser	

1 emerald vein (4 tiles)
2 mauve (6 tiles)
3 dark green (10 tiles)
4 mint green (12 tiles)
5 purple (3 tiles)
6 bright green (12 tiles)
7 candy pink (3 tiles)
8 soft pink (80 tiles)
9 pink vein (3 tiles)
10 green (10 tiles)
11 dark pink vein (2 tiles)
12 green vein (4 tiles)

176

1 Transfer the design onto the skim ply as described on page 218. Cut out the fingerplate using the jeweller's saw for the curves; on the straight sides you will be able to manage with a craft knife and metal ruler. In each corner, drill a small hole 3 mm (⅛ in) diameter to accommodate the screws. Mosaic the main leaf, trying to get a smooth, clean, flowing line for the leading edge. Continue to mosaic the remaining green areas.

2 When you have finished the floral motif, lay a line of the soft background pink tesserae right the way along the edge of the fingerplate.

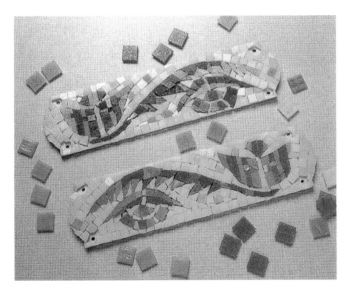

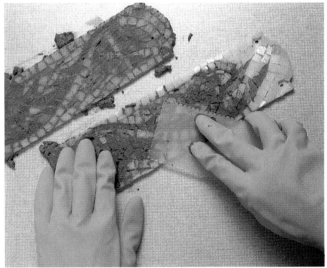

3 Fill in the background. Pepper the soft pink with the occasional mauve tessera to add a little texture. Once you have finished, leave the mosaic to dry for at least three hours, or until the glue becomes clear.

4 Then grout in the normal way. Allow to dry for at least two days before cleaning off the surface scum with the liquid floor cleaner and abrasive pad. When completed, screw or glue the fingerplate to a door.

SIMPLE MIRROR

An easy project for beginners, this mirror will liven up any bathroom. It also provides worthwhile practice at cutting and laying mosaic tesserae. You can either mosaic around the mirror or fit it in at the end when you grout the finished piece, as shown here.

The blue, green and white tiles which have been chosen here will harmonize with almost any bathroom decor, but do not feel that you have to stick to this colour scheme. Simply choose a range of colours that will match your own bathroom.

DESIGNER AND MAKER: SYLVIA BELL
42.5 CM (16½ IN) SQUARE

YOU WILL NEED

Pencil

Ruler

15 mm (⅝ in) thick MDF board measuring 42.5 cm (16½ in) square

Vitreous glass and gold-leafed tiles as shown right

Mosaic nippers

Safety spectacles

Large tweezers

Clear PVA wood adhesive

White grout

Trowel

Bowl of water

Rubber gloves

Grout spreader

Household cleanser

Cloths

Abrasive sponge

Pair of 'D' rings or mirror plates and screws

1	dark green (52 tiles)
2	white (143 tiles)
3	pale blue (44 tiles)
4	gold-leafed (4 tiles)
5	copper-veined dark blue (44 tiles)

1 Draw diagonals from corner to corner across the board to find the centre and mark out the area where the mirror will fit. Place the board on a sheet of scrap paper or newspaper and organize your tiles. Cut triangular tesserae from the white vitreous glass. Run a bead of glue along one side of the board and mosaic the edge with uncut white tiles. Continue around the four edges of the board.

2 Starting with the corners, lay out the border tiles on top of the board, keeping to a strictly geometric pattern and making sure the gold-leafed tiles are correctly placed at the corners.

3 First glue down the coloured tiles, buttering the back of each one carefully and placing it symmetrically in position. Work your way around the frame, mosaicing the whole tiles. Then begin filling in the outer and inner borders with the white triangular tesserae.

4 Continue filling in the borders until the design is complete. You may like to use large tweezers to tweak the tesserae gently into position along the inner border.

5 Use wood glue to fix the mirror in the centre of the design. When set (up to three hours), mix up the grout and water and carefully grout the mosaic area and between the mirror and the mosaic, taking extra care around the edges. Leave to dry for two days and then clean off and polish the mosaic using the household cleaner and water. Fix 'D' rings or mirror plates to the back of the board and hang on your bathroom wall.

SHELL DOOR NUMBER

I think that shell mosaics can look very tacky if the whole area is encrusted with tiny sea molluscs, all vying for attention. My solution here is to minimize the use of the shells, creating a hard sand bed for them to sit in. Sand is mixed with PVA, and as the PVA goes clear when dry, the end result looks like sand alone. Sharp sand has a beautiful, soft white colour. It is important that you do not use sand taken straight from the beach, as the salt content is corrosive which affects the finished mosaic.

At first glance, the procedure opposite looks complicated but, in fact, this is the quickest and easiest project in the book. Once you have assembled your materials, it should be possible to make the whole piece in half a day. If your house number runs into three digits, you may wish to make the plaque into an ellipse instead of the circle shown (see the variation shown opposite).

SIZE: 22 CM (8½ IN) DIAMETER
DESIGNER AND MAKER: MARTIN CHEEK
VARIATION: PAUL HAZELTON

YOU WILL NEED

15 mm (⅝ in) thick MDF measuring 40 x 20 cm (16 x 8 in)	Cocktail stick
	Sheets of newspaper
Large compass or a plate 22 cm (9 in) diameter	Craft knife
	Two-part, slow-setting epoxy resin
Electric jigsaw	Small plastic mixing bowl
1 m (1 yd) of 20 mm (¾ in) thick yachtsman's rope (available from ship's chandlers)	Sharp sand
	One 'D' ring with screws
	Assortment of small sea shells as shown right
Pencil	
Two-part, fast-setting epoxy resin	33 large periwinkles
	37 small periwinkles
Piece of card measuring about 15 x 10 cm (6 x 4 in)	18 'bleeding teeth'
Lollipop stick or modelling tool	1 starfish

180

1 Draw a circle 22 cm (8½ in) diameter using a compass or a plate for a template. Cut this disc out with a jigsaw. Take the rope and run it around the outside edge of the disc and tie a half knot at the bottom of the disc, as shown. Draw around the two crescents made by the knot then untie and remove the rope and cut out these arcs. Replace the rope as before. It should now fit snugly around the MDF disc.

2 In a well-ventilated room, mix up the fast-setting epoxy resin by squirting out equal amounts onto the piece of card. Work on the reverse side of the rope and MDF disc (one side may look more pleasing than the other so choose that one as the top). Place it on a sheet of paper to protect your work surface and check that the two ends of the rope are sticking out equally from the disc. Then, using the modelling tool, run the epoxy resin into the gap between the disc and the rope. Leave to set (15 minutes).

VARIATION
Paul Hazelton's alternative design, below, shows how to adapt to an elliptical base. Paul has chosen to omit the rope and simply coat the edges of the MDF with sand and glue. Larger shells have been incorporated into the design to give a bigger, bolder finished effect.

3 Remove the backing paper and, using a scalpel, cut off any hardened glue that has dribbled through the gap. Now mix up the slow-setting epoxy resin by squirting out equal amounts into the small mixing bowl. Mix together the two parts thoroughly and then slowly add the sharp sand. Spread an even layer of the sand and resin mix onto the board, trying to get it as even as possible.

4 Divide the periwinkles into two piles, large and small. Place a row of the larger periwinkles around the rim of the disc. It is best if you can be assertive in the positioning of the shells and place them firmly into the sand and resin bed and then leave them. However, if you need to, you can use the cocktail stick to finely tweak the shells into place.

Run a second row of smaller periwinkles inside the outer one. Then, with your modelling tool, mark out your house number (I live at Number 21) and carefully form the numbers with the 'bleeding teeth'. I have placed a starfish at the bottom to add a little colour. Finally, fix the 'D' ring to the back of the board and hang the mosaic on your front door or wall.

BEAD BOX

Beads have their own natural beauty and so I thought it best to not completely encrust the box with them, but rather to use them sparingly. However, this makes for a 'knobbly effect', so to compromise I incorporated ordinary vitreous mosaic tiles to meet them half way. The beads are very rich in colour so it is important that the vitreous should be limited. I have chosen only two colours: a dark blue and Sorrento blue which has a metallic veining running through it that echoes the stripes of the beads and sets them off.

Grouting would have been possible, but it seemed somehow inappropriate and would have added unnecessary weight to the box. Instead, we painted the box before gluing down any tesserae so that the areas between would look harmonious. The simple addition of some gold and silver wax gilt, dry brushed onto the surface, complements the sparkle of the beads.

SIZE: 9 X 9 X 9.5 CM (3½ X 3½ X 3¾ IN)
DESIGNER: MARTIN CHEEK   MAKER: SYLVIA BELL

YOU WILL NEED

Mosaic nippers
Beads and vitreous glass tiles as shown right
MDF box 9 x 9 x 9.5 cm (3½ x 3½ x 3¾ in) (see Suppliers)
500 ml (1 pint) pot of white, quick-drying wood primer
Paintbrush
250 ml (9 fl oz) pot of sailor blue high gloss paint suitable for wood and metal (toy paint)
Jar of white spirit
Small pot each of gold and silver non-tarnishing wax gilt
Cloth
125 ml (4 fl oz) wood adhesive in a dispenser
Safety spectacles
Face mask

1-4 various beads
5   Sorrento blue (25 tiles)
6   dark blue (6 tiles)

1 Using the mosaic nippers, break a few of the beads in half. If some shatter, keep the fragments, they too can be used. Play with the beads, arranging them on the lid of the box and use vitreous glass tesserae to help set them off. When you are happy with the result, place the beads and tesserae one by one to one side, keeping the pattern that you have made.

2 Coat the box with white primer and then leave to dry as instructed on the pot. As well as priming the wood, the white colour will give a greater luminosity to the top coat. If the white looks patchy when dry, give the box a second coat of primer and leave it to dry again.

Paint the box with a coat of the sailor blue paint and leave to dry as instructed. Once again, if the finished blue looks patchy when dry, and not very smooth, give the box a second coat and leave to dry. Finally, sparingly apply some of the gold and silver paints with a dry brush and then rub it into the top surface with the cloth until you feel satisfied with the effect.

3 Replace the beads and glass tesserae as before, but this time butter each piece with PVA as you position it.

It is important to use sufficient glue to hold the beads and tesserae, but be careful not to use too much or it will squidge out from underneath them and onto the painted areas between. Remember that the finished mosaic is not going to be grouted this time so any excess glue will show.

4 When you have finished the top of the box, put it to one side and start on the sides. Don't rush it. It is advisable to allow each side to dry thoroughly for an hour or so before turning the box round to mosaic the adjacent side.

5 In the areas where you know you are going to put glass tesserae, you can, if you wish, run a bead of glue onto the box. Continue in this way until you have mosaiced all four sides. Leave to dry for three hours. Fill the bead box with the remaining beads and replace the lid. Your bead box is now finished and ready to use.

GECKO PLAQUE

In hot countries, it is believed that there is a gecko in every happy home and it is regarded as a symbol of good fortune. In Malaysia, for example, where 'chic chic' means 'good luck', it is nicknamed chee cha.

Because a lizard's scaly body looks a bit like a mosaic anyway, they are particularly suitable for this art form. The sensuous movement within their bodies is very appealing and a delight to try and capture. This modern mosaic is tipping a wink at the Romans, who also loved to include lizards in their mosaics.

DESIGNER: MARTIN CHEEK
MAKERS: ALAN WELCOME AND
MARTIN CHEEK
SIZE: 40 X 20 CM (16 X 8 IN)

YOU WILL NEED

15 mm (⅝ in) thick MDF measuring 40 x 20 cm (16 x 8 in)	Face mask
	Rubber gloves
Two sheets of A4 carbon paper	450 g (1 lb) of powdered grout
Template (page 220)	Bowl of water
Sharp pencil	Mixing board for the grout
Tracing paper	Trowel
Sheets of newspaper	Plastic grout spreader
Vitreous glass tiles as shown above right	Cleaning cloth
	Liquid floor cleaner
Mosaic nippers	Abrasive cleaning pad
125 ml (4 fl oz) wood adhesive in a dispenser	Pair of 'D' rings or mirror plates and screws
Craft knife	
Safety spectacles	

1	gold-leafed (2 tiles)	7	pale green (240 tiles)
2	black (3 tiles)	8	dark green (66 tiles)
3	pale blue (6 tiles)	9	mauve (36 tiles)
4	blue (4 tiles)	10	emerald vein (10 tiles)
5	pale green (98 tiles)	11	Sorrento blue (6 tiles)
6	purple (33 tiles)	12	lizard green (53 tiles)

1 Using carbon paper laid ink-side down on the surface you are about to mosaic, transfer the gecko design and the background lines onto the MDF board as described on page 220.

2 Begin by mosaicing the edge of the board. Place a sheet of paper under the board to protect your work surface. Cut some of the green and dark green tesserae in half and run a bead of glue along one side of the board. Fix the tesserae to the side of the board making sure that they adhere firmly. Continue on the other three sides and do not move the board as this may dislodge the tesserae and they may come away from the MDF. Leave to dry for about an hour.

3 Now cut the mauve and purple tesserae for the border. The edge tesserae will be standing proud of the surface of the MDF board, but as you complete the mauve and purple border you will see that the tesserae around the edge become flush with it.

4 Cut the tesserae for the gecko, keeping each colour ready to one side on a separate sheet of paper. Start to mosaic the key line of the gecko's tail, back and neck by buttering the ribbed face of each tessera with glue and fixing it down on the board. Make a clear, flowing line as this will define the entire mosaic. It is rather like a jigsaw puzzle in that you need to select a tessera which fits well. Compare the angle made by the side of the tessera with the outline of the design and select the tile to match that angle. If you can't find a suitable tessera, then nibble one to fit.

5 Continue to mosaic the gecko. When you come to mosaic the toes, nibble a curve onto the tessera. Try to match the design as closely as possible but don't worry if it comes out slightly differently. When finished, cut up a pool of tesserae ready for the background and keep them on one side. Put in the line of background that surrounds the gecko, using the background colour. This *opus vermiculatum* is very important as it delineates the subject and separates it from the flow of the background. Then mosaic the rest of the background.

Once you have finished, leave the mosaic to dry for at least three hours; then tear off the newspaper and, using a craft knife, cut away any excess glue. Pour out the grout onto a board or into a bowl and add just enough water to make a fairly sloppy 'mud pie' mixture, mixing it thoroughly with the trowel. Put a small quantity in the middle of the plaque. Beginning with the sides, spread out the grout evenly, pushing it gently into the gaps.

6 Next grout the top of the mosaic, running the grout in all directions to ensure that the gaps are thoroughly filled.

Wipe off with a damp cloth and, if necessary, remove all excess grout with a craft knife and make sure that no part of any tessera is submerged beneath the grout.

Allow to dry for at least two days before cleaning off the surface scum with the liquid floor cleaner and abrasive pad.

Fix the 'D' rings or mirror plates to the back of the board and hang the mosaic as a picture.

COCK CLOCK

It seemed entirely appropriate to design a clock based on a cockerel crowing loudly at sunrise.

We have chosen a beautiful sunburst to go behind the cockerel, so it is very important that the cockerel doesn't get lost next to such strong bright yellows. For this reason, dark colours were used for the body, and brilliant white for the head of the cockerel, both of which have strong tonal contrast against the yellow background.

Re-assemble the clock by placing the hands back on to the mechanism. To make the hands stand out sufficiently from this busy background, spray them with gold spray paint before assembling.

SIZE: 53 X 36 CM (21 X 14 IN)
DESIGNER AND MAKER: KIM WILLIAMS

Template (page 218)

YOU WILL NEED

Wooden clock kit (see suppliers list)	Rubber gloves
Two sheets of A4 carbon paper	450 g (1 lb) of powdered grout
Template (page 218)	Bowl of water
Sharp pencil	Mixing board for the grout
Tracing paper	Trowel
Sheets of newspaper	Plastic grout spreader
Vitreous glass tiles as shown right	Cleaning cloth
Mosaic nippers	Liquid floor cleaner
125 ml (4 fl oz) wood adhesive in a dispenser	Abrasive cleaning pad
	Black ink
Craft knife	Gold spray paint
Safety spectacles	Pair of 'D' rings or mirror plates and screws
Face mask	

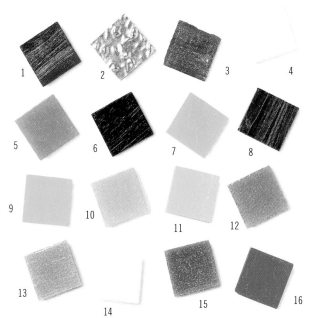

1	russet vein (3 tiles)
2	gold-leafed (2 tiles)
3	copper vein (15 tiles)
4	pale grey (3 tiles)
5	orange (3)
6	black (45 tiles)
7	tangerine (6 tiles)
8	bronze vein (12 tiles)
9	bright yellow (51 tiles)
10	lime green (6 tiles)
11	lemon yellow (36 tiles)
12	green (12 tiles)
13	pale blue (6 tiles)
14	white (12 tiles)
15	blue (8 tiles)
16	bright red (14 tiles)

1 Transfer the design onto the face of the clock as described on page 218. Colour in the design as this will help you attain good colour contrast between the cockerel and the background. Begin by mosaicing the 'key line' from the cockerel's throat, down his breast to his feet. Try to get a good clean flowing line that will clearly define the cockerel from the bright yellow background.

2 Next, add the cockerel's comb and wattle in bright red, followed by his beak and legs in tangerine. Finally, set the blue tesserae that will form the inside feathering of his tail feathers.

3 Fill in the cockerel's face and head. Lay the black key lines that make up his tail feathers and the blue one that forms the base line of his wing.

 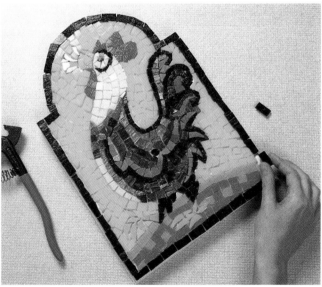

4 In making the eye we chose a tile of copper vein. You, too, *should* be able to find a similar tile to this. By carefully nibbling around this line, a tessera that looked like a closed eye was made. Continue in this way to fill in the body and tail of the cockerel.

Mosaic the hillock on which the bird is standing. Remember that things get lighter towards the horizon, so make the horizon line pale green.

5 Introduce more of the darker green tesserae as you add each successive row, to achieve a blended effect. Mosaic the sunburst in the two shades of yellow. Try to make the tesserae form lines that radiate out from the vanishing point, in this case, where the sun is. Finally, add the row of black tesserae to make the border, leave to set for three hours, then grout and clean in the normal way. When the mosaic is complete, use black ink to paint the fluted wooden edge of the clock, blending it in with the black border. Reassemble clock components.

WAVE PICTURE FRAME

What better way to show off your favourite picture than to mosaic a frame to go around it? Remember that the strong mosaic colours make for a very rich effect which can overpower or even clash with your picture if it has a lively composition. So if your picture is a busy one, choose quieter, softer colours and vice versa.

Here I have chosen a classical Roman 'wave' border based on a traditional Roman design. It was often used to frame huge scenes with swirling fish of all weird and wonderful manner and description. I have used this border many times and have always found it tricky to divide each side into an exact number of waves. Like a lot of the geometric patterns used in Roman mosaics, the look is deceptively simple until you try to do it yourself.

Size: External dimensions
29 x 23 cm (11½ x 9 in)
Internal dimensions
19.5 x 13 cm (8 x 5 in)
Designer and Maker: Martin Cheek

Template (page 219)

YOU WILL NEED

15 mm (⅝ in) thick MDF measuring 29 x 23 cm (11½ x 9 in)	Craft knife
Electric jigsaw	Safety spectacles
Electric drill	Face mask
1 cm (½ in) drill bit	Rubber gloves
Two sheets of A4 carbon paper	450 g (1 lb) of powdered grout
Template (page 219)	Bowl of water
Sharp pencil	Mixing board for the grout
Tracing paper	Trowel
Sheets of newspaper	Plastic grout spreader
Vitreous glass tiles as shown right	Cleaning cloth
Mosaic nippers	Liquid floor cleaner
125 ml (4 fl oz) wood adhesive in a dispenser	Abrasive cleaning pad
	Pair of 'D' rings or mirror plates and screws

1	purple vein (6 tiles)
2	dark blue vein (50 tiles)
3	dark purple vein (27 tiles)
4	navy blue (18 tiles)
5	purple (4 tiles)
6	blue (40 tiles)
7	dark viridian (3 tiles)
8	cyan (16 tiles)
9	pale blue (50 tiles)
10	ice blue (7 tiles)
11	mid-pale blue (13 tiles)
12	grey blue (5 tiles)
13	Sorrento blue (5 tiles)
14	sea green vein (2 tiles)
15	blue (37 tiles)

1 Mark the vertical centre line and cut the inner rectangle out of the MDF. To do this, drill a hole 1 cm (½ in) diameter to get the jigsaw blade through. Transfer the design onto the MDF board as described on page 219. Then mosaic the outer edge of the frame. Place a sheet of paper under the frame to protect your work surface. Cut the various shades of dark blue tesserae in half and run a bead of glue along one side of the frame. Fix the tesserae to the side of the board making sure that they adhere firmly.

Continue on the other three sides – do not move the board around as this will allow the tesserae to come away. Repeat this process for the inner frame using the various shades of light blue tesserae. Leave to dry for about an hour.

Run a bead of glue along the crest of each wave and mosaic down to where it touches the edge of the frame. Repeat with the next wave, then finish off the tail of the previous wave to where it meets the new wave. The reason for doing this is because the crest of the new wave is more important than the tail of the old wave, so mosaic that first.

2 When the inner and outer edges have dried, peel off the backing paper and discard. Cut off any excess glue with the craft knife. Continue to mosaic the waves as described in step 1 until you have gone all the way around the frame. Fill in the triangular areas under the waves – try to echo the flow of each wave as you do so.

3 Now mosaic the sky. Once again, start at the crest of a wave and run a bead of glue along the side of it. Mosaic this line, finishing off underneath each crest in a circular movement.

4 Continue all the way around the frame. Fill in the triangular areas above these sky lines, echoing the flow as you do so. Leave to dry for three hours and then grout and clean. Fix the 'D' rings or mirror plates to the back of the frame, glue your picture in place and hang the mosaic.

CIRCUS PODIUM POT

This simple but attractive pot clearly demonstrates how even the simplest everyday item can be transformed by using mosaic. The shape reminded me of a circus podium – hence the design. However, we chose vivid greens and blues as opposed to circus colours (ie reds and oranges) to echo the natural colours of the plant which it will contain. Dark viridian was chosen for the top and bottom bands so that the design would be 'contained'.

OVERALL DIMENSIONS:
14 X 12 CM (5½ X 4¾ IN)
DESIGNER: MARTIN CHEEK
MAKER: SYLVIA BELL

YOU WILL NEED

Wall-hanging terracotta pot
Coloured pastels or chalks
Vitreous glass tiles as shown right
Mosaic nippers
125 ml (4 fl oz) wood adhesive in a dispenser
Safety spectacles
Face mask
Rubber gloves
450 g (1 lb) of powdered grout
Bowl of water
Mixing board for the grout
Trowel
Plastic grout spreader
Cleaning cloth
Liquid floor cleaner
Abrasive cleaning pad
A 5 cm (2 in) screw

1	dark viridian (43 tiles)
2	mid-green (12 tiles)
3	lime green (23 tiles)
4	cyan (15 tiles)

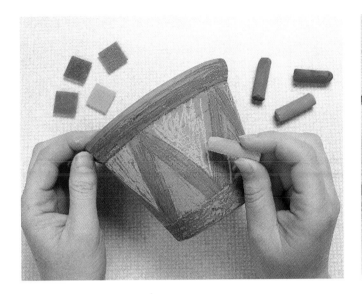

1 Draw the design on the pot using the coloured pastels or chalks. Drawing onto a three-dimensional object is always quite different from a flat piece of paper. You may find that you have to space out the design further than you think.

2 Begin by mosaicing the top rim of the pot with dark viridian tesserae. Leave to dry for an hour or so and then mosaic the top and bottom bands, also in the dark viridian. This may well take time and patience. Our pot, being so small, proved to be a bit tricky. When we turned it round, gravity did its worst and some tesserae dropped off. The obvious, though frustrating, solution is to work in stages, allowing the glue to 'take' for about 30 minutes each time before you turn it.

3 Mosaic the cyan zigzag. The *opus* is diagonal here, so you need to nibble the end tesserae to the correct angle

4 Fill in the remaining triangles alternating the mid- and lime greens. Mosaic in horizontal rows, nibbling triangles where necessary to fit. When finished, leave to set for three hours and grout and clean. Fill the pot with a suitable plant and hang it on a wall in the sun.

PEBBLE MOSAIC PAVING SLAB

Simple designs work best for pebble mosaics. One of the difficulties is getting the pebbles to sit close enough to each other to get the detail you require. For this reason I have chosen the broad curves of a Greek knot commonly used in Roman mosaics. It also has the advantage of being a repeat pattern, so that if you wish, you can mosaic as many as you wish and line them up to form an attractive border to your garden.

We used a large bag of Arran pebbles from Scotland, bought from a builder's merchants. If you live near the coast, it is, of course, possible to use pebbles off the beach, but you should ask permission from the local authorities first.

Pebble mosaics look their best when wet. You will soon find yourself looking forward to a downpour so that you can go out into the garden to admire your work!

Once again, this looks, at first glance, to be a very complicated project. In fact, we were able to complete it to the stage of pouring the concrete in just one day. One of the thrilling aspects of this type of mosaic is that you are never quite certain how the finished piece will look. We had to be patient for a whole week before turning out the mould to find out. The temptation to cheat is always great, but once you have and if, like me, damaged days of work, you soon learn to be patient and let chemistry do its work.

SIZE: 66 X 48 CM (26 X 19 IN)
DESIGNER: MARTIN CHEEK
MAKERS: ALAN WELCOME AND
MARTIN CHEEK

YOU WILL NEED

Piece of brown craft paper measuring 76 x 56 cm (30 x 22 in)	Two 2.5 m (8 ft) lengths of 10 x 2.5 cm (4 x 1 in) timber	25 kg (50 lb) bag of sharp sand	Cocktail stick
	PVA wood adhesive		Plant water atomizer
MDF board measuring 80 x 60 cm (31½ x 23½ in), waxed (see pages 15-16)	Drill	Wooden levelling tool (see page 8)	25 kg (50 lb) bag of cement
	2.5 mm (1/16 in) drill bit	Builder's float (see page 8)	Metal bucket
	Four 5 cm (2 in) no. 8 screws	Paper	One 1 m (3 ft) square board
Roll of 5 cm (2 in) wide gummed brown paper tape	Screwdriver	Pencil	Shovel
	Tub of petroleum jelly (vaseline)	12 kg (24 lb) bag of pebbles varying in size and colour as shown below	Rubber gloves
Template (page 221)	500 ml (1 pint) white spirit		Trowel
		Large pair of scissors	Scrubbing brush

194

MAKING A SIMPLE MOULD

Making a mould and laying the pebbles indirect (upside down) into a shallow bed of sand ensures that the final surface of the slab will be flat and therefore easier to walk on.

Stretch some brown craft paper onto the waxed MDF board and secure with 5 cm (2 in) wide gummed brown paper tape. Leave it to dry (see page 164). Cut the 2.5 m (8 ft) length of 10 x 2.5 cm (4 x 1 in) timber into two lengths of 76 cm (30 in) and two lengths of 56 cm (22 in). Run a bead of glue down the end of each batten where it touches the adjoining piece of wood and glue down the batten onto the area where the brown tape overlaps the brown paper on the board. Screw the adjoining walls together with the 5 cm (2 in) long screws. Run more glue generously along the base of the batten where they touch the board and rub it into the joins with your index finger.

When the glue has set (up to an hour), paint the inside walls with the release agent made from a 50:50 mixture of petroleum jelly and white spirit. You have now made a simple mould. Because the paper is temporarily fixed to the board, the whole mould is easy to dismantle and will fall apart easily when necessary.

Pour sharp sand into the mould to form a bed 12 mm (½ in) deep. The final depth from the top of the pebble to the top of the cement is called the rebate and this is determined by the depth of the sand you initially pour into the mould. Obviously, as you push the pebbles into the sand, so the sand is forced up between the pebbles. Thus the rebate on your mosaic will be about 2 cm (¾ in) deep, depending on the size of the pebbles.

Take the levelling tool (see page 156 for making) and sit it on the adjacent sides of the mould. By running the tool across the top of the mould you can level out the bed of sand.

1 Use the builder's float to make the sand compact and flatten out any rough areas in the top surface of the sand. Then draw the design on page 221 to size on paper. Carefully cut out the shaded areas: the middle circle, the two semi-circles on either side and the four circular triangles between the rings and the border. Keep the smaller cut-out pieces and place on one side and place the larger cut-out piece of paper into the mould. Trace down the design onto the sand using a scalpel, a sawing action will ensure that the surface of the sand stays undisturbed.

2 The smaller cut-out pieces can be used to tidy up the scalpel lines once the main cut-out piece of paper has been removed. Use the sharp edge of the builder's metal float to cut the straight edge lines into the sand.

3 Sort out the pebbles into piles of their various colours: here blacks, greys and browns. Within each pile, separate the larger pebbles from the smaller ones. Using the larger black pebbles, lay the key line that describes the outer edge of the knot. Be positive in your choice and in the placing of the pebbles into the sand. Try to avoid repositioning as this disturbs the sand and results in the pebbles being not so well supported. It helps if the sand is kept moist; use a plant water atomiser and occasionally give the surface of the sand a quick spray. If you do disturb the surface of the sand, use the trowel to repair the damage, sprinkling in a little more sand if necessary. Push the pebbles into the sand until they are touching the brown craft paper. Remember that the surface of the paper will eventually become the top surface of your pebble mosaic.

4 Lay a second line of pebbles alongside the key line. Try to choose pebbles that fit snugly between where the first row of pebbles touch. Pack the pebbles as tightly as you can. You will find that the process of inserting the pebbles gets progressively easier as they begin to prop each other up. You can check that the depth of the sand is consistent by using a cocktail stick as a simple depth gauge. You will find that you can work surprisingly quickly, covering a large surface area in a relatively short space of time.

5 Continue mosaicing the knot. Try to blend in grey pebbles with the black ones so that you achieve some shading. This is especially important where the curves cross over and under each other. Wetting the mosaic will make it easier for you to judge the subtle differences in the shade of the pebbles. Mosaic in the dark centres with black pebbles and, working inwards, fill in the remaining loop with brown pebbles. Mosaic the outside edge with dark pebbles.

6 Continue to mosaic the border. We managed to get two rows of brown and one row of dark grey before touching the knot. Fill in any gaps with thin pebbles of the same colour. Then complete the mosaic by filling in the small triangular areas with brown pebbles.

7 Mix a 1 litre (1¾ pints) solution of
cement and water only, to the consistency
of thick cream. Pour slowly and evenly over
the pebbles. This is to fill any small gaps that
the sand and cement would be too thick to
flow into. Leave the cement solution to dry to
the consistency of putty. (About an hour or so
depending upon the temperature.) This will
also help to hold the pebbles in place when
the heavy sand and cement mixture is poured
on top of them.

8 Thoroughly mix together the sand and
cement 3:1 at the dry stage before adding
any water. Make a volcano and slowly add the
water, mixing thoroughly with a shovel. The
final sand and cement mixture should have the
consistency of a thick mud pie. Carefully add
the sand and cement in small quantities to the
mould using a trowel so as not to disturb the
pebbles. Level out the surface with the trowel.
Leave to harden. The concrete will take about
three weeks to fully harden. After a week it is
set hard enough for you to unscrew the walls of
the mould and knock them away from the slab
with a hammer.

9 With a strong friend to help you, carefully
turn the slab over onto its back. Remove
the wooden board – this should come away
easily because it was waxed – and brush away
the sand. This is the most exciting part as it is
a bit like archaeology as you brush away the
sand to reveal what lies beneath the surface.

   Finally, wash and scrub the mosaic with a
scrubbing brush. If the cement has 'seeped'
through onto any of the pebbles, you could
scrape off the offending cement with a chisel.
However, don't worry too much about this,
once *in situ*, the overall effect will be
wonderful – especially when it rains!

ROMAN PAVING SLAB

This geometric paving slab is based on an ancient design. The Romans loved interlacing patterns, and this one can often be seen as part of a border or elsewhere on a large Roman mosaic floor.

This mosaic is made indirect, in other words laid in reverse and fixed onto paper with a water-soluble glue. By using a simple wooden mould to contain the sand and cement, a paving slab can be made. The sand and cement, once hardened (this takes at least a week), is ideal for any patio or garden.

SIZE 46 CM (18 IN) SQUARE
DESIGN: MARTIN CHEEK BASED ON A TRADITIONAL ROMAN DESIGN
MAKERS: ALAN WELCOME AND MARTIN CHEEK

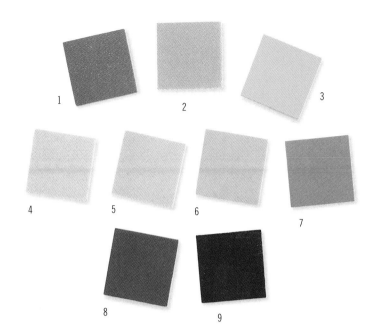

1 dark grey (24 tiles)

2 pale grey (23 tiles)

3 dark yellow (24 tiles)

4 pearl (95 tiles)

5 rose (23 tiles)

6 pale yellow (21 tiles)

7 gold (75 tiles)

8 brown (24 tiles)

9 black (273 tiles)

1 Stretch some brown parcel paper onto a waxed MDF board. Draw the design to size on tracing paper. The design is symmetrical about two axis, so you only need to trace a quarter of the full design. Transfer the design to the paper as described on page 220. By drawing a horizontal and vertical line through the centre, the design can be traced down onto the paper in four stages, turning the tracing through 90 degrees at each stage. Then colour in the design using colouring pencils as close in colour as you can get to the Cinca tiles. This may seem unnecessary, but it allows you to concentrate on the mosaicing without having to constantly worry about whether you are using the right colour.

2 Begin by gluing down a pearl tessera in the middle of the design. Remember that the finished surface of the mosaic will be the one that touches the paper. Cinca tiles don't have a right and wrong side so you can flip them over if you wish. Add the four black lines that spin off this central tessera. Place down complete half tiles where you can; where this is not possible, cut down one tessera and place it in the middle of the line, where it will not be so obvious. Leave a small gap of 1 mm (¹⁄₁₆ in) between each tessera. When grouted, these gaps will delineate the tesserae and emphasize the geometric quality of the design.

3 Working outwards, mosaic the four central rectangles. Look at where the bands overlap and aim your mosaic line so that it lines up with where it reappears. This is easier said than done! It is helpful to use a ruler to make sure that you are still on line when you come out on the other side. If the lines are wobbly here the final effect won't be as good, so it is worth taking care and spending time to get the lines neat.

4 Put in the next eight pearl tesserae. If you have worked neatly so far, these will line up, forming a neat grid. Working outwards, continue to mosaic the knot until it is completed.

5 Finish off 'papering' the mosaic by laying down the black and pearl border and the surrounding black background area. When you have finished the mosaic, make a mould around it to contain the concrete. Prepare the surface with a releasing agent.

6 Sprinkle a small amount of fine silver sand onto the top surface of the mosaic and carefully brush into the interstices. The sand acts as a barrier and prevents the concrete from flowing under the tesserae onto the surface of the mosaic. Make sure that there is no sand left on the top surface of the mosaic as this will prevent the cement from keying.

7 Cut a piece of chicken wire to the same size as the slab. Place it in the mould to make sure it fits snugly. Any extra wire can be bent over and squashed down. When you are satisfied, remove the wire from the mould. Then mix the sand and cement in their dry state. Make a well in the mixture and gradually add the water until the sand and cement are well mixed and of thick mud pie consistency. Slowly, pour this into the mould and when you have covered the surface of the mosaic, add the chicken wire. Top up the mould with the remaining sand and cement.

8 Leave to harden for at least a week, then unscrew and remove the wooden battens by gently tapping them away with a hammer. Because they are only glued to the brown craft paper they will come away quite easily. Turn the slab over and remove the MDF board.

Soak off the paper (if the board has been properly waxed, the paper should peel away very easily), and using a toothbrush sweep away any excess sand that is still lying in the interstices. Grout and clean.

SUNDIAL

Smalti are beautiful, both to work with and to look at. The rippled surface of this hand-made glass catches and plays with the light that falls on it, so what better thing to make with it than a sundial? I wanted to show how even when used very simply, it still enlivens and enhances the piece. The octagonal shape of the slab suggested that all I needed to do was to radiate alternating bands of orange and yellow smalti around the top surface of the dial and over the sides to create a jolly sunburst effect.

OVERALL DIMENSIONS: 40 X 40 X 8 CM (16 X 16 X 3½ IN)
DESIGNER AND MAKER: MARTIN CHEEK

1	yellow tesserae 1.5 kg (3 lb)
2	orange tesserae 1.5 kg (3 lb)

1 The base of the sundial I bought was cast concrete which had brickwork effect indentations on the side. To create flat sides, I filled these groves with a rapid set floor and wall tile adhesive. Use a grout spreader to achieve a smooth flat surface and leave to set.

2 Using pastels or chalks, divide the octagonal top surface into its eight segments. Colour each segment in orange and yellow alternately. To break this up I made the central line of each segment the opposite colour, ie a yellow strip through the centre of each orange band, and vice versa.

3 Mix the waterproof tile adhesive with water to the consistency of smooth porridge. Begin mosaicing by applying an even layer of the adhesive to a segment with the metal modelling tool or a lollipop stick. Lay the two diagonal outer lines and the vertical central line of smalti first. The lines on either side of the central line are also vertical, mosaic these next. If a piece of smalti does not fit exactly, trim down the last piece to size; it looks better if this smaller piece is in the middle of the line and not at either end. Now work from the diagonals inwards to meet the central lines. Nibble the angle of the two end tesserae of each diagonal line to the same angle as the sundial.

4 Continue in this way, alternating the colours on each successive segment until you have completed the top surface of the sundial. Then mosaic the sides by running vertical lines of smalti down the edge of each segment. Try to match the vertical lines to those on the top surface of the sundial.

Continue on each successive side until the sundial is completely covered in smalti. Leave to harden for 24 hours, then place the sundial in the middle of your favourite flower bed, where it can catch the sun.

BROKEN CHINA TERRACOTTA POT

Even the simplest shapes can be useful to the mosaic artist. By using china, which has a very intricate design, you can get away with using quite large tesserae as the pieces are intrinsically interesting. Indeed, if the pieces are too small, you can't appreciate the delicacy of the patterns or the subtle shading of the colours within the china itself.

You do not need to grout the finished mosaic since the adhesive is forced up between the pieces of crockery and so 'self grouts' as you work.

Once again, this is a project that looks complicated, but isn't. We completed the entire mosaic in a morning. Before attempting a larger, more complicated structure using broken ceramic, as, for example, the bird bath on pages 214-217, it would be a good idea to have a go at a small pot with a simple shape like this one.

Having finished this pot, we thought that the white adhesive looked a bit stark and did not set off the pieces of crockery. To remedy this, I stained the adhesive with a waterproof blue ink. It did the trick. It would, of course, have been better to colour the adhesive at the dry stage with powder paint!

OVERALL DIMENSIONS: BACK SEMI-CIRCLE:
21 X 16 CM (8 X 6½ IN)
DISTANCE FROM FRONT TO THE BACK OF THE
POT: 13.5 CM (5 IN)
DESIGNER AND MAKER: SYLVIA BELL

YOU WILL NEED

Assortment of broken plates and china as shown right
Plastic bag
Hammer
Mosaic nippers
5 kg (11 lb) rapid set floor and wall tile adhesive
Bowl
Trowel
Rubber gloves
Cleaning cloth
Liquid floor cleaner
Abrasive cleaning pad
Waterproof blue ink

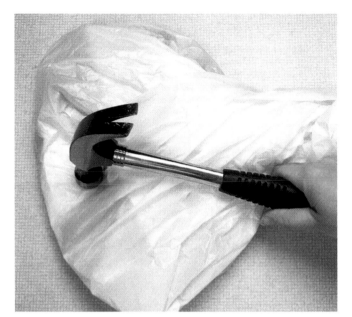

1 Roughly break up the plates by putting them in a plastic bag and hitting it with a hammer. Then use the tile nippers to break up the pieces still further. Sort out the darker, stronger colours in one pile and the more delicately shaded ones in another. Mix up the rapid set floor and wall tile adhesive with water until it is the consistency of porridge.

2 Begin by mosaicing the stronger blue bands at the top and bottom of the pot. As you break up the plates, you will notice that some pieces have cut sides and others, the ones taken from the edge of the plates, have a rounded side. It looks neater and gives a better finish if you can place the uncut, rounded edge along the top and bottom of the pot.

3 Mosaic in the flower. Place the centre first and then add the petals around it.

4 Continue mosaicing this remaining centre band until the entire surface is covered, apart from the flat area at the back of the pot where it rests against the wall.

FROG SPLASHBACK

This design is derived from a series of frogs that Sylvia and I made for a swimming pool. Sylvia liked him and thought he would make a good splashback. This project was made indirect so that the final mosaic surface would be flat and easy to clean. The finished surface of the mosaic is the one that touches the paper, so remember to lay the tesserae flat-side-down. This is very important when making an indirect mosaic using vitreous glass, which has a 'right' and a 'wrong' side.

Make sure that the pale underbelly of the frog stands out well enough from the background. We have chosen a white background to ensure this, but you may prefer to use various blues to create a watery-effect. If so, make sure that you use a dark blue tile against his light green underbelly and a light blue tile against his dark green back when placing the opus vermiculatum to achieve significant contrast.

SIZE: 53 X 36 CM (21 X 14 INCHES)
DESIGNER: MARTIN CHEEK   MAKER: SYLVIA BELL

YOU WILL NEED

Brown craft paper	Rubber gloves
Roll of 5 cm (2 in) wide gummed paper tape	Building sand and cement
Wooden board measuring 80 x 60 cm (31 x 24 in), waxed	MDF measuring 53 x 36 cm (21 x 14 in)
Tracing paper	Two-part fast setting epoxy resin
Pencil	Piece of card measuring about 15 x 10 cm (6 x 4 in)
Template (page 221)	
Carbon paper	Lollipop stick or modelling tool
Wallpaper paste or water-soluble gum	Grey grout
Bowl	Trowel
Vitreous glass tiles as shown opposite	Builder's float (see page 8)
Mosaic nippers	Squeegee
Safety spectacles	Cloths and sponges
No. 8 paintbrush	Bowl of water
Craft knife	Liquid floor cleaner
Cement	

1 copper (30 tiles)
2 black (3 tiles)
3 pale pink (8 tiles)
4 green (30 tiles)
5 emerald green vein (4 tiles)
6 dark green (30 tiles)
7 sage green (63 tiles)
8 pale green (13 tiles)
9 white ceramic (320 tiles)
10 white (2 tiles)
11 marbled white (7 tiles)
12 brown (2 tiles)

1 Stretch some brown craft paper onto the waxed MDF board. Leave to dry for 3-4 hours, depending on room temperature. Then transfer the frog design onto the paper as described on page 218. Remember that the design will eventually be reversed, so you need to trace down the image the 'wrong' way round. Colour in the frog so that you are happy with the tonal values within his body. Try to create a good clear contrast between his dark back and his soft underbelly. Begin to prepare the tesserae.

2 Mix up the wallpaper paste or use any water-soluble paper gum. As the pasting down is only a temporary measure, only use a small amount of paste. The paper will eventually be soaked off by dissolving the glue. In this sort of mosaic it actually helps if you allow a small gap of, say, 1 mm ($\frac{1}{16}$ in) between each tessera. When grouted, these gaps will delineate the tesserae and emphasize the flow of the design. Begin by mosaicing the frog's eyes. Then, working outwards, put in the key line along the frog's back. Try to get this line neat because it is the outside edge and it will give the frog its shape.

3 When you have finished the frog's dark green head, mosaic the line that describes his underbelly. Try to describe the roundness of the belly by working in neat, curved rows. Continue to mosaic the frog until he is completed.

4 Place down the *opus vermiculatum*: the line of tesserae that surrounds the frog. It delineates the subject and is very important as it prevents the background tesserae from 'crashing' into the subject, in this case, our frog. Now mosaic the border using dark green and copper tiles.

5 Finish off the splashback by mosaicing the surrounding white background area. Echo the 'line of action' of the frog's movement. This is called *opus musivum* and is one of the most dramatic and striking of all the forms of *opus*. Leave to dry for three hours or so, depending on room temperature.

6 Take the 53 x 36 cm (21 x 14 in) piece of MDF and 'seal' it with a coat of PVA diluted 50:50 with water. Leave to dry for an hour or so, depending on room temperature. Then cut the mosaic from the waxed board using a scalpel; it will slide off easily if you have waxed the board properly. Keep the board, it can be reused.

Mix the cement with the trowel so that it is the consistency of thick cream. The cement should not be too thick as it needs to fill the gaps between the tesserae. With the grout spreader, carefully butter the surface of the mosaic, trying not to disturb any of the tesserae. Position the buttered mosaic, cement side down, onto the sealed MDF and leave to dry for 24 hours.

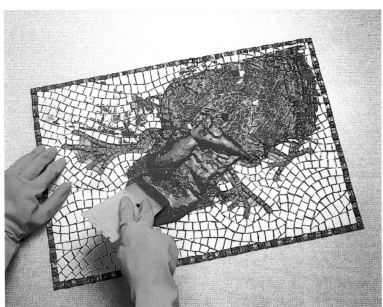

7 The next day soak the paper off the mosaic using warm water. Wipe the water onto the paper and give it a few minutes to soak in. The paper should peel away quite easily, but do this slowly. If any tesserae are loose and come away, put them to one side and glue them back into place using the fast setting two-part epoxy resin mixed in a well ventilated room. Finally, grout and clean the mosaic in the normal way.

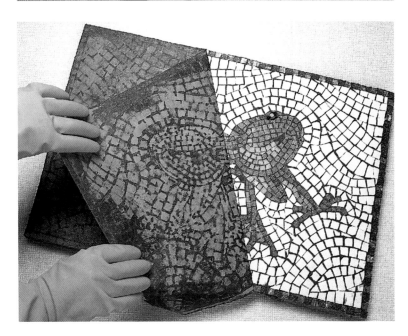

TO FIX A MOSAIC ONTO A WALL

First prepare the surface of the wall where the mosaic is to be fixed. Clean it so that it is free of dirt and grease and then seal it with a coat of PVA diluted 50:50 with water. Leave to dry for 1-2 hours, depending on room temperature.

Then render the area of the wall where you want the mosaic to be with a coat of cement. Use the trowel to smooth the rendering, getting it as flat as possible – the mosaic is only a skin and will only be as flat as the wall. When satisfied, key the surface and leave to harden for 3-4 hours.

'Butter' the ribbed side of the mosaic with cement. The cement should not be too dry as it needs to fill the gaps between the tesserae. Apply the mosaic to the rendered wall. Use a builder's float to push the mosaic and flatten it against the wall.

Leave the mosaic to harden for a few days and then soak off the paper and grout the mosaic in the normal way. Two days later, polish off any scum on the surface using floor cleaner and a damp cloth.

FISH DISH

The durability of mosaics means that they are suitable for kitchens and bathrooms and, because of this, fish are an ever popular choice of subject.

I bought this plastic, fish-shaped platter many years ago, attracted to the way it looked in a shop window. These days, many department stores sell similar ones as picnicware. When I decided to mosaic the dish, I chose a warm, fiery red fish: the lyre-tailed sea bass. The white underbelly is in stark contrast to the deep red back of the fish. It is important to harmonize the top and bottom by gradually blending in yellows through to oranges and finally to the reds.

The eye was made to stand out from the strong red behind it by separating it with a dark ring of brown followed by a light ring of white. If you don't like this effect, then an alternative idea would be to make the colour of the fish's body a softer colour so that there is a good tonal contrast and the features stand out better. We cut long, thin tesserae to achieve the delicacy necessary for the fins.

SIZE OF PLATE: 40 X 30 CM (16 X 12 INCHES)
DESIGNER: MARTIN CHEEK
MAKERS: MARTIN CHEEK AND ALAN WELCOME

YOU WILL NEED

Vitreous glass tiles as shown opposite	Trowel
Plastic fish-shaped picnic plate	Plastic grout spreader
Mosaic nippers	Rubber gloves
125 ml (4 fl oz) wood adhesive in a dispenser	Craft knife
Cocktail stick	Cleaning cloth
Safety spectacles	Liquid floor cleaner
Face mask	Abrasive cleaning pad
Rubber gloves	Large 'D' ring with screw
450 g (1 lb) of powdered grout	Two-part, fast-setting epoxy resin
Bowl of water	Piece of card measuring 15 x 10 cm (6 x 4 in)
Mixing board for the grout	

1   black (3 tiles)
2   marbled pink (4 tiles)
3   brown (2 tiles)
4   yellow (26 tiles)
5   soft pink (75 tiles)
6   scarlet (32 tiles)
7   tangerine (32 tiles)
8   orange (60 tiles)
9   white (3 tiles)
10 bright red (44 tiles)
11 mauve (8 tiles)

1 I started this project by mosaicing the fins of the fish. Because the tesserae here are thinner, these areas will take longer to mosaic. I like to start on the slowest part of the mosaic and get that bit done, so that I can finish on a 'home straight'. By cutting the tiles into long thin strips you can emphasize the delicacy of the veil-like fins compared to the more solidly mosaiced body of the fish.

Because the plastic surface is slippery, initially lay a few key lines and allow them to set. For the same reason, place the centre of the eye in position, nibble a circle, cut it in half and wedge a thin white triangular highlight between the two halves. You may find it helps to use a cocktail stick to finely position the pieces. Nibble a tiny circle for the fish's nostril and glue it in position.

2 Once fast, the key lines will act as buffers against which you can place the adjoining rows of tesserae. Fanning outwards from the centre, mosaic the top dorsal fin in the various reds, orange, tangerine and yellow. Repeat for the other fins. Mosaic the key line that forms the jowl of the fish.

3 To run the yellow ring around the eye, cut a large circle out of one tile, cut it into quarters and then nibble the centre out of each quarter. Arrange these tesserae around the black centre to re-form the circle. Keep working outwards adding a brown, then white and finally a red and orange ring to the fish eye. The brown ring will delineate the yellow one, the white ring will make the whole eye stand out from the red body, and the red and orange ring will act as an *opus vermiculatum* (see page 165) stopping the tesserae of the body from 'crashing' into the white ring.

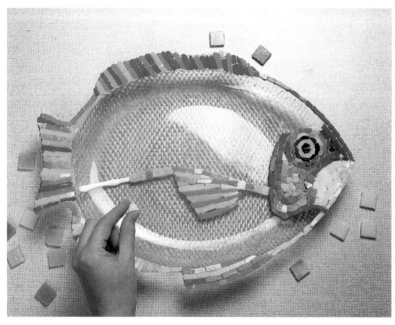

4 Continue to mosaic the head of the fish. Try to get a good, strong, clear line between the line of the red upper lip and the line of the white lower lip which form the mouth. This will help give the fish its particular expression. Run the white key line along the middle of the fish's body and allow to dry.

5 Fanning outwards from the centre, mosaic the fish's upper body. As you work upwards with each row, use a little less yellow, replacing it with tangerine, then a little less tangerine, replacing it with orange, and so on, slowly blending in each colour as you go. By the last row you should be using predominantly scarlet with the occasional piece of bright red.

6 Mosaic the lower part of the fish's body using a predominance of soft pink tiles. Pepper the pink with the occasional yellow and mauve tessera. The final few rows where the plate slopes up are particularly tricky to mosaic. The remaining gaps always appear to want larger tesserae than they actually need. Be patient and, if necessary, spend time nibbling each tessera to fit.

7 Continue in this way until you have finished the fish's entire body. Leave to dry until the PVA goes clear, taking up to four hours. (This is longer than usual because whereas MDF is absorbent which helps the drying process, this plastic plate isn't.)

8 When the glue has set, grout and clean the mosaic in the normal way. Although the squeegee is useful for applying the grout to the flatter areas of the plate, you will find that you have to use your fingers (wearing rubber gloves) to grout the curved edges. When you have finished cleaning and wiping off the excess grout, prod with your craft knife to check there are no tesserae hidden beneath the bed of grout (pay particular attention to the curved sloping sides during this operation). Then allow to dry for at least two days before cleaning off the surface scum as usual.

When it is cleaned and dry, you can, if you wish, hang your plate on an interior wall. Glue a large 'D' ring to the back of the plate using fast-setting two-part epoxy resin in a well ventilated room. Scratch the surface with your craft knife first so that the glue will key to the plastic surface.

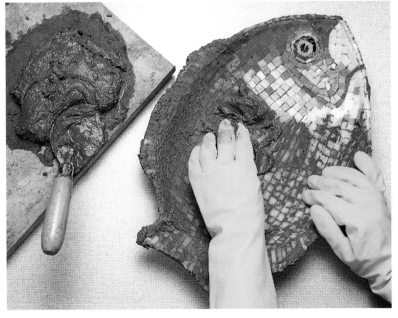

BIRD BATH

One of my favourite designers is the Victorian, William de Morgan. Reproductions of his tiles are still manufactured and are widely available. The cost of these exquisite pieces would normally be beyond the pocket of the average mosaic artist, but I was lucky enough to get hold of some seconds.

In designing this project, I wanted it to be obvious that I had used the William de Morgan tiles, so I tried to keep the overall feel of the piece in keeping with the designs on the tiles, grouping the different motifs – the peacocks, ships and fish – together in their own area.

This method is quick by comparison to ordinary mosaic. The individual pieces can be quite big and large areas can be covered in a relatively short time. This project was completed by Sylvia and me in just one day. Using broken tiles or china is an excellent way of recycling an attractive material that would otherwise be thrown away. There are 'ceramic dumps' where you can pillage such trophies. There is no specific list of tile requirements here since, for obvious reasons, it will not be possible to reproduce this design exactly.

OVERALL DIMENSIONS: BIRD BATH: 42 X 42 X 5 CM (16 X 16 X 2 IN)
PLINTH: MOSAIC AREA CONSISTS OF FOUR TRAPEZIUMS:
13 X 27 X 47 CM (5 X 10½ X 18 IN) HIGH
DESIGNER: MARTIN CHEEK
MAKERS: MARTIN CHEEK AND SYLVIA BELL

1 Using the tile nippers, break up some of the tiles and arrange them in an interesting way on the top surface of the bird bath. (You may want to wear rubber gloves to do this as the tiles can be sharp.) Use some of the most attractive tiles for this surface as this is the one that is seen the most. You will get a neater finish if you use the straight glazed machine edge of the tile for the edges of the birdbath. When you are happy, transfer these tiles to a board and put them aside.

215

2 The William de Morgan tiles are very thick (6 mm [¼ in]) and as you mosaic each surface you leave the thickness of the tile showing on the adjacent surface. In order to disguise this as much as possible, it is important to start on the underside, then the sides, and finally the top surface of the bird bath, mosaicing over the edge of the tiles in each successive case. So, beginning on the bottom of the bird bath, cut the tiles to size and butter each piece with the rapid set floor and wall tile adhesive before finally placing it down. Leave to dry.

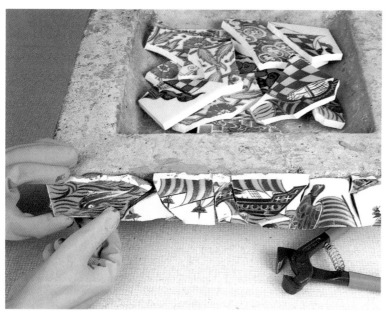

3 Now mosaic the four sides, making sure that you cover over the edges of the tiles on the underside. The William de Morgan ship designs had dolphins swimming along the bottom edge. If you are extremely skilful (or lucky!) you will be able to cut these out and place them on the corners of the bird bath.

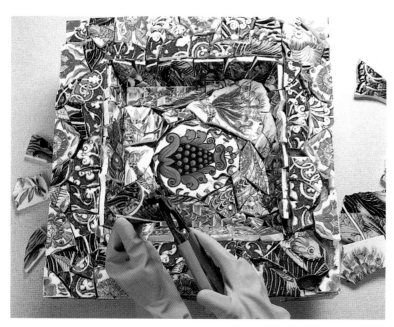

4 Bring back the board with the pre-sorted tiles on and stick these down. Once again, cover the edges of the tiles on the sides. You will be aware that the gaps between the tesserae are much bigger than in any other type of mosaic, this is the nature of working with broken tiles and/or china. Continue until you have covered the entire top surface. We tried to keep the colours together for certain areas, such as reddish tiles with peacock feathers for the inner edge contrasting with darker blue tiles on the uppermost inner edge.

5 Grout the completed bird bath. Because the gaps are large, use a wide gap grout. You may find it easier to squidge the grout in with your fingers than use the grout spreader. Be generous with the grout, filling in any crevices, as this will strengthen the final piece. Wipe off the excess grout. The next day, use a piece of broken tile as a scraper to remove any excess grout that is obscuring any glazed area of tile. This is easier and quicker than it sounds.

6 Now start on the plinth. Our plinth had attractive fluting on it which I didn't want to lose. There were also ribbed bands with tight curves that would have proved difficult to mosaic. I decided to leave these areas unmosaiced and blend the grout into the curves to incorporate it into the overall design. If your bird bath is basically square and plain, it may well be better to mosaic over the entire surface.

Once again, I chose a large blue flower as the centrepiece for each side and the poppies for the corners of the central panel. Try to create contrasts between the neighbouring areas.

7 Continue in this way until you have covered all of the mosaic areas. Grout and clean up the plinth in the same way as the bird bath. Rub some grout into the untiled areas to blend them in with the tiled areas. In this case, the grouting process goes a long way towards achieving a harmonious whole to the finished piece. Allow to dry for at least two days before cleaning off the surface scum with the liquid floor cleaner and abrasive pad.

TEMPLATES

SIZING THE DESIGN

The easiest way to enlarge any of the designs featured on these pages is to use a photocopier with an enlarging facility. If you don't have access to such a machine, use the square method. Draw a grid of small squares over the outline and then draw a grid with much larger squares on a blank piece of paper. You will then be able to transfer the design, square by square.

TRANSFERRING THE DESIGN

To transfer the design onto your mosaicing surface, whether it be MDF, skim ply, acetate, or any other material, place a sheet of carbon paper, ink side down, on the board or mosaic surface (if the area is a large one, you will need to use more than one sheet of carbon). Tape or pin down your sized template and trace off the design onto tracing paper and place it on top of the carbon paper. Firmly trace over the design with a sharp pencil to transfer it onto the mosaicing surface.

Trivet (see page 174)

Cock Clock (see page 188)

Fingerplates (see page 176)

Wave Picture Frame (see page 190)

*Roman
Paving Slab*
(see page 198)

Gecko Plaque (see page 184)

*Pebble Mosaic
Paving Slab*
(see page 194)

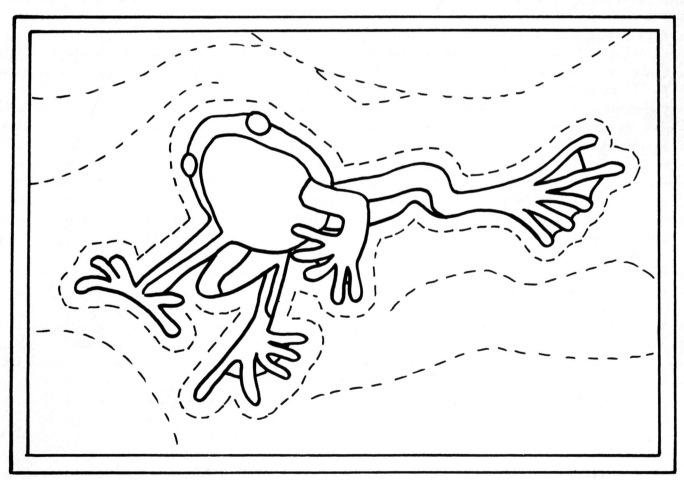

Frog Splashback (see page 206)

PAINTING GLASS

Moira Neale and Lynda Howarth

INTRODUCTION

Decorating glassware has been a popular craft for centuries and indeed some of the glass in this book has been inspired by old Venetian work. Now that there are so many excellent products on the market, glass painting is enjoying an enormous revival and every craft magazine on the newsagents' shelves contains yet more ideas and designs.

We have inspired, supported, amused and entertained each other for almost twenty years. On many occasions our children have been reared in the inevitable chaos associated with combining our talents in creative ventures. We both became interested in glass painting when a new product, Porcelaine 150, became available which has very good dishwasher resistance and is safe to use with food — this idea really appealed and has revolutionised the craft. It means that as well as making purely decorative items or ones needing careful hand-washing, everyday glassware may be painted which will stand up to tough washing.

During the past few months we have been busy painting, stencilling, sponging, marbling and etching any and every glass item in our homes, our friends' and parents' homes. Our craving to embellish has included anything from humble jam jars and wine bottles to carafes and glasses, mirrors and even window panes ... nothing has escaped the Lynda and Moira treatment. It has led to our homes being filled with glasses no-one is allowed to drink from in case they dare drop them before this book is printed!

Trips for the weekly food shop have taken on a new appeal. Never mind what the product is, tastes like or costs — what will the bottle look like given a coat of paint? This has led to severe confusion. Just what IS that strange yellow stuff in that jam jar in the fridge? Is it mustard dressing, lemon and honey vinaigrette or custard? And how long does it keep for? If only we had labelled things before parting the mysterious contents from their beautiful containers!

And as for Jim, Lynda's husband — he became increasingly bewildered that the sponge cloth used for washing the dishes was getting smaller by the day (it was a truly marvellous discovery when we found just how good they are for sponging glassware)! All we can say is thank you Jim for putting up with us, our mess, our glass, our experiments and our masterpieces! It has certainly spared Tony, who, as anyone who has read *Dough Craft in a Weekend* will know, has a strong aversion to Moira and her mess!

We have had enormous fun putting together all the ideas in this book and we hope that you will be inspired by them. No particular artistic skill is required as we have described, step-by-step, how to arrive at the finished designs. We have provided templates and patterns where necessary but you will see from the gallery shots just how much stylish glassware can be made with just a few simple brushstrokes and dots of outliner.

Have fun!

Moira and Lynda... partners in design

GETTING STARTED

One of the greatest advantages of painting on glass is that the craft requires very little in the way of specialised tools or equipment – just a plentiful supply of new or old glassware which can be picked up for very little money. You will probably discover that much of the equipment listed below can be found around the home. This chapter explains the different paints and demonstrates the basic decorating techniques used in the projects that follow later in the book. Once you have mastered these, you will be able to create a wide range of effects and finishes and adapt them to make your own patterns.

EQUIPMENT AND MATERIALS

Your local hobby shop, paint outlet or mail order company will be able to supply the glass paints and other basic materials to get you started. Begin with just a few colours and add to them gradually as your skill and enthusiasm grow. The other equipment you will need to begin is listed in detail in the middle column of this page.

As soon as you have bought your glass paints you will be inspired to make a start. Do not be surprised if your first efforts look very amateurish as it can take a few projects to master this skill. It is therefore a good idea to start off with a really simple design on a jam jar in order to become familiar with the texture of the paint and its application.

It will not be long before you have exhausted your own supply of plain glass and will be requesting friends and relatives to collect empty containers for you too. Everyday packaging suddenly becomes remarkably interesting once the labels are removed and a little imagination is employed!

Interesting jars, bottles and glassware
Good quality brushes, no 2 and 4
Glass paints according to the project required. Some are solvent-based and suitable for decorative items. For more durability, choose oven-bake water-based paints
Outliner in a variety of colours
White spirit
Jam jar
Kitchen paper towels
Low-tack masking tape
Pencil
Scalpel with no 11 blade or craft knife
Tracing paper
Cocktail sticks (toothpicks)
Sponge or fur fabric
Cotton buds
Cellophane
Hairdryer
Apron
Newspaper, to protect your worksurface
Additional useful items for styling your finished work include raffia and florist's wire

SOURCING GLASSWARE

If, like us, you are delighted to have an excuse to go to a car boot fair or a jumble or garage sale, glass painting gives you the perfect reason! So much beautiful old glassware is available in an abundance of shapes and sizes at very reasonable prices. Even a batch of dissimilar glasses can be united into a set simply by painting them with the same colour or design motifs.

Look for unusual items such as goldfish bowls, old perfume bottles, engraved glasses, picture frames, clip frames, mirrors and vases.

Make sure you clean your glass very thoroughly before you begin painting. Really stubborn stains inside bottles may be removed with denture cleaner dissolved in hot water. Sticky labels can often be removed by rubbing with a drop of nail varnish remover on a pad of cotton wool.

TIP

To keep the mess down, once you are ready to begin, protect your workspace with layers of old newspaper or an old tablecloth as some of the paints are solvent-based and may damage some surfaces.

If children are going help with the painting, make sure they are also well covered up.

SAFETY NOTES

There is no reason why children cannot enjoy the hobby of glass painting as well as adults. Make sure that they are supervised at all times and choose water-based paints for them to use. Store paints and brush cleaner in a cool place, well out of the reach of prying hands when not in use.

Always follow manufacturers' specific instructions regarding the baking process if it is required (see facing page for more details).

mainly transparent and quick drying. Replace the tops to prevent evaporation. Brushes need to be cleaned using a compatible solvent, generally white spirit. These paints are flammable and should not be used near a naked flame nor should children use them unsupervised. Make sure your work area is well ventilated.

> ### SAFETY NOTE
>
> Please refer to manufacturer's specific user and safety instructions regarding all glass paints. As a general rule, never paint any surface which is to come into contact with food unless the paint is non-toxic (this is why we decorated the backs of the plates) and as an extra precaution, avoid the lip line on glasses which are going to be functional and not simply used as decorations.

A collection of glassware ready for painting

GLASS PAINTING PRODUCTS

There are many paints available on the market for painting on glass. They tend to fall into several categories:

1 Water-based paints. These do not need baking and are ideal for items which will not require washing. These are perfect for children to use too.

2 Water-based paints. These need to be baked at 200°C/400°F/gas mark 6 for 30 minutes. Items using this paint are hand-washable. The colours are bright and dense and easy to apply.

3 Porcelaine 150, Pébéo's water-based paints. These are baked at 150°C/300°F/gas mark 2. These are completely safe when in contact with food and have good dishwasher resistance. These are ideal for tableware and glasses and we have used them extensively in this book. They are available in a huge range of colours, both transparent

and opaque, and once baked feel wonderfully smooth. Practice may be needed with these, as indeed with all paints, to achieve the density of cover required. It is often better to sponge on two light coats, allowing the first to dry before applying the second. There is a matt medium in the range which, if used alone, gives a wonderful, frosted effect. Used with the other colours in the range as instructed, it gives a matt finish without affecting the colour.

4 Pébéo's water-based gel paints. A new product on the market is a water-based gel which allows three-dimensional colour to be applied to glassware direct from the tube or with the aid of a palette knife. Glass nuggets, tiny mirrors and other items may then be embedded in the gel before it sets for an exotic effect. This enables you to imitate various blown glass effects, as well as creating stylish jewellery. Available in a range of colours, the gel liquifies when shaken or stirred so may also be applied with a brush.

5 Solvent-based paints. These tend to be the paints associated with the traditional stained glass look and are

OUTLINING

The outliners used in this book are water-based, although there are some which become permanent with baking. They can be difficult to control, so practise on jam jars or cellophane before embarking on the real thing.

Have a sheet of kitchen paper ready to catch any blobs of outliner from the tube which may appear as soon as the top is removed. Start by making a row of dots and you will soon realise how little pressure is required on the tube. Progress to circles, squares, triangles and lines ①, using the practice templates on page 290. You may find you get a halo effect at times — do not worry as

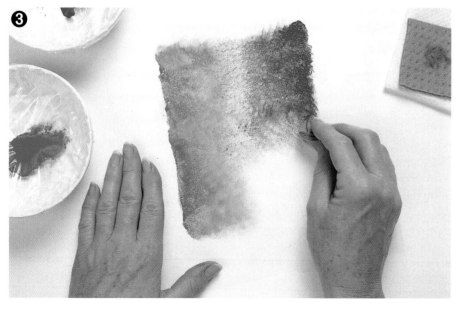

this can be salvaged once the outliner has dried and can be eased back into place with the scalpel. A hairdryer is useful for speeding up the drying times of both outliners and paints but needs to be kept at least 15 cm (6 in) away from the surface to avoid damage.

USING THE GLASS PAINTS

Within about five minutes the outliner will be dry enough to apply the paint. A soft brush is essential for smooth application of the paints ①. Try filling in some of the shapes you have made with the outliners. Apply the paint with even strokes. Keep a cotton bud nearby to correct any errors and a small jar of water or solvent for brush cleaning.

SPONGING

Sponging gives a soft, delicate effect and is a very quick and easy way to apply glass paints.

Tip a few drops of the paint into a saucer (covered with cling film to reduce the cleaning up). Gently dip in your sponge pad and wipe any excess off against the edge of the dish and then test the effect on a piece of cellophane or an old jam jar before starting on your project.

One colour can be used on its own to produce a graded effect just by applying more paint onto the lowest part of the item, reducing the pressure and contact as you move up ②. A graduated effect is achieved by using several colours in succession, allowing each one to merge into the next ③.

TIP

Thin sponge dishcloths are ideal for glass painting as they can be cut up into small pieces and discarded after use. Fine fur fabric also produces an even sponged finish but the rough edges should be folded in before use to prevent any fibres migrating onto the surface of the glass.

SPONGE DOT APPLICATORS

A really simple way to apply uniform dots to a project is to make your own applicators. Peel a foam dishcloth into two and then cut it into 2 cm (¾ in) squares. Bind each one over the end of a cocktail stick or toothpick using fuse wire. Make several as you will find them a useful addition to your equipment kit!

STENCILLING

This is a good way to decorate glassware with a regular repeat pattern. It is particularly useful if you intend to sell your finished items as it is very quick to do once the initial stencil cutting has been done.

To make your stencils, photocopy the required template (see page 284), use adhesive mount to attach it to the card you are using and allow the glue to dry for about ten minutes before attempting to cut it. Protect your worksurface with a cutting mat, cork mat or a thick layer of newspaper before you start. Use a metal ruler as a guide for cutting straight lines ①. Avoid trying to cut around angular designs in one go; instead, make several shorter cuts ②.

It is worth taking care in order to get good, professional results and the initial investment in a craft knife or scalpel and plenty of spare blades is worthwhile. For one-off stencils to decorate flat surfaces, thin card is ideal or even a good quality paper. If you are using your stencil on a curved surface, you may need to use either thin paper or specialist adhesive stencilling film which moulds more easily to the contours of the glass.

USING STENCILS

Lightly spray the back of the stencil with aerosol glue and press it onto the object to be decorated. On cylindrical items you may also need to secure the stencil with a couple of rubber bands.

③ Pour a little glass paint into a saucer and use either a piece of old

reinforcements or indeed any shape you care to cut out of paper.

Use aerosol adhesive mount to apply your own shapes to the glass. Masking tape, torn strips of newspaper and very thin tape available from art shops can also be used. Squares, oblongs, stripes of varying widths and harlequin designs are all possible this way, producing very effective results ①, ②.

It is so easy to produce fabulous glassware with minimal artistic ability using these ideas. If you wish, the masked off area can later be embellished with outliner to add a relief pattern, such as the veining on a leaf. This method can also be used to add a regular pattern, for example to the outer edge of a plate.

Simple, Shaker-style stencil, ideal for beginners

sponge or fur fabric to apply the paint. It is always worth experimenting at this stage and we found that fur fabric works wonderfully well for a fine, even texture. Sponge will give a rougher, less even texture which is more suitable for rustic style projects ④.

MASKING AND REVERSE STENCILLING

Many different objects can be used to mask out clear areas on the glass before you decorate with sponging or marbling. Stick on shapes like stars, hearts, flowers, initials, ring

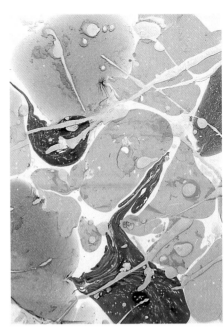

ETCHING

This is a very good way to add embellishment without having to use another colour. It is perfect for adding details like feathers, scales on fish, eyes and so on as well as creating abstract designs on a sponged surface. You will need to etch the design as soon as the paint has been applied and there are several ways of doing it. Use a cocktail stick or toothpick for very fine designs or for details on tiny items. A typist's 'pencil' type of rubber is ideal for chunkier etching and may be sharpened with a knife or pencil sharpener depending on the effect required ①. Knitting needles work well too.

MARBLING

A wonderful range of patterns may be produced using this technique which involves floating coloured solvent-based glass paints on a suitable medium. We have kept the procedure simple and have avoided the use of specialist marbling mediums in preference for water and wallpaper paste. You will need to use a bowl larger than the size of the item to be marbled and cover the worksurface with plenty of paper before you begin.

One of the projects in this book has marbling as one of the stages of producing the final item. Refer to page 274 for fuller instructions.

Sponged and etched snowflake plate

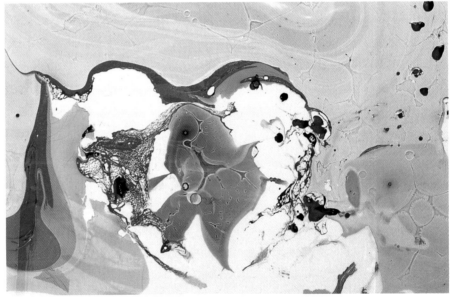

An exotic effect created by marbling a
simple piece of glass

TRANSFERRING DESIGNS

The easiest way to transfer a design onto glass is to trace it. Tape the design to the inside or back of the object to hold it firmly against the glass. If the surface is curved, make many small vertical slits to enable the pattern to conform to the glass. Trace over the pattern with outliner.

NARROW NECKED BOTTLES

It is impossible to tape the design to the inside of narrow necked bottles but there is a simple solution. Make sure the bottle is dry inside and then, on a piece of paper, cut out the design to the height of the bottle. Roll up the paper, push it into the bottle, then pour in pasta or lentils right up to the top and the design is perfectly anchored! ①

❷

❶

EMBELLISHMENTS

The addition of those lovely shiny glass nuggets available in a myriad of colours gives a very splendid finish to an otherwise ordinary item. Tiny rhinestones and sequins may be used too and they are available from craft shops or mail order companies ②.

Apply them to your glassware before the paint using a specialist glass glue to

REVERSE PAINTING TECHNIQUE

This is a very handy way to decorate the back of a glass plate so that the cutting surface will not become damaged when the plate is used. It is also useful if you wish to use paints which are not safe when in contact with food. A little planning is needed before you begin because the details, normally left until last, must be painted on first. Just think in reverse and remember to reverse any text too!

These iridescent nuggets inspired this floral design

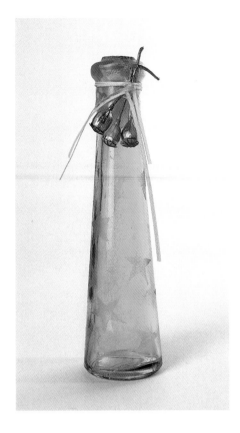

Matt medium was applied over a star stencil for this subtle effect

ensure good adhesion. If you are giving a filled, decorated bottle to a friend as a present, spend some time adding a label, a pretty stopper or sealing wax. See our gallery pages for more ideas. Remember, a beautifully presented item will quickly lead to orders if you want to sell your glassware.

INSPIRATION FOR DESIGNS

Wrapping paper, gift cards, colouring books, curtain fabrics, flower and bulb catalogues are good sources of inspiration. Do remember, however, that you may not sell any work using other people's designs.

For a baby gift you could use the nursery wallpaper design to inspire the edge of a mirror or picture frame. Glasses, jugs and carafes decorated to match existing crockery or table linen make excellent gifts for adults and may be themed to celebrate a special occasion, such as a milestone birthday or anniversary.

If you enjoy museums, why not visit one and get inspiration from old Venetian glassware? We found some fascinating pieces where much of the design is made up of dots and swirls – very easy to reproduce as you will see in our Historical Gallery on page 246.

This design was adapted from traditional East European glassware

PROJECTS AND GALLERIES
FOR PAINTING GLASS

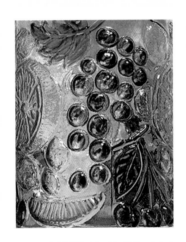

GOLDFISH PLATE

A shoal of golden fish swim around this plate which is both practical and attractive. You could use it to brighten up your bathroom, and could decorate other items such as a soap dish or toothbrush mug to match. As the plate is decorated on the underside, it may be used for serving food.

1 Wash the plate in hot soapy water and dry carefully. Start by sponging the edge of the plate on the underside with the gold paint, applying it densely around the outside. Allow the paint to look feathery on the inner edge. Use the paper towel and white spirit to clean any paint from the front of the plate.

YOU WILL NEED

A glass plate

Solvent-based glass paints in gold and white

Fine sponge or fur fabric

White spirit

Kitchen paper towels

No 2 paintbrush

Cellophane to practise on

Kitchen paper towels

Fish and surf templates (page 284)

Sticky tape

Paper

Pen

Scissors

Cocktail stick (toothpick)

Aerosol spray mount

Saucer covered with cling film

VARIATIONS

This plate could be painted using oven-bake paints if you want to preserve the pattern during frequent use. It seems a pity to hide it away in a cupboard when not in use, so why not store it on a plate display stand?

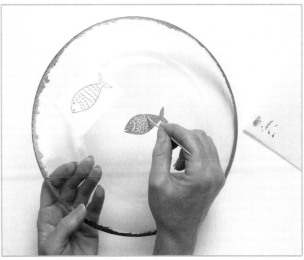

2 Copy the large fish template and tape it to the inside of the plate, positioning it centrally. Working on the back of the plate, paint the fish gold, but do not apply the markings at this stage.

3 Remove the template and use it as a guide to etch in the details of the scales and gills using the cocktail stick. Keep the tip clean with the paper towel.

4 Paint the shoal of tiny goldfish next. This time have a practise run on cellophane first as it is easier to copy the tiny shapes we have given you. Use the cocktail stick to etch in the details after every third or fourth fish. For a bit of fun, paint one little fish swimming the wrong way! Allow the plate to dry for about an hour while you make the surf template for the next stage.

5 Draw around the plate onto a piece of paper. Cut out the circle and then fold it in half four times to make 16 equal sections. Open it out flat and mark 1 cm (½ in) in from the edge all the way round. Trace the surf template onto each marked section. Pour some of the white paint onto the saucer, dip the sponge into it and wipe the excess off on the edge. Sponge the surf design all around the plate. Remove the template and quickly soften the edges of the wave design by carefully sponging over it. Turn the plate over every now and then to check what it looks like from the front. Leave the plate upside down to dry for 24 hours before use.

OLIVE OIL BOTTLES

This project would make an ideal present. After painting the the olives and leaves on the glass, we filled the bottles with finest quality olive oil and attached a small pastry brush by drilling through the handle and attaching a length of wire. Choose a brush which is slightly shorter than the bottle.

1 First, wash and dry the bottle thoroughly inside and out. Trace or photocopy the template and cut it out close to the edge of the design. Tape a piece of ribbon or string to the top for easy removal from narrow necked bottles. Push the template into the bottle. Fill the bottle with pasta to anchor the paper in place and then stopper it firmly.

YOU WILL NEED

A tall bottle (ours is 27 cm (11 in) tall) with a cork stopper	Solvent-based glass paints in brown, emerald green, yellow, red and blue
Template (page 284)	Saucer covered with cling film for mixing colours
Paper	White spirit
Pen	Cocktail stick (toothpick)
Scissors	Kitchen paper towel
Sticky tape	Wooden pastry brush (optional)
Ribbon or string	Drill (optional)
Pasta, baking beans or similar	Florist's wire (optional)
No 2 paintbrush	

——— VARIATIONS ———

This bottle would make a lovely gift for anyone to display in their kitchen. Use this idea for salad dressings too. Artistically minded people will have fun decorating bottles of flavoured oil or vinegar with sprays of chillies or a variety of herbs.

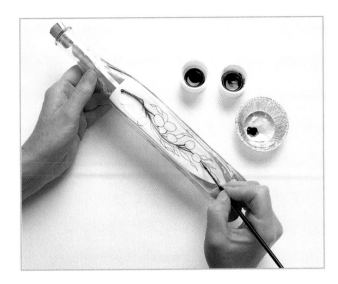

2 Start by painting the olive branches using the brown paint darkened with a little blue if necessary. You may find it easier to rest your hand on something of similar height (we found a paper towel roll works very well as a cushion to steady the wrist).

3 You need to mix emerald green with a little brown and yellow to achieve the leaf shade we have used. Test the colour on cellophane but remember it does not have to be botanically correct! Paint in the leaves using the illustration as a guide. Use the white spirit to keep your brush clean and to remove mistakes.

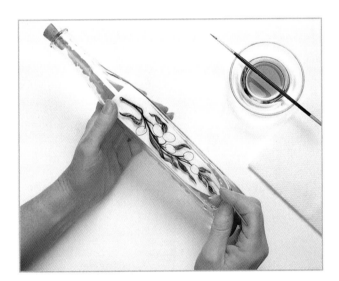

4 Etch in the details of the leaves using a cocktail stick. It is best to do this as soon as possible before the paint has time to dry. This technique really does bring the leaves to life. Alternatively, paint in the veins using a darker shade of green.

5 Finally, paint in the olives using a mixture of red, blue and brown. If you are happy with your work, allow it to dry thoroughly. If not, remove it and start again! To give the bottle a rustic appearance, add a hook made from wire which is then twisted around the neck of the bottle. Fill the bottle with extra virgin olive oil and then firmly wire the cork stopper in place.

YELLOW GALLERY

'Volcano' oil burner
This has been etched and over-painted.

Orange slices jar
A citrus effect was achieved by applying the paint with a very small brush and fine brushstrokes.

Tall yellow bottle
This elegant bottle has been stencil-frosted for a pretty finish.

Shallow yellow platter
A very simple gold border was painted around this dish for a striking effect.

Cup and saucer
Luscious apricots were painted on this cup using opaque glass paints.

Shaped glasses
One glass has been painted with simple bands of yellow and gold and the other given an iridescent effect by being lightly sponged first with gold and then with a clear yellow. A simple band of gold dots was added later.

1940s' style glass dessert dish

Bottom: The embossed lines on this dish made it very simple to decorate with yellows, orange and gold.

Perfume bottle

Matt medium was used on this little bottle first and then the yellow paint applied, making the glass appear transparent again.

Hexagonal jar

Bottom: Low-tack tape was used to mask off alternate facets before marbling with yellow, orange and gold. Gold outliner dots were added later.

Tall, pale yellow glass

The bowl of this glass was made from pale lemon glass but a deeper colour was overlaid using clear yellow paint.

Copper glass

This glass was frosted with matt medium first before a coat of copper was sponged over the bottom section.

Stripy frosted glass

Strips of paper were used to mask off areas and matt medium then sponged on to give a frosted look.

MILLEFIORI LANTERN

This lantern was inspired by the wonderful range of colours found in millefiori beads. It is surprisingly easy to reproduce the design but can only be successfully done on a flat surface. As the panels of this lantern are removable, it is ideal for decorating in this way and candlelight enhances the rich colours.

1 Clean the panels of glass using glass cleaner, being very careful of the sharp edges. (Wear the leather gloves for protection.) Lay your glass onto a sheet of paper and draw round it and then use small coins as templates as shown. If you prefer, use the template on page 285.

YOU WILL NEED

Lantern
Glass cleaner
Old leather gloves for handling the glass
Paper
Pencil
Small coins or template (page 285)
Oven-bake outliners (we used Porcelaine 150) in green, blue, red, yellow and orange
Kitchen paper towels
Cocktail stick (tooth pick)
Domestic oven

— VARIATIONS —
Faceted bottles and jam jars may be decorated using this method but make sure that your chosen item is kept completely level at all times until baked.

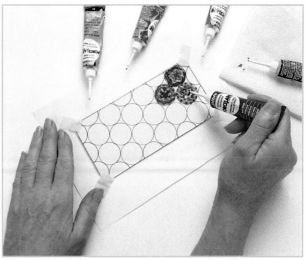

2 Lay the panel of glass onto the pattern and remove the lids from all the tubes of outliners before you begin. It is best to work on just three circles at a time and vary the colour combinations using an equal amount of colour overall. Begin with the red. The fluid nature of the outliners make them ideal for this project.

3 Continue to add more colours in circles and dots in an effort to achieve a star or floral effect. Note how well the colours look juxtaposed to the nearest colour in the rainbow, i.e. red, orange, yellow, green and blue. This stops complementary colours (e.g. orange and blue) merging and becoming sludgy within each 'bead'. Aim to use all the colours on each one and do not worry if your work looks blobby at this stage.

4 Once you have completed three of the 'beads', use the cocktail stick to start the feathering. Drag the colours in and out all the way round each one to create a spider's web effect and encourage the colours to blend and bleed into one another.

5 Continue to work down the panel of glass towards yourself to avoid smudging your work. The paint looks very dense and opaque at this stage until it is thoroughly dry. When you have finished the panel, set it aside and start the next one. Note how all the colours continue to bleed into each other. This will continue to happen as the panels are left to dry flat for at least the next 24 hours. Bake following the manufacturer's instructions. Allow to cool and then fill in the spaces with solvent-based glass paint if you wish. Leave to dry thoroughly before reassembling the lantern.

RUBY AND GOLD SUNDAE DISHES

The inspiration for this design comes from Middle Eastern tea glasses and if you are able to find any plain glasses, the design may be adapted to suit them.
If you are feeling adventurous, why not make a complete dinner service using this design?

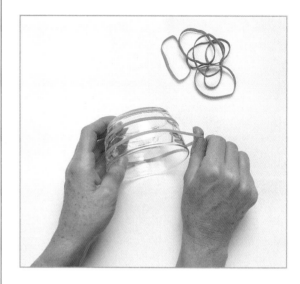

1 Wash the glassware in hot soapy water, rinse and dry thoroughly. Cover your work area with paper before you begin. Use the rubber bands to mask off a parallel strip around the dish. The width may be varied depending on the size of your dish, but be sure to make them all equidistant.

YOU WILL NEED

Set of sundae dishes

Rubber bands 5 mm (¼ in) wide

Solvent-based glass paints such as Vitrail in ruby and gold

No 2 paintbrush

White spirit for brush cleaning

Kitchen paper towels

Template (page 284)

Scalpel

Cellophane for practise runs

VARIATIONS

The dishes could each be painted in a different colour as long as each is strong enough to contrast with the gold. Practise first before going on to the real thing. The central band would make an attractive decoration on wine glasses too.

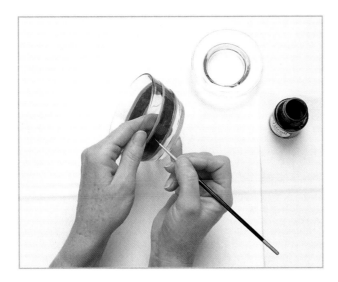

2 Fill the masked off area with the ruby paint, keeping the bowl clear of the work top to avoid smudging. Keep a paper towel to hand for brush cleaning before moving on to the next step.

3 The narrow gold bands are added next, along with the wavy gold line which forms the basis for the leaf and tendril design. Have a practise run on cellophane first using the template (see page 284) as a guide.

4 Once you are confident painting the leaf and tendril design, paint them on the bowls. If your artistic ability is not up to it, try painting little groups of three dots or simple tendrils instead.

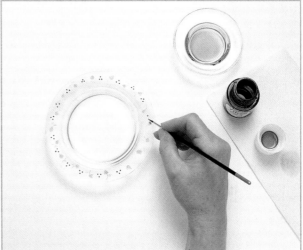

5 Finally, work on the saucers. The leaf design is echoed around the edge in gold, followed by groups of three red dots in between.

HISTORICAL GALLERY

Spotted 1950s' style glass

Bottom: Use a fine brush to apply spots in a variety of colours.

Miniature perfume bottles

These little bottles are surprisingly cheap to buy and very quickly decorated with simple brushstrokes and outliner.

Hexagonal jar

Bottom: Simple brushstrokes were used for the flowers and gold and white leaf shapes decorate the edges.

Old jam pot

The engraved design on this delightful old jam pot has been highlighted with gold, with fuschias delicately painted around the top.

Venetian-style bottle

The simple brushstrokes on the edges of this bottle were inspired by old Venetian glassware. The lady was painted first with an opaque white and then the green and red clear paints applied on top.

Art Deco bottle

Simple lines and clean colours inspired by the Art Deco movement.

Champagne glass

Bottom: Red and green were drizzled down this old fashioned champagne glass and dots of colour added too.

Recycled perfume bottle

This beautiful lady in her crinoline dress is definitely for the more artistic reader!

Heraldic goblet

This is a good example of allowing the shape of the glass dictate the style of the embellishment. Here, the design has been added in black, white and gold.

Thistle glass

Bottom: This engraved bargain buy has been transformed with the use of colour.

Hexagonal boxes

Simple Art Nouveau motifs have been applied in gold and black.

ANTIQUED ETRUSCAN-STYLE VASE

The little stoppered jug used for this project started life filled with salad dressing which has now become one of the anonymous substances in the fridge! The idea can be adapted to any bottle or jug you can find either hiding at the back of your cupboard or on your next trip to the supermarket. Several pieces may be decorated in a similar way to make an interesting and original display.

1 Sponge the top half of the vase with the green paint allowing it to fade around the middle. The sponging can look quite rough as you are aiming for an aged look. Leave for a few minutes to dry between this and the next three steps.

4 Highlight the edges of the vase with the gold, including the rim and handle. The idea is to make the worn surfaces look metallic.

YOU WILL NEED

Glass jug (ours was filled with salad dressing which is now in a jam jar!)	No 2 paintbrush
	Kitchen paper towels
Oven-bake paints such as Porcelaine 150 in pale green, slate blue, pewter and gold	Pewter outliner
	Fine sponge
	Domestic oven
Matt medium	

2 Using the blue paint, sponge from the bottom upwards and over the first coat. Allow the paint to fade out as you work upwards.

3 Antique over the base of the jug with the pewter, adding light touches of the metallic colour to the neck of the jug and the handle. Again, precision is unimportant as a rough look is more authentic.

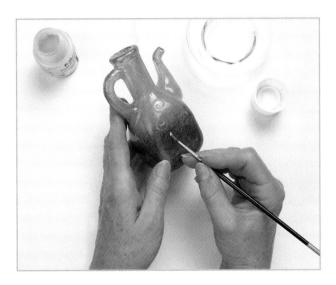

5 Paint swirls of matt medium at random on the vase. The paint looks milky when it is applied but dries to a very subtle finish.

6 Echo the swirls using the pewter outliner. This dries to give an extra dimension to the vase. Leave the vase to dry for 24 hours before baking following manufacturer's instructions.

VARIATIONS

Try making a collection of glassware using this technique. Similar glassware is readily available and very quick to decorate in this way and several pieces could be painted at the same time.

FIFTIES STYLE CARAFE AND TUMBLERS

This really is a 20-minute project! It is brilliantly easy to do and as the shapes are so simple, they require no artistic ability – if you can write, you can reproduce them once you have mastered using the paints.

1 Copy the template on page 285 and lay the cellophane over it in order to have a practice run if you are not sufficiently confident to start straight onto the glassware. Keep a sheet of paper towel to hand and use it to keep the nozzle clean before drawing each motif. Apply the paints sparingly as they will spread slightly over the next ten minutes.

YOU WILL NEED

Carafe and six tumblers
Patterns (page 285)
Cellophane to practise on
Oven-bake outliners, such as Porcelaine 150, in green, magenta and black
Kitchen paper towels
Scalpel or craft knife
Domestic oven

--- **VARIATIONS** ---

Why not decorate the backs of glass plates and bowls to make a complete table setting?

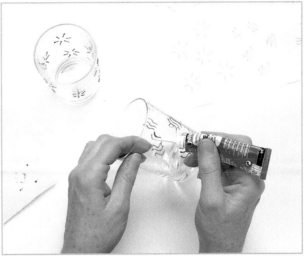

2 Once you are ready to start on the glasses, wash them with hot, soapy water. The black squiggles are fun to do and it is best to do these freehand in order to get a flowing line. The black diamond design is easiest to work in two stages, working from the top to the bottom of one side and then the next.

3 Magenta sunbursts are worked from the outside inwards, making up the six spokes. The second magenta design of three wavy lines is then worked on the next glass.

4 The green triangular design is worked next and then the green dot design. Finally, transfer all the designs to the carafe, starting with the black, followed by the magenta and then the green. The groups of three dots can be added last of all as they are small and make good 'fillers'.

5 Leave all the glassware to dry for 24 hours and then use the scalpel to ease any stray outliner gently into place before baking following the manufacturer's instructions. Wash the glassware before use.

STAINED GLASS MIRROR

The colour selection of red, blue and green has made this simple mirror look quite exotic! The outline shapes could also be used as a solid design to decorate a wine bottle or jam jars with great success. It is easy enough for children to be able to imitate as long as they are carefully supervised, and a myriad of effects can be obtained depending on the colour selection used and the size of each shape.

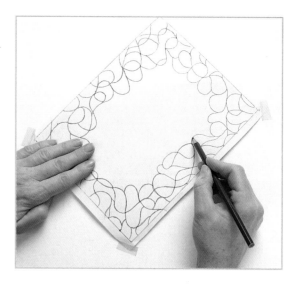

1 Use glass cleaner to remove all traces of grease from the mirror before you begin. Cut the carbon paper to the size of the mirror and lay it face down onto it. Make a copy of the template, enlarging or reducing it as required and lay it over the carbon. Tape it in place. Use the coloured pencil to copy the outline onto the mirror so that you can see what you have already traced.

YOU WILL NEED

Mirror 23 x 18 cm (9 x 7 in)
Glass cleaner
Carbon paper
Scissors
Template (page 286)
Sticky tape
Sharp coloured pencil
Paper for protecting your work top
Solvent-based paints such as Vitrail in ruby red, blue and green
No 2 brush
White spirit for brush cleaning
Hairdryer (optional)
Lead effect outliner
Kitchen paper towels
Scalpel

TIP

The beauty of this project is that precision is unimportant so do not worry too much when you are copying the outlines! You may want to have more or less of the mirror showing than we have and it is easy to adjust this in step 1 by altering the size of the template using a photocopier.

2 Now the fun begins. Load the paintbrush with red paint and allow it to flow onto the mirror. Apply the paint quite thickly to produce a rich colourful effect. Paint about a quarter of the shapes this way. Clean the brush with the white spirit and allow the red areas to dry before using the next colour. This may be speeded up with the use of a hairdryer if you wish.

3 Apply the green to a further quarter of the shapes. It does not matter if the edges of your painted areas are uneven as the outliner will hide a multitude of sins!

4 Finally, use blue glass paint to fill in all but a quarter of the shapes. These remaining plain mirrored spaces can be embellished with the addition of rhinestones, glass nuggets or sequins, securing them in place with glass glue, or left plain as we have done.

5 Now use the outliner to trace over the pencil line in the mirror. Apply even pressure to the tube and have a paper towel to hand to keep the nozzle clean Finally, edge the mirror with the outliner to give a finished look. Allow the mirror to dry for about 24 hours before use, and polish off any fingerprints.

TASSELLED CHAMPAGNE GLASSES

Here is an imaginative idea to transform a set of champagne glasses into unique and expensive-looking tableware. As just one colour is used, there is little financial outlay and the results are stunning.

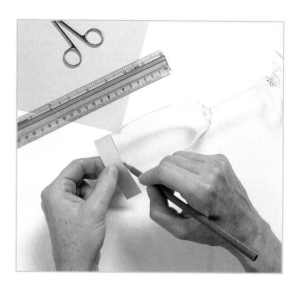

1 Wash the glasses in warm soapy water or clean them with spirit. Start by cutting a piece of paper about 2 cm (¾ in) wide and long enough to fit around the top of the glass and, if necessary, use a pencil to mark the cutting line. This is the template which will determine the height of the tassels but you can adjust it if you wish provided you keep the painted design clear of the lip line of the glass.

YOU WILL NEED

Champagne flutes
White spirit or warm soapy water
Paper
Pencil
Ruler
Scissors
Elastic band
Tassel and rope template (page 285)
Tube of gold Porcelaine 150 outliner
Kitchen paper towels
Domestic oven
Empty jam jars or cellophane (optional)

TIP

Before you begin you may like to experiment with the flow of the paint by testing it on a jam jar or cellophane first. As it is water-based it is easy to wipe off and start again and again until you are proficient. It is a good idea to keep the paper towels at hand to blot the nozzle before each attempt. You will find that the paint tends to spread slightly over the next ten minutes so it is best to avoid applying it too thickly.

2 Fold the paper into five, open it out and then secure it around the glass using an elastic band as shown. This is a quick and easy way to space the tassels evenly as each fold indicates the position of a tassel.

3 Use the glass paint to make five tiny dots around the glass to mark the position of the tassels as shown. Remove the paper and repeat on each glass.

4 Cut the template to fit inside the glass and hold it in place while tracing off the tassel with the gold outliner. (Remember to clean the nozzle with a paper towel before starting each one.) Move the template around and paint all five tassels.

5 Finally, link each tassel with the rope motif. Leave in a safe place for 24 hours to dry and then bake following manufacturer's instructions.

VARIATIONS

This design is equally suited to embellish a straight-sided jug and matching tumblers. As the design is so quick and simple to do, it could be used to decorate a large number of glasses for a special celebration. Why not use silver outliner for a 25th wedding anniversary for example?

BLUE, GOLD AND SILVER GALLERY

Heart
Bottom: These little hanging plastic hearts were decorated using silver and gold outliners.

Snowflake plate
The silver edge was sponged first, followed by the blue. A typist's rubber was used to etch the snowflake shapes.

Tiny storage jar
Below: This little jar has been decorated with a variety of shells and a star fish and is an ideal container for beads.

Old-fashioned sweet jar
This bottle was first sponged with white over the top part of the bottle and then, once dry, blue was sponged up from the bottom giving this wintry effect. Snowflakes were added using outliner.

Simple spiral designed glass
This delightful old glass has been brought right up to date with the simple addition of gold and blue banding.

Triangular blue bottle
Right: There is so much interestingly shaped and coloured glassware on the market now which can be decorated with opaque colours.

Tiny perfume bottles
Tiny hearts and a cherub have been painted on these little bottles using a fine brush and gold paint.

Frosted glass bottle

Bottom: This bottle started life filled with salad dressing! It was too pretty to throw away and has been transformed by being sponged with blue and silver and then decorated with silver snowflakes.

Marbled plate, bottle and jar

Blue, white and gold paints were floated on water and gently swirled to create these marbled patterns.

Storage jar

Here is a simple way to brighten up plain storage jars using deliberately uneven brush marks based on squares.

Wheat vase

Twenty minutes is all you need to add this simple wheat design in gold.

Small storage jar

Above: Use simple flowers, dots and scrolls to make this storage jar suitable for a bedroom or bathroom.

259

SUNFLOWER PLATE

This moulded plate lends itself to being painted as a sunflower. If you are unable to buy a similar one, the design could be applied to the back of a plain plate if you make a simple template first by folding a circle of paper into equal segments. Draw a circle for the centre of the flower and then stick the template onto the inside of the plate before you begin.

1 Lightly brush the petals and centre of the design with the gold. Use it sparingly so that the other colours, to be applied later, will shine through. Set aside to dry.

YOU WILL NEED

Glass plate — ours is 27 cm (10½ in)
Oven-bake paints such as Porcelaine 150 in gold, two shades of yellow, orange, black and brown
Cellophane
No 2 brush
Water
Domestic oven

2 It is time to experiment now while the gold paint dries. Use a piece of cellophane to work out the colour density you want to achieve before working on the plate. Use delicate brush strokes.

3 Use the palest shade of yellow first and brush it evenly, following the direction of the petals. Work the second yellow over it, working about two-thirds of the way up the petals so that the outer edges are paler.

4 Use the orange to darken from the centre of each petal to about half way down, using the brush almost dry to give a light, feathery look.

5 The centre of the sunflower is stippled using a mixture of brown, black and orange to give the appearance of seeds. Leave the plate to dry for 24 hours before baking according to the manufacturer's instructions. It may then be used and washed frequently without damage.

STARRY OIL BURNER

These beautiful, simple glass burners are perfect for decorating with glass paints and can be painted, etched or sponged to suit any occasion. They are available in several different shapes and sizes and are economic to run. No more dripping candle wax! Make sure you use oven-bake paints to prevent any lamp oil coming into contact with the surface and dissolving your creation.

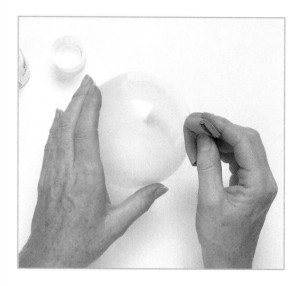

1 Remove the wick and holder from the burner and plug the hole with adhesive putty. Wash the burner in hot, soapy water and dry thoroughly. Sponge the matt medium over the entire surface. Put some of the matt medium on the jam jar too as it will be useful in step 5. The paint looks transparent when it is first applied but it dries quickly. When dry, apply a second coat. A hairdryer will speed up the process.

YOU WILL NEED

Round glass oil burner
Jam jar
Re-usable adhesive putty
Small piece of sponge
Oven-bake paints such Porcelaine 150 in pewter and matt medium
Porcelaine 150 pewter outliner
No 2 paintbrush
Water
Hairdryer (optional)
Large and small star templates (page 287)
Metal ruler
Scalpel with a 11 blade
Cutting mat
Pencil
Paper towels
Domestic oven

SAFETY NOTE

Always follow the manufacturer's instructions supplied with the lamp and never leave it unattended at any time, particularly if you have children or cats in the house.

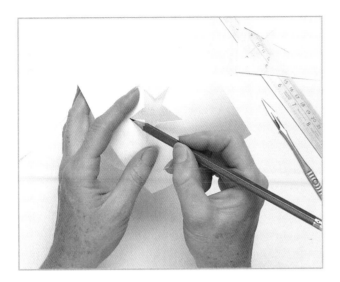

2 Cut out the star templates using a metal ruler, cutting mat and scalpel. (Refer to the techniques section.) Use the pencil to draw the star outline onto the globe using the photograph as a guide for the spacing. Keep the motifs equidistant.

3 Paint the marked stars using the pewter paint. The matt base coat is a wonderful surface to paint over. For a really good cover, a second coat is needed.

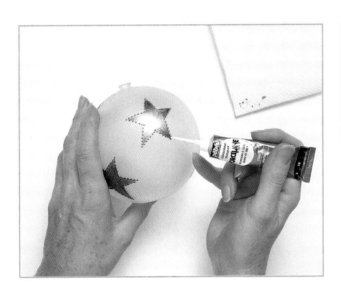

4 Use the outliner to make rows of tiny dots round each star. Be careful to use the outliner sparingly as it continues to spread. Allow the globe to dry thoroughly before moving on to the next step.

5 The tiny stars are etched out using the scalpel and the template pattern provided. It is a good idea to practise on the jam jar first before starting on the real thing. Leave the globe to dry for 24 hours before baking following manufacturer's instructions. Once the globe is completely cool, fill it with lamp oil using a tiny funnel to avoid any getting onto the matt surface. Replace the wick in the bottle and light.

——— VARIATIONS ———

Use different coloured lamp oils to make the burner look festive or spring-like. It will look wonderful as a table decoration surrounded with ivy but make sure leaves are kept well away from the flame.

BLACK, SILVER AND GOLD GALLERY

Etched cork-stoppered jar
Bottom: This jar was frosted with matt medium with the design etched out afterwards.

Oak and acorn glass
Bottom: This design was stencilled on and the detail etched out with a cocktail stick.

Jug
Bottom: As simple as ABC! Letters were drawn on the jug and black dots added around the top.

Black plate
These stunning white brushstrokes look very oriental but are, in fact, simple random strokes.

Cocktail glass
Two coats of gold on the outside of this glass were followed by random black spots for a stylish finish.

Marbled plate
Here black, white and gold paints were floated on water and the design picked up on the back of the plate.

Frosted carafe
Oak leaves have been stencilled on this carafe using matt medium.

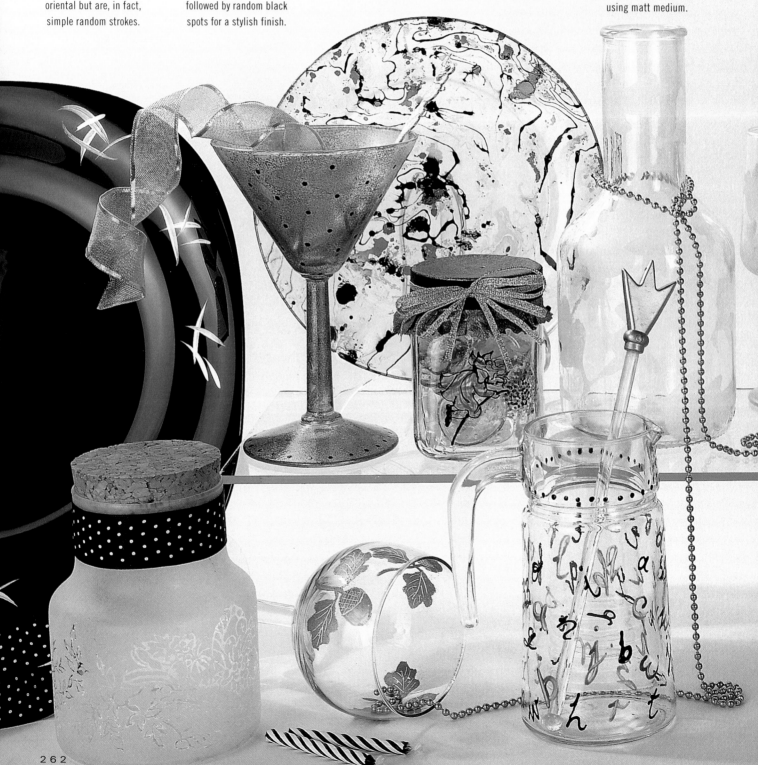

Art Deco jar

Bottom: This jar has been decorated very simply with stylised deer.

Glasses

Below: It is so easy to unite several dissimilar glasses like these with a common colour scheme. Black, gold and white paints and outliners were used to apply the designs.

Christmas bauble

Not even the humble bauble can escape decoration! This one was patterned with outliner.

Art Deco perfume bottle

Centre: This bottle was sponged with silver and gold before the stylised design was added in black.

Black and white dappled plate

Blobs of black and white paint were dropped onto the back of the plate and then spread and etched with a cocktail stick.

Perfume bottle

Bottom: This bottle embellished with trefoils was decorated in the same way as the project on page 264.

Gold and black glass

This glass was made in the same way as the set of decorated glasses with bands on page 244.

PERFUME BOTTLE

Have you ever thought what a pity it is to throw out your empty perfume bottles, especially when they are often such lovely shapes? Here is the answer. The design can be applied to any size or shape of bottle and a group of dissimilar bottles can be united in this way to make an attractive collection for the bedroom or bathroom.

1 Wash and dry the bottle thoroughly before you begin. Cover the entire surface by sponging it with the pewter paint. Apply two or three light coats, allowing the paint to dry between coats. In this way you will build up a really deep, lustrous surface. Allow to dry for 24 hours and bake following manufacturer's instructions. This will make a much better surface to work on and mistakes can be easily removed.

YOU WILL NEED

Small decorative bottle or empty perfume bottle

Oven-bake glass paints such as Porcelaine 150 in pewter, black and ivory

Fine sponge

Trefoil pattern (page 286)

Cellophane for practice runs

No 2 paintbrush

Water

Kitchen paper towels

Domestic oven

2 It is a good idea at this stage to have a practice run at painting the trefoils. To copy the pattern, lay cellophane over the template and paint as many as you need using one colour until you feel sufficiently confident to paint them freehand.

3 Check the spacing of the trefoils by laying the cellophane over your chosen bottle. This will give you an idea of how and where to place the shapes.

4 Now you are ready to start on the bottle. Paint all the ivory shapes in first, remembering to leave room for the other two colours.

5 Paint the black trefoils next and then fill in the gaps with a silvery mix of black and pewter. Leave to dry for a further 24 hours and bake again.

DECORATED WINE GLASSES

Here is a really clever way to decorate glasses and a matching carafe simply with the help of a few rubber bands. Use this technique to mask off sections which are then sponged in one colour. Neat rows of dots add a finishing touch. The perfect project for the non-artistic!

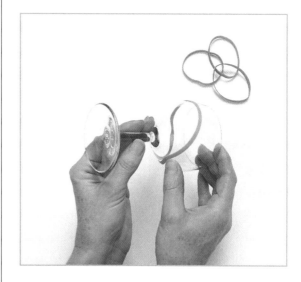

1 Wash all the items in hot soapy water and dry thoroughly. Place a rubber band around the glass 1 cm (½ in) from the top on one side to the same distance from the stem at the bottom. Take time to adjust the band evenly for best results. The width of the band will determine the space between the coloured areas; the band measurement given is the minimum you should use. It is advisable to avoid the lip line if using a paint other than that specified.

YOU WILL NEED

Set of glasses and carafe

Jam jar for practice runs

3 x 5 mm (¼ in) rubber bands for each item to be decorated

Porcelaine 150 glass paints in your choice of opaque colours

Porcelaine 150 outliner

Small piece of fur fabric or fine sponge for each colour being used

Saucer covered in cling film to speed the cleaning up process

Scalpel

Domestic oven

VARIATIONS

Add a matching carafe to the set using a different colour in each section to unite it with the glasses. Experiment with different colour combinations and outliners. This idea can be adapted to make little candle holders decorated with solvent-based paints to give a stained glass effect.

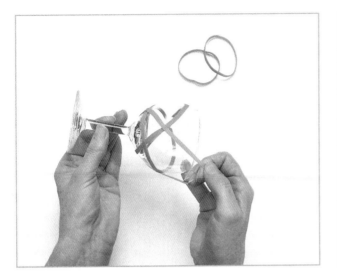

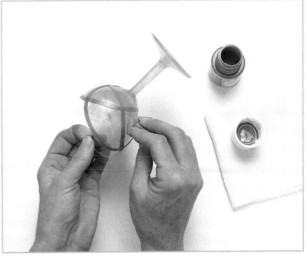

2 Repeat with the second and third rubber bands aiming to spread them equally around the bowl of the glass so that all the sections to be painted are roughly the same size. If you are planning to decorate a carafe to match the set, add bands to it as well.

3 Pour a little paint into the saucer and then sponge the spaces between the bands with your chosen colour. Apply the colour lightly and evenly for best results. We painted all six areas the same colour on each glass but you could use six different colours. Paint the stems too, as we have, or leave them plain. Leave for 24 hours to dry before being tempted to go on to step 4!

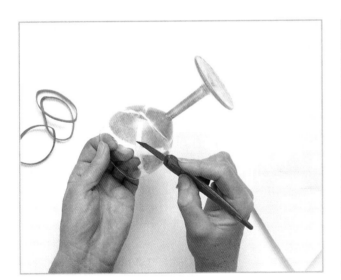

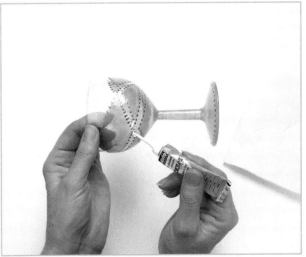

4 Remove the bands and you will find that the paint has seeped under the rubber where they cross. Use a scalpel to neaten up the edges.

5 Using the outliner, apply tiny dots around each block of colour to give a really neat finish. Remember that the outliner tends to spread slightly so leave space between each dot. (It might be worth practising first on a jam jar.) If you are happy with the result, leave for a further 24 hours before baking following manufacturer's instructions. If not, wash the design off and start again! Wash the glasses before use.

FROSTED GLASS WINDOW

Here is a cheap but attractive alternative to frosted glass. It is also a good substitute for net curtaining at windows where you need a little extra privacy. The painting may be done on the inside of an existing window if self-curing paint is used, or on a sheet of glass cut to size as we have done, in which case oven-bake paints may be used for scratch resistance. Use a photocopier to enlarge or reduce the pattern to suit any size of window.

1 Enlarge the pattern using a photocopier to the size required if necessary. Use aerosol mount to attach it to the thin card (if using). Leave to dry for at least ten minutes before cutting the stencil. Place the pattern onto the cutting mat and use the scalpel to cut out the design carefully. Keep the cockerel for step 3.

YOU WILL NEED

A piece of glass (ours is 22 cm (8½ in) square)	Opaque white glass paint such as Vitrail or Porcelaine 150 matt medium
Template (page 287)	
A sheet of paper or card the same size as the glass if you wish to reuse the template	Paintbrushes
	Water or white spirit, depending upon paint used
Scalpel with a no 11 blade or craft knife	Saucer covered with cling film to make the cleaning up process easier!
Cutting mat or thick newspaper to protect the worksurface	
Aerosol adhesive mount	Scrap of fine sponge or fur fabric
Glass cleaner or warm, soapy water	Typist's rubber or halved cocktail stick (toothpick) for etching
Old leather gloves for handling the glass	Cotton bud
	Domestic oven
Offcut of coloured fabric or paper	

VARIATIONS

If you omit the cockerel, this design would look good as a frame for a mirror. With the addition of a few more squares, the pattern can easily be elongated and a row of cockerels added!

2 Thoroughly clean the glass with warm soapy water or glass cleaner and make sure it is completely dry before sponging. Lay the glass onto a piece of coloured paper or fabric so that you can see what you are doing. Use a light spray of adhesive mount on the back of the stencil, leave to dry for a few seconds and then position it centrally on the glass.

3 Pour some opaque white paint into the saucer and use the sponge or fur fabric to apply the paint evenly over the outer design. Hold the glass up to the light to check for even density. Sponge the cockerel last and then remove the stencil with great care and admire before quickly moving on to the next stage!

4 Use the typist's rubber or cocktail stick to etch in the eye, wing and other details of the cockerel using the template as a guide.

5 Finally, remove any stray paint which has managed to work its way under the stencil using a cotton bud and then leave to dry for at least 24 hours. Alternatively, use a scalpel to remove the paint once it is completely dry. Bake if appropriate.

TIP

If using oven-bake paints, remember to use a pane of glass which will fit inside the oven.

FLORAL ROUNDELS

These roundels make a refreshing change from the usual stained glass versions that are now seen everywhere. They are a perfect way to brighten up a window and look attractive when the sunlight shines through them.

1 If your roundel is not the same size as ours, use a photocopier to enlarge or reduce the template to the required dimmensions. Lay the template on the worksurface and tape the roundel over it, being careful to position the tape over plain areas of the pattern.

YOU WILL NEED

Glass roundel — ours is 13 cm (5 in)

Template (page 288)

Masking tape

Black outliner

Craft knife or scalpel

No 2 paintbrush

Solvent-based paints such as Vitrail in ruby and chartreuse

Cellophane for practice runs

White spirit

Kitchen paper towels

Hairdryer (optional)

— VARIATIONS —

These designs could be used as jam pot covers if the designs were worked on cellophane using black paint instead of outliner. Enlarge or reduce the design according to the size of the jar and use white tissue underneath it to show off the design.

2 With the outliner, carefully follow the outlines of the flowers and leaves using steady, even pressure. Start at the top and work towards yourself to avoid smudging. Keep a paper towel to hand to remove any blobs of outliner from the tip of the nozzle. Leave to dry or speed up the process with the hairdryer.

3 If there are any imperfections in the outlining they can be salvaged at this stage. Use a scalpel to scratch off any rough areas and use the paintbrush to gently brush loosened outliner away from the surface.

4 Practise your brush stokes on cellophane using the ruby paint. Once you are confident, start working on the flowers and brush the petals from the centre outwards to obtain light, feathery strokes.

5 Finally, paint the leaves with the green paint varying the density of the paint for a more realistic effect and to build up depth.

TURQUOISE GALLERY

Stoppered bottle

White lilies have been painted on this bottle with silver used for the stamens. Look through flower catalogues for similar ideas.

Tall turquoise vase

Gold outliner has been applied to give a 'punched' look in simple spirals and curves.

Floral jar

Bottom: Green and silver paints were used to brighten up this jam jar. A little white was added to the silver for the outer parts of the petals and the white dots of paint applied last.

Goldfish jar

Below: This would be fun to fill with bubble bath as a gift for a child. The fish were painted with outliner first and then with a coat of clear yellow glass paint.

Fish platter

Gold was lightly brushed on the back of this plate and then a variety of blues, greens and turquoises painted over it.

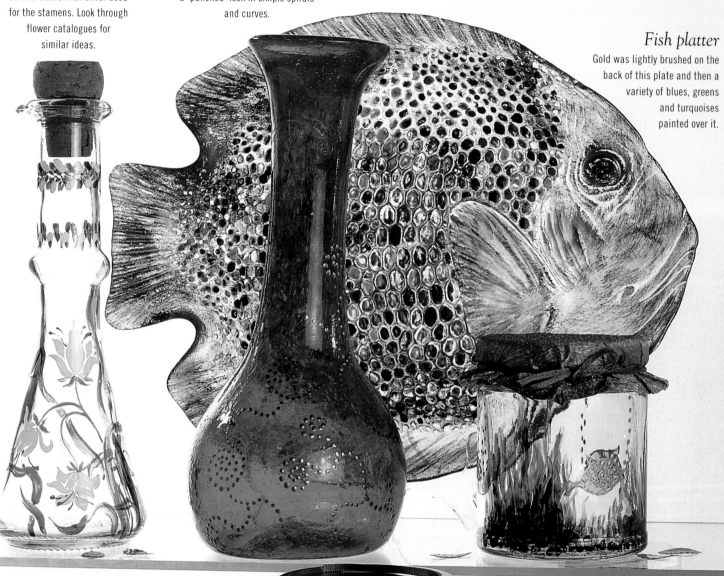

Two-tone glass

Bottom: Transparent oven-bake paints in green and blue were sponged onto this little glass to give a graded effect.

Marbled plate

The edge of the plate was painted with gold and allowed to dry before turquoise, green, purple and gold paints were floated on water, and the plate marbled with them.

Cup and saucer

Below: Just imagine sipping fruit tea from this cup, beautifully painted with blackcurrants. Why not make a set featuring a variety of fruits?

Multi-faceted jug

This old jug was picked up at a junk shop and transformed by being sponged with a range of oven-bake paints. Pewter outliner was then dotted around each colour.

Tall vase

Simple brushstrokes in shades of blues, greens and gold make this a very quick and easy project.

Turquoise tumbler

Left: The black lines were applied first and then green, white and gold paints to fill some of the spaces.

Clip frame

Black outliner was allowed to trail in wiggly lines around the frame. Once it was dry, some of the spaces were filled with green, gold and purple paints.

Encrusted bottle

Chunky glass nuggets were glued in place on this bottle and the design worked around them. The bottle has been worked in both of paints and outliners.

MARBLED PLATE

Decorate the back of a glass plate with this attractive combination of techniques to produce designer tableware. You may be lucky enough to have one of these plain glass plates, so popular in the 1960s, at the back of your cupboard. If not, they are still readily available in department stores.

1 Run the tape around the plate about 5 mm (¼ in) from the edge and then use this as a guide to paint the silver rim. If you have a steady hand you will be able to do this freehand. Leave to dry thoroughly before removing the tape.

TIPS

Before you begin the marbling, cover the worksurface with plenty of protective paper. Line the bowl with a polythene bag, if you wish, and fill with water to within 2.5 cm (1 in) of the top. We found that this makes the cleaning up process very easy! Be warned, however, that lining the bowl with PVC cling film and certain plastics can prevent the colours from spreading. We learnt the hard way and experimentation is essential.

Instead of using cellophane or paper to clean the surface of the water (see step 5), use a jar or small bottle to pick up the paint. You might end up with a really interesting piece!

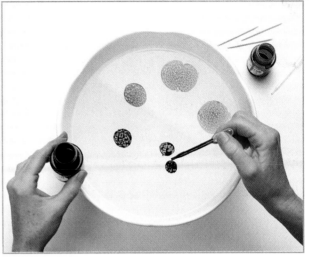

2 The fine silver detailing is added at this stage using the outliner. Once the paint has been 'anchored' on to the rim of the plate at one side, the tube is lifted up into the air and the paint allowed to flow backwards and forwards across the plate in fluid lines. Occasionally it may break but do not worry too much – it all adds to the character of the design! Allow to dry.

3 Drop the purple paint onto the surface of the water or wallpaper paste using a pipette or cocktail stick and it will spread immediately. About 5 drops will be enough. For best results, speed is of the essence now.

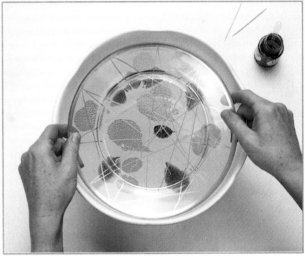

4 Using the pipette, add a few drops of the second colour and then use the cocktail stick to swirl the colours gently into a pleasing pattern.

5 If you are not happy with the pattern you have created, remove it by lifting it off the surface using cellophane or paper towels and start again. When you are pleased with the result, pick up the plate at the very edges, position it over the marbled pattern and then tip it towards you slightly and down onto the marbled surface. Carefully rock the plate away from you so that it picks up the pattern on the surface of the watery solution. Turn it upside down and stand it on a small tin or similar item. Use brush cleaner on a paper towel to remove any paint which has found its way onto the front of the plate and then leave it to dry for 24 hours.

TIP

Store marbled plates with sheets of silicone paper between them to protect the pattern. The plate can be washed as long as it is not immersed in water which will damage the marbling. As there is no paint on the cutting surface, it is ideal for occasional use.

PASTA JAR

Brighten up your pasta jar with these colourful Italian flags. This project is perfect for a beginner as no artistic ability is required! Tie a large bow around it and fill with spaghetti for an attractive inexpensive present.

1 Wash the pasta jar thoroughly in warm, soapy water and dry thoroughly. Cut the greaseproof paper to fit around the jar and cut off about 5 mm (¼ in) down one side. Stick the paper lightly to the jar. Stick the string to the top of the jar and then wind it around and around the jar before taping the string in place at the bottom of the jar. Aim for about three rotations. Using the string as a guide, draw a continuous line onto the paper.

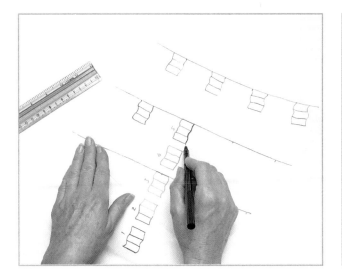

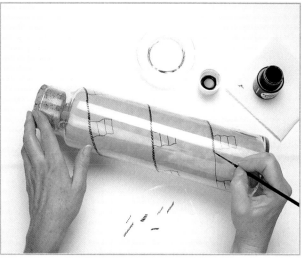

2 Remove the string and lay the paper flat. Place the flags equally on the line by measuring even gaps between them. Use the five variations of flags given and draw them along the line. You now have a pattern which will fit snugly into your pasta jar.

3 Place the pattern into the jar and fill it with pasta to hold it in place. Paint the line with the black paint using either a straight line or a rope pattern if you are more adventurous, but experiment first on a piece of cellophane. Use the hairdryer to speed the process if you are impatient.

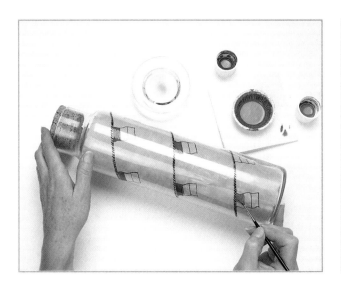

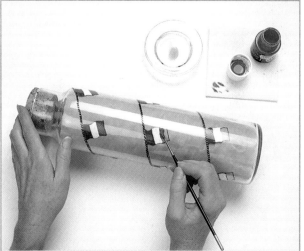

4 Paint the green section on each flag next, again allowing the colour to dry before moving on. If necessary, mix a little blue with the green to achieve the correct shade.

5 Change the water and clean your paintbrush very well before painting the white part of each flag. Allow it to dry and then finish with the red and leave for 24 hours to dry before baking following the manufacturer's instructions.

TEXTURED FRUIT TUMBLERS

There is no need for a template when the design is embossed in the glass as it is in these tumblers. This makes it ideal as a beginner's project. The tumblers are made from recycled glass and similar glassware is widely available. Use the idea on embossed jugs and wine bottles too, and choose jewel-like colours to produce a luscious look.

1 Thoroughly wash and dry the glasses in hot soapy water to remove any trace of grease and then dry them in a cool oven. Choose the colours you want to use and test them on a sheet of cellophane before starting on the glassware. Start by painting the lemons and orange slices with the yellow paint.

YOU WILL NEED

Embossed glasses

Porcelaine 150 glass paints in orange, pink, purple, yellow and green

Cellophane

No 2 paintbrush

Water

Kitchen paper towels

Domestic oven

TIP

You can easily unite a collection of mismatched textured glassware by painting it in the same colours.

2 Using the orange paint, highlight the citrus slices to give them depth and a rich, fruity look. You may wish to build up colours by using two or more coats of paint.

3 We have chosen a cerise pink for these cherries but if you prefer a brighter look, use a strong red or even a really dark mix of purple and red paint to imitate juicy black cherries.

4 The grapes are painted using the purple. Do not worry if the paint does not lie flat on the surface of the grapes as the nature of the paint is such that it has an uneven effect. In this project this is of benefit as it reflects the natural bloom of the fruit.

5 Finally, paint the foliage green. Leave the tumblers to dry for 24 hours and then bake according to manufacturer's instructions. Wash the glasses before use.

RED GALLERY

Sundae dish

Below: The top part of the dish was sponged with red, while gold was used for the lower part. Once dry, tiny spots of gold outliner were added as a decorative pattern.

Fleur de lys jar

Bottom left: Flat-sided jam jars are ideal for decorating. This one was sponged first and then the design added with gold outliner.

Triangular red bottle

Bottom: Sponging forms the basis of the pattern on both these bottles. Outliner has been used for the relief patterns.

Valentine platter

Simple and sweet for the one you love!

Faceted jar

This design was inspired by old glassware and could be used very effectively in a range of colours on a set of sundae dishes or tumblers.

Octagonal dish

Positive and negative stencilling has been used to decorate this dish with heart motifs.

Heart-shaped crown bottle

Bottom: Coloured glass bottles are widely available and are easy to decorate. This one features simple but effective designs.

Bow glass

The bottom part of this glass was sponged with gold. Once dry, the bow motif was stencilled on. You could cut your own stencil or use a commercial one.

Strawberry cup

Bottom: You do need some artistic skill to reproduce this design, but it could be simplified or even stencilled. Why not paint a set of glass cups with a selection of fruits and use them to serve fruit teas?

Faceted jug

This wonderful old jug was found at a local junk shop. It lends itself to this kind of decoration and similar pieces of glass are easy to find. A combination of painting and relief work has been used.

Spotty bottle

Mineral drinks come in a superb range of shapes and sizes and are ideal for revamping and re-using.

CHRISTMAS PLATTER

It seems a pity to cover the design on this Christmas plate but it is perfect for serving up hot mince pies on a wintry day. The pattern is on the back, making a series of these plates ideal as special dinner plates if they are washed with care. Christmas trees or ivy leaves could be substituted for holly.

1 Make the reverse stencil for the gold edging by folding a piece of paper in half and then into quarters. Fold in half diagonally twice so that you have 16 layers of paper with the fold lines radiating out from the central point. Use the ruler to measure the radius of the flat base of the plate, and then mark this measurement on the paper from the central point outwards. Cut the 'V' shape as shown in the photograph. Open out the paper (you should have a circle with a pointed edge) and lightly spray with aerosol mount. Leave for a few seconds and then stick to the back of the plate.

YOU WILL NEED

Glass plate — ours is 25 cm (10 in) in diameter
Ruler
Paper
Pen or pencil
Scissors
Scalpel with no 11 blade
Cutting mat
Holly leaf and star patterns (page 290)
Aerosol adhesive spray mount
Solvent-based glass paints in gold, red and green (we mixed emerald and chartreuse for the holly)
Fine sponge or fur fabric
No 2 paintbrush

VARIATIONS

Why not make a complete set of Christmas glasses to match the plate? The holly design could be reduced on a photocopier and the holly and berries painted around the glass bowl. Sponge gold on the base, stem and bottom of the bowl.

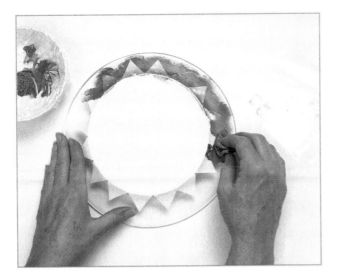

2 Pour a little of the gold paint into the saucer and then sponge over the edge of the template all the way round. Apply the paint densely at the edge of the template to give a sharp outline and less densely near the rim of the plate. Remove the template and leave to dry.

3 Meanwhile, cut the holly stencils using the holly patterns given on page 76. As the points of the leaves are very fine, it is worth using a new scalpel blade before attempting to cut them. Cut out the stars too. Use a cutting mat to protect the worksurface and leave a border of about 1 cm (½ in) around each one. Lightly spray the backs with the aerosol adhesive.

4 Stencil the gold stars in the centre and allow them to dry. Mix the green paints to achieve the desired colour and then stencil about three leaves around the base of the plate using the sponge. Use the photo as a guide and vary the angle of the leaves as you go. We have given you three different leaf sizes to make it look more interesting. Use the cocktail stick to etch in the veining details of each leaf before stencilling the next three.

5 Use the paintbrush to fill in the gaps with the holly berries. We have mixed a rich ruby red colour for them. Leave to dry thoroughly before using.

TEMPLATES

The templates shown here are actual size. They may be easily enlarged or reduced on a photocopier to suit the size of the glass to be decorated.

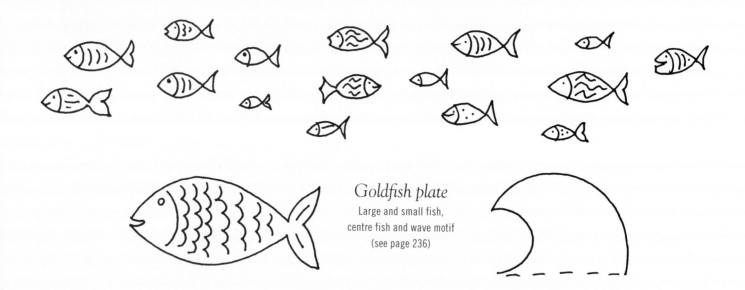

Goldfish plate
Large and small fish, centre fish and wave motif
(see page 236)

Olive oil bottle
Olive spray (see page 238)

Ruby and gold sundae dishes
Leaf and tendril design (see page 244)

Millefiori lantern
(see page 242)

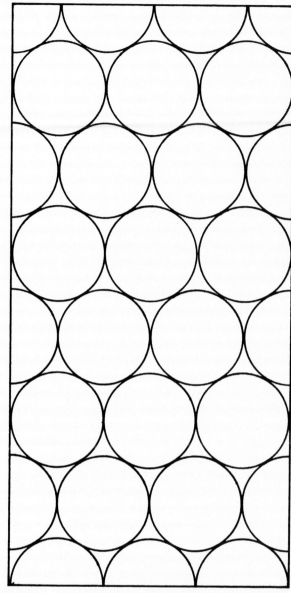

Tasselled champagne glasses
Rope and tassels (see page 254)

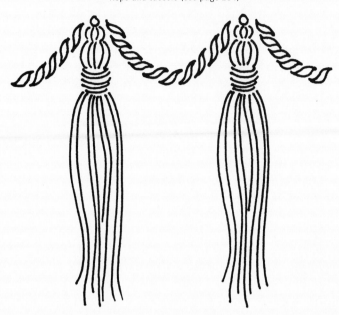

Fifties-style carafe and tumblers
Six different motifs (see page 250)

Stained glass mirror
(see page 252)

Perfume bottle
Trefoil motifs
(see page 264)

Frosted glass window
Cockerel, heart and blocks pattern
for stencil making
(see page 268)

Starry oil burner
Star shapes (see page 260)

Floral roundels
(see page 270)

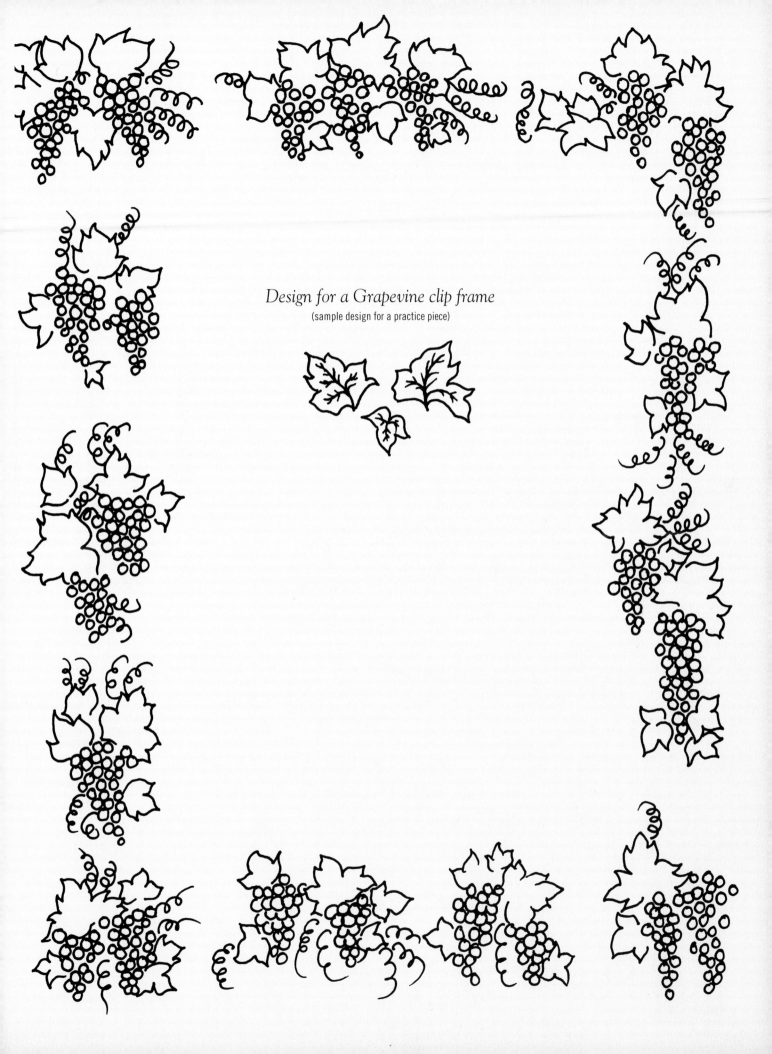

Design for a Grapevine clip frame

(sample design for a practice piece)

Pasta jar (see page 276)

Christmas platter (see page 282)

Practice patterns for getting started (see page 227)

Design for a Floral border
(sample design for a practice piece, repeat
the design for each corner using both sides of
the tracing)

Getting started heart stencil design
(see page 229)

PAINTING CERAMICS

Moira Neale and Lynda Howarth

INTRODUCTION

It all started when we were sunning ourselves in the garden on a hot summer's day, looking forward to seeing the first copy of our previous book, *Painting Glass in a Weekend*, when we suddenly decided it was time for a new challenge. On such a hot day most normal people would be dreaming of diving into a cool swimming pool or having a water fight. Thankfully all you compulsive craft workers reading this will completely understand our need to get motoring on a new challenge. Having had so much fun writing our glass painting book, we simply could not wait any longer before embarking on this new project.

We discovered that painting ceramics can be even more fun than glass because the opacity of china allows you to achieve completely different results and, in the case of bowls, cups, mugs and so on, there are two surfaces to paint instead of one. Now you can paint a range of china to match your hand-decorated glassware. The other exciting development is the availability of new paints which are both washable *and* completely food-safe which takes the craft into a new dimension. All you need is a domestic oven and your items can be patterned for life.

It is always great fun to be creative and find new ways of doing things, but while trying our various designs for this book we became very frustrated at being unable to paint perfect concentric circles on our china. In desperation we resorted to using Tony's hifi ... he was out at the time! The results were brilliant, but for some reason he failed to share our enthusiasm and was most relieved when Jim appeared with an ancient record player which is now well splattered with paint!

The only problem with china painting is that it does become compulsive, particularly when there are two of you egging each other on, and much practise and experimentation is required on anything and everything you can lay your hands on. We had to laugh during a recent painting session. Jim came into the kitchen to make some coffee and exclaimed, 'Hang on ... this was just an ordinary cup and saucer the other day'. Yes, this is true. The cup and saucer he was talking about now take pride of place between these pages and can never be referred to as ordinary again.

We hope that you will enjoy our book and that you too will no longer have cupboards full of ordinary china, but bursting with colourful creations that you will be proud to own. When the shelves start to overflow with your designer china, which they surely will, you will know it is time to start wrapping them up and giving them away as presents.

Have fun!

Moira Neal.

Lynda Howarth

Moira and Lynda, partners in design

GETTING STARTED

Like so many crafts, all that painting on ceramics requires is some basic equipment, lots of enthusiasm and a willingness to try something new. You will find the projects featured in this section are all quite straightforward, but take a moment first to read through this chapter which explains the various techniques involved. We have developed several new techniques for you to try and the majority of them do not require any special ability. Rest assured that it really won't be long before you are ready to try the projects. Once you have followed a few of them, allow your own creative powers to take over and develop your own designs and colour combinations.

EQUIPMENT AND MATERIALS

Apart from the paints and brushes, you will probably find that you already have much of the equipment listed here. There are several different types of ceramic paints now on the market (see right). These will be available either in your local craft or hobby shop, or via mail order (see page 374 for suppliers).

The other obvious requirement is a good supply of china. You will probably need to have a few practise runs before tackling your first project, so acquire a collection of plain china at boot fairs, garage sales and charity shops for trying out new paints and different techniques. Always wash the china in hot soapy water to remove any dust or grease before painting.

Additional useful items include rubber resist paint, rubber shaper brushes for etching, aerosol glue and an old record player (useful and fun if you fancy being creative!). Refer to page 299 for more details on this unusual painting method.

A selection of china
Ceramic paints (see right for more details)
White spirit (if using solvent-based paints)
Good quality paintbrushes in a variety of sizes; see individual projects (good brushes are quite expensive but a worthwhile investment, so put them on your birthday or Christmas wish list)
Container for water or white spirit
Outliners compatible with the paints being used
Palette or plate for mixing colours
Kitchen paper towels
Cocktail sticks (toothpicks)
Cotton buds
Sponges of various densities and textures
Masking tape
Scissors
Paper
Chinagraph pencil
Newspaper to protect your worksurface
Apron
Domestic oven (if using oven-bake paints)

CERAMIC PAINTING PRODUCTS

There are many ceramic paints now available. They fall into several categories:

1 Water-based paints which do not need baking and are ideal for items which are not going to be washed. They are also perfect for children to use, although children should be supervised at all times.

2 Water-based paints which need to be baked at 200°C for 30 minutes. Items decorated with this type of paint must be washed by hand. The colours are bright and dense and easy to apply.

3 New generation water-based paints which are baked at 150°C and are said to have good dishwasher resistance. These are ideal for tableware and

TIP

To keep the mess down, once you are ready to begin, protect your workspace with layers of old newspaper or an old tablecloth as some of the ceramic paints are solvent-based and may damage some surfaces.

If children are going to help with the painting, make sure they are also well covered up.

SAFETY NOTES

There is no reason why children cannot enjoy the hobby of ceramic painting as well as adults. Make sure that they are supervised at all times and choose water-based paints for them to use. Store paints and brush cleaner in a cool place, well out of the reach of prying hands when not in use.

Always follow manufacturers' specific instructions regarding the baking process if it is required (see facing page for more details).

OUTLINING

There are various types of outliner on the market and it is important to select one compatible with the paint you are using. If using an oven-bake paint, the outliner must be the same.

Outliners are slightly tricky to use at first and so it is worth practising to perfect your technique. Have a piece of kitchen towel to hand to wipe the tip clean before you begin. You will find that very little pressure is required and the aim is to produce an even finish. The projects show that outliners may be used to produce a variety of finishes to your work. Photographs ① and ② show how their application onto basic painted shapes, such as the plate, or masked off areas can be very effective.

A collection of china ready for painting. Broken or unwanted items can be used as test pieces.

glasses and we have used them extensively in this book. They are available in a huge range of colours, both transparent and opaque, and once baked feel wonderfully smooth. Practice may be needed with these, as indeed all paints, to achieve the density of cover required. It is often better to sponge on two light coats, allowing the first to dry before applying the second. There is a matt medium in the range which, if used alone, gives a wonderful frosted effect. Used with the other colours in the range as instructed, it gives a matt finish without affecting the colour. Items painted this way must be fully baked to ensure good adhesion of the colour and a more permanent design.

4 Solvent-based paints which are perfect to use on china not intended for food use and may be hand-washed with extreme care. They are available as transparent or opaque shades and are quick drying. Brushes need to be cleaned using a compatible solvent, generally white spirit. These paints are flammable and should not be used near a naked flame nor should children use them unsupervised. Make sure your work area is well ventilated and well protected with plenty of newspaper.

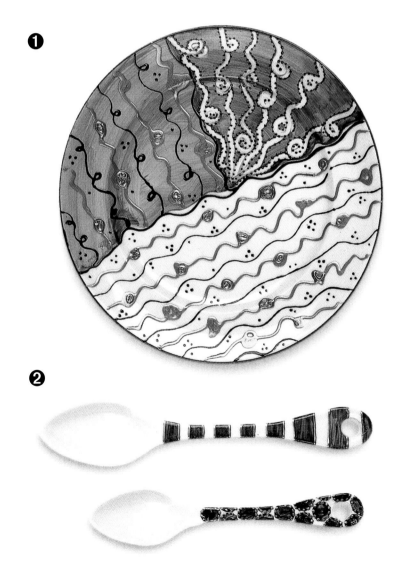

3

They may be used on their own to produce a series of dots, stitch effects, solid and broken lines and cross hatching as well as in conjunction with paints to give emphasis or detail to a design ③.

PAINTBRUSHES

We have been busy experimenting with different types of paintbrush and have been delighted with the results. It is certainly well worth investing in a new brush occasionally. A good quality brush gives the best results and here we tell you about some really useful types.

• **WIDE, FLAT PAINTBRUSHES**
Here is the perfect way to create broad even bands of colour on your china. These brushes are available in a number of sizes but we have found the 2 cm (¾ in) brush to be the most useful. A tartan effect is easily achieved by laying on bands of colour and then overlaying in the opposite direction with the same or contrasting colours ①. Allow plenty of time for the first colour to dry before applying the next. Later, fine lines may be added using a conventional paintbrush or outliner. Look in the tile gallery on pages 326-327 for some more ideas.

This type of brush may also be used to produce a series of parallel lines which looks very effective. A simple daisy type floral design is made by painting five or six lines in a circle, leaving the centre free to paint in a different colour. A number of different shades could be used to build up a more sophisticated type of flower design, depending on your confidence and the effect you want.

• **FAN HEADED PAINTBRUSHES**
These are very useful items for edging plates in the 1930s' style with feathery brush strokes ②. Load the brush very lightly with paint and flick the brush from the outside of the plate towards the centre, making the strokes as long or short as you wish. This is also a good way to achieve a grass effect.

①

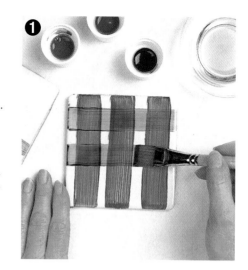

②

Contemporary swirls are easy to paint, too, by lightly rotating the brush on the surface, from just a few turns to a full 360 degree swirl.

3

• ANGLED PAINTBRUSHES

These provide yet another simple way to apply paint in an interesting way. We have used this type of brush to edge tiles in the gallery and also to finish the edge of the bowl on page 320. One, two or more colours may be used alternately to produce an interesting edge. It is also very easy to paint chevron stripes with this brush ③.

A good, long angled dagger brush can give a perfect leaf or petal shape with just one stroke and a little practise to get the angle right ④.

• COTTON BUDS

These can also be used for painting ⑤. The tip holds sufficient paint to be able to draw simple outline shapes, such as the fish shape shown. They are perfect too for painting leaves and frondy seaweed. Cotton buds are also ideal to use for making one or a series of dots in the centre of a flower for example. They produce an interesting texture and can be used to create geometric shapes such as diamonds, crosses and squares made up of a row of dots. The lamp base project on page 330 has been partially decorated with this method. Try combining painting and dotting together. If the cotton buds are used on very freshly applied paint, they may be used to create etched designs and to add etched detailing, to a leaf for example.

RECORD PLAYER PAINTING

Here is a great idea for those of you who are feeling adventurous. As well as being fun, it is a practical method of applying paint evenly to a circular object and works very well on a plate. Find an old record player for this – not a 78 r.p.m. as you will have no control at all! Scrunch up some tin foil into a circle which will fit around the central metal knob on the record deck and then lay the plate on top. Turn the record player on to a slow speed and take time to centralize the plate. Apply the paint to the plate with a large soft brush or sponge until it is evenly covered. If you wish to etch into it, do this immediately with a cotton bud, rubber shaper brush or finger. See the plate gallery on page 342 for examples of this technique.

ETCHING

This is a very good way to add emphasis without having to use another colour ①. It is perfect for adding details like leaves, feathers, scales on fish, eyes and so on as well as creating abstract designs on a sponged surface. You will need to etch the design as soon as the paint has been applied.

Use a cocktail stick for very fine designs or for details on tiny items. A cotton bud or typist's pencil-style rubber, which may be sharpened with a knife or pencil sharpener depending on the effect required, are both ideal for chunkier etching ②. There are some wonderful new rubber-tipped 'shaper' brushes on the market now specially designed for etching which we have found very useful.

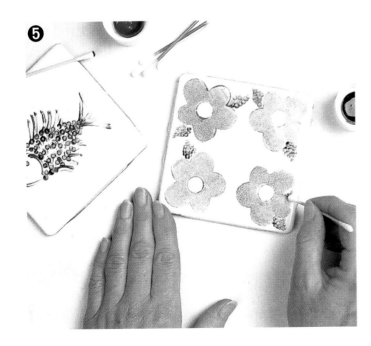

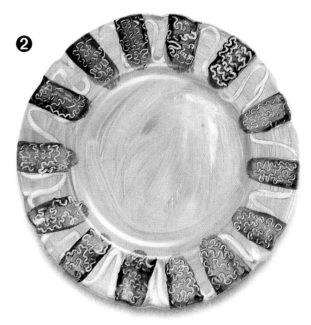

need to resort to thin paper or specialist adhesive stencilling film which will mould more easily to the contours of the china and can be used several times.

You can make your own stencils by photocopying your chosen pattern first. Paper is fine for one-off designs, otherwise use adhesive mount to attach the pattern to the card you are using and allow the glue to dry for about ten minutes before attempting to cut it. Protect your worksurface with a cutting mat or a thick layer of old newspaper before you start. Use a metal ruler as a guide for cutting straight lines and avoid trying to cut around angular designs in one go.

USING YOUR STENCILS

Lightly spray the back of the stencil with aerosol spray mount to hold it in place. On cylindrical items you may also need to secure it with a couple of elastic bands, too.

Pour a little ceramic paint into a saucer or the lid of the pot of paint and use a piece of old sponge to apply the paint ②. It is always worth

STENCILLING

This is a good way to decorate china with a regular repeat pattern or a single bold design. It is particularly useful if you intend to sell your ceramics as it is a very quick process once the initial stencil cutting is out of the way.

It is worth taking great care at the beginning in order to get good, professional results and the initial investment in a craft knife or scalpel and spare blades is worthwhile ①. For one-off stencils to decorate on flat surfaces, thin card or even a good quality paper is ideal. If you are using the stencil on a curved surface, you may

experimenting at this stage. Natural sponge will give a coarser, more rustic look than synthetic sponge which gives a more even finish.

Torn paper stencils can be very effective and are quick and easy to make ③. For example, to make a heart simply fold the paper in half and then draw the shape on as a tearing guide. Carefully tear along the drawn line, then open out and use as above.

MASKING AND REVERSE STENCILLING

There are several ways to mask areas of china before sponging. Stick on shapes like stars, hearts, ring reinforcements or indeed any shape you care to cut out. Use aerosol adhesive mount to apply your own shapes. This method can also be used to add a regular pattern to the edge of a plate for example. Masking tape, torn strips of paper and very thin tape available from art shops can also be used ④. Squares, oblongs, stripes of varying widths and harlequin designs are all possible this way. The masked off area can later be embellished with outliner to add relief pattern, such as veining on a leaf.

For a chequered effect, simply stick lines of low-tack tape onto the china. Sponge the gaps with several colours and then allow to dry completely before removing the tape and reapplying it in the opposite direction and repeating the process. Clean up any rough paint edges with a scalpel.

MASKING FLUID

Rubber solution masking fluid is a very useful addition to your kit ⑤. Use an old paintbrush to paint it over a ready marked design. (Wash the brush immediately to prevent it being ruined.) Allow the fluid to dry for a full 24 hours before being tempted to paint or sponge over it. When the paint has dried, use the tip of a cocktail stick to remove the rubber mask. If used over chinagraph, the marks will be removed with the rubber solution.

SAFETY NOTE

Dispose of broken and worn scalpel blades safely by wrapping in cardboard or placing in an old film canister.

STAMPING

A mosaic effect is very simple to achieve by cutting up thin kitchen sponge into squares and then lightly dipping into paint. Also try some of the many commercially available stamps too. These are ideal when working on a flat surface ①. Apply the paint to the stamp with a brush.

Potato printing is great fun and children will especially enjoy doing this. Cut out simple shapes from the potato to make repeat patterns and use biscuit (cookie) cutters to cut larger shapes like trees, hearts, stars and so on. The finished effect is fairly rustic but worth experimenting with ②.

SPONGING

Sponging is a quick and easy way to apply ceramic paints and a variety of finishes can be achieved. Practise on an old tile first. Anything from natural sponge to make-up sponges or thin sponge dishcloths can be used. Natural sponge gives a coarse, rustic effect, while synthetic sponge results in a finer finish. A graduated effect is made by gradually decreasing the pressure on the sponge as you work down the object or around the rim of a plate. A multicoloured, graduated finish is achieved by using several colours in succession, allowing each one to merge into the next ③.

We had fun sponging large dots with commercially available sponges; a similar effect can be made by cutting sponge into a circle.

You can either use paint straight from the pot or tip a little onto a saucer which has been covered in cling film first to make the cleaning up process quicker and easier.

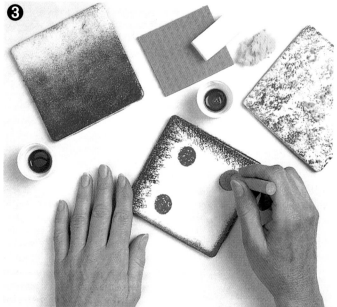

PRINTING WITH LEAVES

Fresh leaves may also be used to take a print from. Use a sponge to apply a very small amount of paint to the veined reverse side of the leaf, then lay it in place on the china and press over it with damp cloth. Peel off the leaf immediately, taking care not to smudge the paint.

Use a range of green shades, or autumnal browns, rusts and a touch of gold for a stunning result. The edge of a plate decorated in this way could be sponged with gold. You could add berries painted freehand in bright red.

COLOURWASHING

For this technique, paint is thinned down slightly and applied with a large soft brush ①. Stipple the paint on and merge colours into each other to produce a soft watercolour effect 'canvas' on which to base your design. Once the colourwash is completely dry, detailed painting may be worked on top as in the Dufy style jug on page 314.

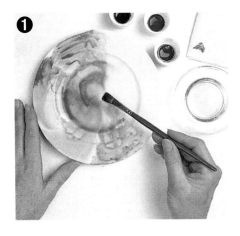

CLEANING OFF UNWANTED PAINT BEFORE BAKING

It can be difficult to wash off the paints once they have dried but the quickest method is to wear rubber gloves and make up a hot solution of dishwasher detergent. Allow the object to soak for a few minutes and the design will wash off very easily.

TRANSFERRING DESIGNS

Unlike glassware, where the design is so easy to tape on the inside and to trace through, transferring onto china needs more thought. One way is to trace the design onto paper ② with a soft 2 or 3B pencil, then turn the paper over and tape in place on the surface of the china. Draw over design on the reverse side of the paper and the outline will be lightly transferred onto the china ③. Chinagraph pencils may also be used to mark out design but we have been careful to use chinagraph as a guide only as it may act as a resist if you try to paint over it. It will also show through light colours.

You can re-size any of the designs we have provided in the back of this book with a photocopier in order to tailor the size to your own china.

EMBELLISHMENTS

There are many ways in which to embellish your china but much depends upon how washable it needs to be. Shiny glass nuggets may be used to give a rich jewel-like finish to an exotic vase, for example, and should be held in place with a two-part or specialist glass glue. Sequins are easy to apply and come in a multitude of shapes and colours. The addition of cellophane wrapping and a pretty bow make your object into a very presentable gift.

INSPIRATION FOR DESIGNS

Wallpapers and borders, wrapping paper, gift cards, colouring books, curtain fabrics, and flower and bulb catalogues are good sources of inspiration. Do remember, however, that you may not sell any work using other people's designs.

For a baby gift you could use the nursery wallpaper design to inspire the design on the edge of a picture frame. Glasses, jugs and carafes decorated to match existing crockery or table linen make excellent gifts for adults and may be themed to celebrate a special occasion such as a special birthday or anniversary. If you are looking for ideas for floral designs, seek out fabrics, handkerchiefs and decorated papers as well as gardening magazines.

If you enjoy museums, why not visit one and get inspiration from old china? We found some fascinating pieces and there are so many styles that may be used for inspiration. The brightly coloured Clarice Cliff designs can inspire your own ideas based on similar colours and simple shapes. Old Moorcroft pottery with its beautiful raised texture can be emulated by piping on outliner to give an extra dimension. Be sure never to copy anything exactly. Instead, loosely base your designs on what you have seen, taking shapes from different sources. This ensures that your work will always be original.

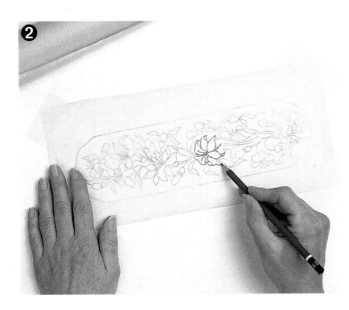

PROJECTS AND GALLERIES
FOR PAINTING CERAMICS

HARVEST TABLEWARE

Here is a really simple project to get you started on ceramic painting. We have used a set of embossed tableware which features apples, figs, grapes and plums but if you cannot find the same china, simply use the idea shown here to embellish any type of fruits, shading them as shown. This project is designed to look hand-painted, so don't worry if your brush strokes show.

1 Wash the china in hot soapy water. Then pick out the apples with the scarlet paint, painting one side rosier than the other for a realistic ripening effect and graduating the paint so that it fades towards the middle.

YOU WILL NEED

Embossed tableware either matching or assorted

Porcelaine 150 paints in scarlet 06, Havana 34, garnet 11, amethyst 13, peridot green 30 and green-gold 31

No 2 sable brush

Kitchen paper towel

Small bowl of water

TIP

If you want to vary the colours, be sure to use the transparent paints from the range. You may find it useful to keep all the paints out while you are working as you will need to mix the paints as you go along, moving them around you as you work.

VARIATIONS

Why not paint a set of embossed glasses to complete your set? The same oven-bake paints can be used to paint on glass too.

2 Fill in the apples and plums with Havana. Then, working clockwise if you are right-handed, paint the twisted rope edging with the same paint, wiping any excess paint off the brush with a piece of paper towel if necessary. You do not need to clean the brush.

3 Dip the brush into the garnet and pick out the figs. Also paint the grapes using the garnet, then clean the brush in the water and dab it dry on the paper towel.

4 Use amethyst paint to build up the colour of the grapes and to add the shadows to the other fruits where they touch. Change the water, if necessary.

5 Working clockwise, paint the foliage using peridot green, applying the colour slightly unevenly to add an impression of depth. Darken the centres of the leaves and add the veins to finish the natural look. Use the green-gold to add highlights to the leaves. Leave the crockery to dry for 24 hours and then bake it following manufacturer's instructions.

COLOURWASHED COOKIE JAR

This is a wonderful free technique which could be applied to a multitude of surfaces. Enlarge or reduce the design to suit the size of the object being decorated. We have also decorated a jug to match.

1 Wash the jar in hot soapy water. Load a number 4 brush with water and then dip the tip into the first of the four colours. Apply the colour with a very free, washy technique making it more dense in the centre of each area. Repeat on the lid.

YOU WILL NEED

White cookie jar or other white china washed in hot soapy water
Porcelaine 150 paints in ruby 07, citrine 01 (yellow), emerald green 19, lapis blue 16, petroleum blue 22 and abyss 41 (very dark blue)
No 4 paintbrush
No 1 fine liner brush
Small bowl of water
Kitchen paper towels
Template (see page 356)
Sheet of cellophane

VARIATIONS

This technique can easily be adapted and used as a springboard for your own ideas. You may prefer to apply the colourwash all over as we have done on the adjacent jug.

2 Continue with the other colours, spacing them out to fill the surface. Leave some areas of white as we have or merge the colours into each other until you have a base you are happy to work on.

3 It is useful to practise the designs provided by laying a sheet of cellophane over them and following the lines using the fine liner brush. This type of brush makes it easier to produce long, sweeping strokes. If you are not too confident with your painting ability, it is a good idea to bake the jar at this stage for about 15 minutes, following the manufacturer's instructions. This will be long enough to 'set' the base coat so that any mistakes may be safely washed off.

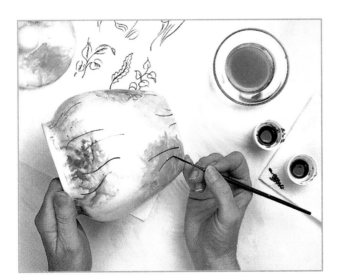

4 When you are ready to commit the pattern to the cookie jar, start by painting a skeleton of long, sweeping lines to represent plant stems, distributing them around the jar. Leave some of the white areas free from design.

5 Now add leaves and flowers using all six varieties shown on the template. Work freely and confidently to achieve a really flowing finish. Once you are happy with the result, leave to dry for 24 hours, then bake following the manufacturer's instructions.

BARGE-WARE POT

Black china provides the ideal background for this colourful paint technique. Here we have used acrylic deco paints for a greater density of colour. These are water-resistant when dry and can withstand occasional, careful hand-washing. The beauty of this style of painting is its flexibility and the way the different roses, leaves and little flowers may be arranged to suit the container you are working on.

1 As brush strokes are an integral part of this design, it is worth taking time to practise each stage of the design first. Build up the petals of the red, yellow and white roses by starting with the central petals and working outwards with sweeping brush strokes.

YOU WILL NEED

| Black china |
| Pattern (see page 357) |
| Tile or plate to practise on |
| Acrylic paints such as Pébéo Deco in red 06, yellow 03, blue 12, antique green 28 and white 41 |
| No 2 paintbrush |
| Small bowl of water |
| Kitchen paper towels |

VARIATIONS

Use this painting style to recycle old tinware as well as ceramics. It is traditionally used to decorate kettles, teapots, watering cans and tinware plates. The background for the design should be red, bottle green, navy or black.

2 Next, paint the little blue flowers with five dots of paint each. The pattern is flexible enough to adapt at this stage as long as you keep it roughly symmetrical in character with the traditional look.

3 Now paint the leaves with two brush strokes each. Again, practise this technique on the tile first. The definition is added at a later stage when the paint has completely dried.

4 Add definition to the small flowers by outlining with the white. While you have white on the brush, add the tiny white dots around the outside of the leaves and then paint the stamens on the red roses.

5 Paint the centres of the little flowers with the red along with the stamens on the white and yellow roses. Add the yellow brush strokes to the leaves and a few random brush strokes to the background to fill in any spaces. Wash out all brushes very thoroughly as acrylic paint can spoil them if allowed to dry. Leave the pot to dry for several days to allow the paint to harden completely before being tempted to use it.

JAZZ JUG

Capture the simple style of the 1950s with this stylised design. Stripes of various widths are decorated with simple outlines of musical notes, treble clefs and a variety of different instruments which are characteristic of the beatnik era.

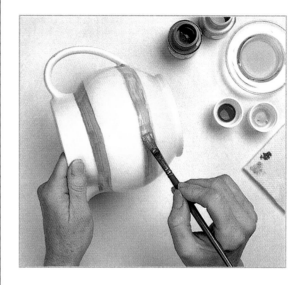

1 We mixed the Ming blue with a little ivory to soften the colour slightly before we started. Using the flat wash brush, paint bands of blue and green onto the jug. The number of bands and their thickness is variable and will depend upon the size of your jug and the effect you want. Also paint a band of colour down the handle.

YOU WILL NEED

Ceramic jug
Porcelaine 150 paints in Ming blue 1, ivory 43, opaline green 24 and abyss blue 41 (very dark blue)
1 cm (⅜ in) flat brush
Dagger paintbrush or no 4 paintbrush
Fine liner paintbrush
Template (see page 357)
Old tile or plate to practise on
Kitchen paper towels
Container of water
Scalpel

VARIATIONS

Instead of a musical theme, you could choose to use simple trees and flowers or birds and fishes.

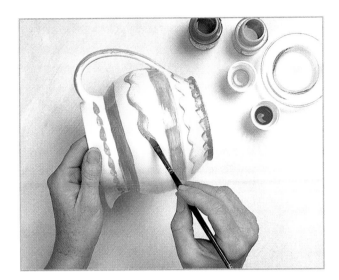

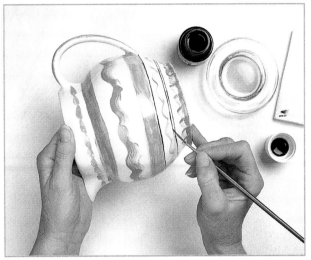

2 Next, add some wiggly lines with a dagger brush if you have one. If not, a similar effect is possible if you use a no 4 paintbrush. We have used just two colours for our jug but you may want more and now is a good time to add a third colour if you wish. Soft pink would work well with the colours we have used.

3 Use a fine liner brush and the dark paint to place a few fine lines in between the others. You could use black outliner if you prefer, although this would give a far heavier feel to the jug.

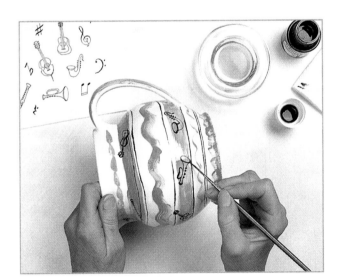

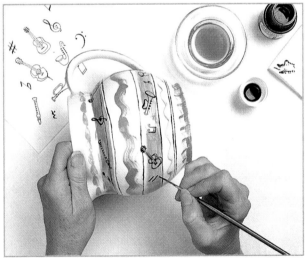

4 We have provided a number of musical notes and instruments to copy. There is no need to use them all and the ones you choose will depend on your artistic ability to copy them! We suggest you practise first on a tile or plate before applying them to the jug. If you wish to use any of the instruments, paint them at this stage. If you are nervous about making a mistake, simply bake the jug for about 20 minutes according to the manufacturer's instructions. This will set the surface well enough to wash off any errors.

5 Fill in some of the gaps with simple musical notes and signs but be careful not to over-complicate the design. If there are any irregularities in your work that you are not happy with, simply use a scalpel to neaten them up. Finally, once you are happy with your work, allow the jug to dry for 24 hours, then bake according to the manufacturer's instructions.

OLIVE DISH

The addition of a few sprays of olives has transformed this simple partitioned dish into a stylish piece of tableware perfect for serving olives, nuts, crisps and other nibbles. It would also make a very welcome gift for any occasion.

1 Wash the dish in hot soapy water before you begin. Use a pencil to copy the pattern onto the dish. If you are a confident painter you may not need to do this and simply have the pattern beside you to use as a guide as you work.

YOU WILL NEED

Partitioned dish
Template (see page 358)
Pencil
No 1 fine liner paintbrush
Porcelaine 150 paints in mummy brown 39 (dark brown), peridot 30, bronze 28 (leaf green), green-gold 31 and amethyst 13
Old tile or plate, for mixing paint
Kitchen paper towels
Small bowl of water

VARIATIONS
We have decorated a similar dish with holly. See the Christmas gallery on page 352 for further details.

2 Next, with the fine liner brush and the dark brown, paint the stalks of each of the three olive sprays. Use long flowing brush strokes working from the bottom of the spray upwards.

3 Before you start painting the leaves, make an olive green by mixing the two greens and a touch of brown. Paint the leaves with this mixture, working towards the tip of each one.

4 Now work into the leaves, extending the centre stem definition with the brown. To make the leaves appear folded in places, run a light coat of brown paint down the edge of each leaf.

5 Make a mix of the amethyst and brown and use this to paint the olives. Apply the colour fairly thinly working from the outside of each olive to achieve the characteristic shine. Allow the dish to dry for 24 hours, then bake following the manufacturer's instructions.

CLEMATIS DISH

This pretty dish looks good filled with fruit, vegetables or salad but would work equally well as a stylish bathroom accessory holding soaps or shells. We have made it deceptively easy to copy.

1 Wash the bowl in hot soapy water. We have painted seven flowers but you can change this number to suit the size of your bowl. The easiest way to divide it up accurately is to run some masking tape around the rim and cut it to the exact circumference. Then lay it out, measure it and divide by seven, then mark the spacing on the tape. Place the tape back around the bowl and make a mark with the chinagraph pencil for the position of each flower. Remove the tape.

YOU WILL NEED

Bowl
Masking tape
Ruler
Chinagraph pencil
Scissors
Porcelaine 150 paints in lapis blue 16, abyss blue 41(very dark blue) and bronze 28 (leaf green)
Plate for mixing the colours
No 4 brush
Small bowl of water
Kitchen paper towels
Template (see page 358)
Cotton buds
Angle tipped brush (1 cm or ⅜ in)

VARIATIONS

Create a two-colour saw tooth edging by painting alternate brush strokes in a different colour. Try yellow and blue and paint the flowers on the outside the opposite colour. See the Getting Started section for further details.

2 Pour a little of the two shades of blue on the mixing plate and start painting the petals using two brush strokes per petal. Using the pattern as a guide, paint five petals for each flower using the lapis blue on its own for some of them, and a mix of the two shades for other petals to create depth of colour. Work on the centre of the dish only at this stage and once all the steps have been completed, start on the outside.

3 Next, using the leaf green paint and the no 4 brush, link the flowers with the stalk and tendril design using a very free flowing technique. Use the pattern provided as guide.

4 Use the abyss blue and the no 4 brush or a cotton bud to make a number of small dots on the centre of each flower. Use the cotton bud to remove the tiny chinagraph marks to ensure good adhesion of the paint once the dish is baked.

5 Finally, load the angle tipped brush with the lapis blue to create the saw tooth edge to the bowl making each brush stroke about 1 cm (⅜ in) long. Allow the bowl to dry for several hours before repeating the whole process on the outside, reversing the pattern. Note that the tendril design is reversed to give the bowl balance. Allow the bowl to dry completely for 24 hours, then bake following manufacturer's instructions.

FLORAL FINGER PLATES

Protect the woodwork of your doors with these finger plates decorated with a stylish design of lilies. You could also adapt this design quite easily to paint matching ceramic door knobs.

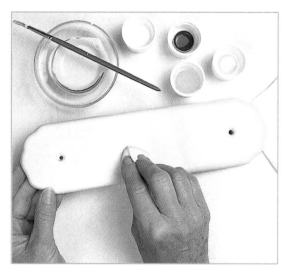

1 Wash the finger plate in hot soapy water. Mix up a pale cream background (or one to match your own decor) from the matt medium, ivory and yellow. When you are happy with the shade, sponge it evenly all over the surface. Allow it to dry, ideally for 24 hours, then bake following manufacturer's instructions. This means that mistakes are easily rectified in the next steps and you can relax as you paint!

VARIATIONS

Co-ordinate finger plates to your own decor by using designs from your wallpaper or borders. Remember you cannot sell any work copied in this way but it is fine for your own use and gives the room a co-ordinated look.

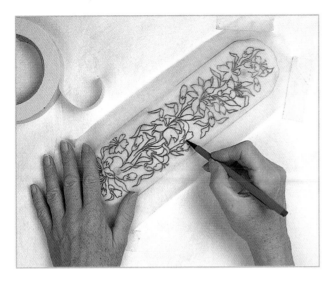

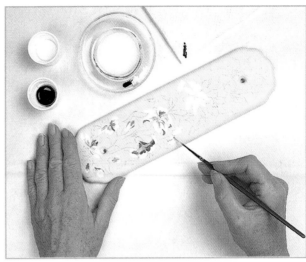

2 The finger plate now has a smooth, matt surface which is easy to work on and takes the paint well. Trace the pattern provided using the pencil. Turn the tracing over and position it centrally on the finger plate. Tape it in position before carefully drawing over all the lines, thus transferring the design to the plate.

3 The lilies are painted first using the ivory, and then the darker areas added by mixing the ivory with a touch of black. Use very delicate brush strokes and make some areas slightly darker to add shadows. Paint the buds in the same way.

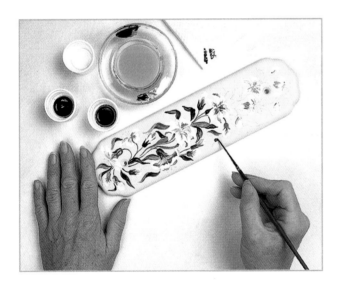

4 Build up a base of green stems and leaves by using the green in a variety of mixes with the black and white to create depth to the design. Allow the green to dry before being tempted to move on to the next stage.

5 Finally, add very fine stamens using the same brush and light brush strokes. Allow the finger plate to dry for 24 hours, then bake following the manufacturer's instructions.

STARRY BREAKFAST CUP AND SAUCER

Just the thing to fill with hot milky coffee for a lazy breakfast, or even a hearty soup on a cold winter's night! This idea could easily be adapted to use on something of lesser proportions – simply reduce the size of the templates on a photocopier.
Less dramatically, the design would work equally well on plain white china.

1 Wash the cup and saucer in hot soapy water. Using the gold paint, lightly sponge around the edge of the cup and saucer, allowing the gold to fade out with a slightly uneven finish. Leave them to dry for a few hours before continuing with the next step.

YOU WILL NEED

Large cup and saucer
Sponge
Porcelaine 150 paint in gold 44
Paper
Scissors
Template (see page 358)
Aerosol glue
Porcelaine 150 outliner in gold
Kitchen paper towels
Scalpel or cocktail stick (toothpick)

───── VARIATIONS ─────
This design would look good around the edge of a serving bowl brimming over with festive treats!

2 Copy a number of both sizes of stars onto paper, cut out and lightly spray with glue on the back. Position the stars around the cup alternating between large and small to create a random effect.

3 If you have not used outliners before, it is a good idea to practise first. Have a piece of kitchen paper to hand to catch any blobs before you begin start outlining the stars. Use the templates as a guide only and make sure that the outliner does not touch them. Allow the outliner to dry for several hours before being tempted to remove the paper shapes with the scalpel or cocktail stick.

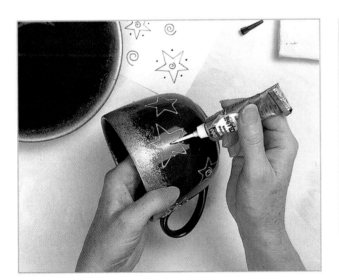

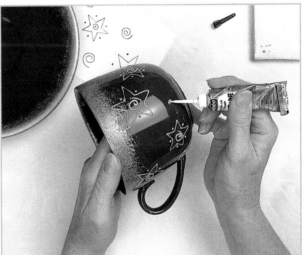

4 Use the template as a guide to add the dots and whirls to the centre of each star. Carefully tidy up any uneven paint with a scalpel.

5 Finally, fill in the gaps between each star with the whirl motif. Alternatively, you could use a different design at this stage such as groups of three dots or crosses. Allow to dry for 24 hours, then bake following manufacturer's instructions.

327

FISH TILES

Plain tiles destined for the bathroom or kitchen wall can easily be decorated with ceramic paint. Once baked, they can be wiped clean using a damp cloth and non-abrasive cleaning fluid. This is a very easy project – you can either work freehand or use the template provided. We have painted two fish, but to build up a larger tableau, paint the fish swimming in different directions on a selection of tiles.

1 Wash the tiles in hot soapy water. Lay out all the tiles you want to decorate, but only work on one at a time as the paint dries very quickly. Using the 2 cm (¾ in) wash brush and emerald green, paint four wavy lines down the first tile.

YOU WILL NEED

Fish template (see page 360)

White ceramic tiles

Porcelaine 150 paints in emerald green 19, Ming blue 17 and abyss blue 41

2 cm (¾ in) wash brush

No 1 paintbrush

Kitchen paper towels

Small bowl of water

Cocktail stick (toothpick)

TIP

Save any slightly chipped or cracked tiles for practising the brush techniques.

VARIATIONS

We have teamed our fish tiles with a really simple, wide stripy design. The fine line was added last. Just imagine how different the same design would look painted in yellows and oranges with golden highlights. Experiment with colour!

2 While the paint is still wet, fill in the gaps with the Ming blue to produce a wavy effect. Blend the colour slightly as you go in order to produce a more natural, watery effect.

3 It is a good idea to practise painting the fish several times on a spare plain tile first to get a really flowing look. Once you are confident, paint each fish with Ming blue using two simple brush strokes as shown. Either do this freehand or use the template as a guide.

4 Define the outline of the fish using the fine paintbrush and the abyss blue to create a smooth, continuous line. Add fin and gill details using the template as a guide. Finally, add a few bubbles to the background and wavy lines to simulate the movement of the water.

5 To further define and emphasize the fish shape, use a cocktail stick to scrape the paint off parts of the outline. If you are not happy with the result, repaint the outline with abyss blue and repeat. Allow to dry for 24 hours and then bake according to manufacturer's instructions.

MEXICAN-STYLE LAMP BASE

The combination of five toning shades of warm browns and gold combine to produce this magnificent patchwork of colour. Although it looks very impressive, it is easy enough for a beginner to tackle.

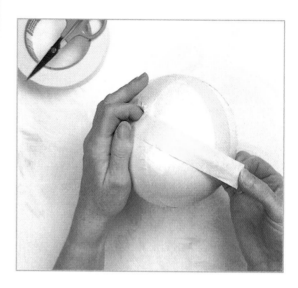

1 If you are using oven-bake paints as we have, it is important to remove all the wiring first. Then wash the base thoroughly in hot soapy water before you begin. Use the masking tape to mask off areas at random but leaving shapes large enough to decorate.

VARIATIONS

There are a number of design ideas here which may easily be used to transform a set of coffee cups. Each one could be slightly different or an alternative selection of colours.

2 Sponge the exposed areas of the lamp base with a selection of shades. We have used all the colours listed at this stage, but you could use just one or two colours if you prefer. Allow the base to dry for a few hours before carrying on. Carefully peel away the masking tape and clean up any messy areas before continuing.

3 Now, using the wide wash brush and smooth continuous strokes, fill in the white areas with the esterel paint. Allow the paint to dry for another 20 minutes or so and then add some narrower lines with the angled brush and the dark brown.

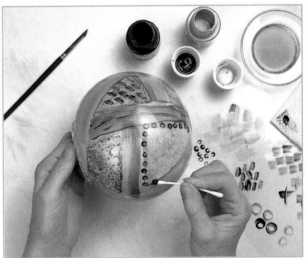

4 Experiment with brush strokes on a piece of cellophane as we have to create various textural designs. We used herringbone, basketweave effect and circles which only require simple strokes. Use a variety of these effects on the sponged areas of the lamp base.

5 Finally, add further embellishment to the design with stitch effect brush strokes in gold, and add dark brown spots by dipping a cotton bud into the brown paint. Allow the base to dry for 24 hours, then bake following the manufacturer's instructions and reassemble the lamp.

CHEQUERED VASE

Just imagine this vase sitting on a sunny windowsill brimming over with colourful sunflowers or cheerful gerbera! We have worked out an exceptionally easy way to apply the colour evenly in case your painting skills are still rather shaky.

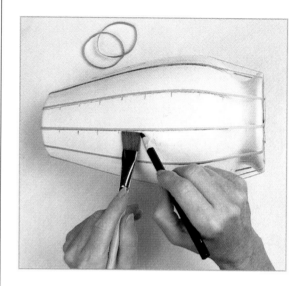

1 Wash the vase in hot soapy water. Taking one rubber band at a time, stretch it around the vase, making sure that it lies flat and is even. The number of bands used will determine the width of the checks. When you are happy with the spacing, make tiny marks the width of the wash brush with the chinagraph pencil along the side of each band.

VARIATIONS

Try masking off a large area on the front of the vase while you paint the checks. Later, remove the mask and fill the area with a single large flower head in yellow or gold to complement the pot. Experiment with other colours for the fine lines too.

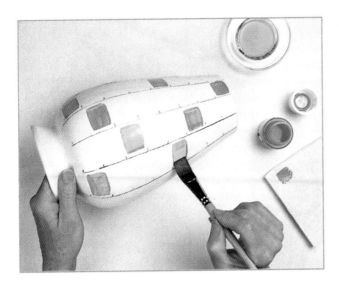

2 With the wide wash brush and using the grid as a guide only, paint wide bands of orange randomly around the vase, filling about a quarter of the spaces. Try to avoid letting any of the paint go over the chinagraph lines which are there as a guide only.

3 Continue to build up the checks, using the other colours, again placing them randomly around the vase until all the spaces are painted. Use each colour to fill about a quarter of the spaces. It is a good idea to allow the paint to dry for a few hours before moving on to the next step.

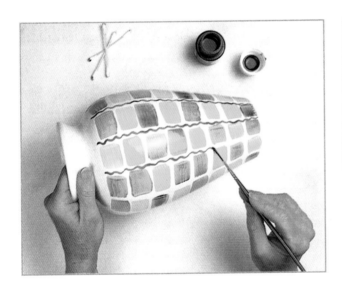

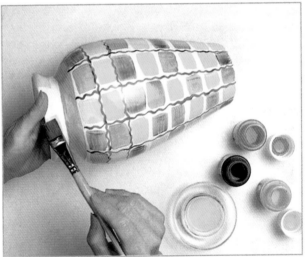

4 Use cotton buds to remove the chinagraph lines completely. With the fine liner brush, apply the emerald green in long wavy lines both vertically and horizontally to create a grid around the coloured blocks.

5 Complete the vase by painting bands of colour around the top with the wide brush using the photograph as a guide. Add a band of emerald to delineate the colours. Allow the vase to dry for 24 hours, then bake following the manufacturer's instructions.

CHERRY COFFEE CUPS

Here is a delightfully simple way of cheering up a set of plain white coffee cups and saucers. We have just used cherries to decorate our set, but apples, oranges, lemons or pears would look just as good, as would a variety of different coloured backgrounds.

1 Wash the china in hot soapy water. Work out the size of 'window' you would like on the front of each cup. Ours are 28 x 25 mm (1⅛ x 1 in). As this idea would also work well on coffee mugs, the whole design can be enlarged. Cut a paper mask for the front and back of each cup and use the glue to hold it lightly in place.

VARIATIONS

Instead of sponging around the window stencil, you could paint colourful stripes or bands of colour. The more confident you are, the more adventurous your ideas and design will become. Remember, it is easy to wash the paint off and start again!

2 Now, using the fine sponge and the parma violet, apply the paint evenly over the entire surface working quickly as the paint dries very fast when sponged on. Leave the centre of the saucer plain.

3 Remove the mask and clean up any rough edges if necessary. Remove any residue of glue that may remain on. Using the pattern as a guide, paint the leaves and stalks green with smooth, even brush strokes.

4 Now paint the cherries with the rich etruscan red and put the cups on one side to dry completely before continuing. Part-bake at this stage if you wish.

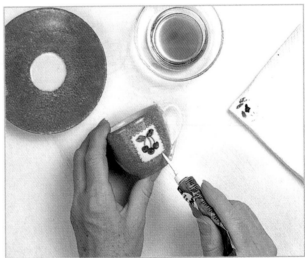

5 Finally, use the outliner to add neat dots all around the outside of the 'window'. You will see from the main photograph that we have also used straight lines which overlap at both ends as well as a corkscrew design. Allow to dry for 24 hours, then bake following the manufacturer's instructions.

PLAYING CARD EGG CUPS

Sponging the gold into the insides of these plain white egg cups makes them look very luxurious but is quick and simple to do. This attractive design could also be adapted to decorate tableware or ceramic storage jars.

1 Wash the egg cups in hot soapy water. Use a tiny piece of sponge to apply a coat of gold paint to the inside of each egg cup and to the bottom outer edges. Leave the egg cups to dry and repeat if necessary until the gold reaches the required density.

YOU WILL NEED

Set of egg cups, any size
Sponge
No 4 paintbrush
Porcelaine 150 paints in gold 44, and ruby 07
Porcelaine 150 outliner in gold
Scissors
String
Chinagraph pencil
Template (see page 360)
Sheet of cellophane
Kitchen paper towels
Small bowl of water

VARIATIONS

Why not paint matching side plates to stand the egg cups on? We painted all our suits red but of course you may prefer to paint the spades and clubs true to form in black. See the egg cup gallery for other ideas.

2 In order to space the motifs equally, you will need to mark the egg cup using the chinagraph pencil. We found that the easiest way to do this is to cut a length of string to fit around the rim, then simply fold it into four, marking it with the chinagraph and then transferring the markings onto the egg cups.

3 We have provided templates for you to copy onto the egg cups. There are several ways you can do this. The simplest is to practise on cellophane with the pattern underneath or as we have done here, simply using the pattern as a guide. When you feel confident with your work, transfer the suits onto the egg cups. You could cut stencils and sponge the design on if you wish.

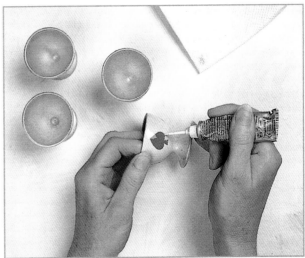

4 Now start working directly onto the egg cups using the no 4 brush and allowing the paint to flow quite thickly for a really good depth of colour.

5 Once the motifs have had several hours to dry, use the outliner to apply dots evenly around the edge of each one. Leave to dry for 24 hours and then stand the egg cups on a plate before baking them following the manufacturer's instructions.

CHEQUERED FRUIT PLATES

These bright and colourful plates are fun, easy to paint and are perfect to use for serving fruit on at the end of a meal. We have painted just three fruits, but there are many other fruits or vegetables you could add to the range.

1 Wash the china in hot soapy water. Start by painting two wide blue bands around the outer rim of the plate using the wash brush as shown. Do not worry if your painting is a bit uneven as this will add to its rustic charm. Leave the plate to dry for about 20 minutes.

YOU WILL NEED

Side plates

2 cm (¾ in) wash brush

Nos 6 and 2 paintbrushes

Sponge

'Spoke' template (see page 361)

Porcelaine 150 paints in lapis 16 (bright blue), agate 04 (orange), bronze 28 (leaf green), scarlet 06 and mummy brown 39 (dark brown)

Cocktail stick (toothpick) or rubber shaper brush

Kitchen paper towels

Small bowl of water

TIP

For perfect circles on the edge of the plate, use an old record player! See page 11 for further details.

VARIATIONS

Try painting cherries in a rich burgundy colour with purple edging or for something really spectacular, paint the fruits in gold, and band the plates with black.

2 Lay the plate over the 'spoke' template and using the no 6 brush, paint from inside the rim outwards towards the edge using the template as a guide for spacing. Alternatively, paint the spokes freehand leaving a gap of about 1 cm (⅜ in) between them.

3 Gather up a small piece of sponge into a round ball and use this to sponge the orange. Work from the centre outwards, dabbing the sponge with a circular motion to achieve the peel effect. If the paint is applied unevenly, the orange will appear to have more depth.

4 Use the no 2 brush and the dark brown to paint in the stalk and to add a tiny bit of detail to the bottom of the orange to make it look more realistic.

5 Finally, paint the leaf with the no 2 brush and green paint, allowing the paint to flow more thickly near the edges. Immediately etch in the detail of the leaf veins using the shaper brush or cocktail stick. Leave the plate to dry completely for 24 hours, then bake following manufacturer's instructions.

ANEMONE PLATE

Enjoy the beauty of these gorgeous flowers all year round by reproducing them on a plate as we have done. The secret is to use as many intense yet harmonious colours as possible – the larger your palette of colours the better. A set of eight with matching side plates would make a unique designer dinner service.

1 Wash the plate in hot soapy water. Copy the pattern onto the tracing paper and cut it out. Tape the tracing upside down onto the plate to hold it in place while you carefully draw over the lines in order to transfer the design onto the plate. Alternatively, use a coin to rub the design onto the plate. The result is a faint outline which will help you to place the flowers.

YOU WILL NEED

| Dinner plate – ours is 28 cm (11 in) |
| Template (see page 362) |
| Tracing or greaseproof paper |
| Pencil |
| Scissors |
| Masking tape |
| Coin |
| No 6 paintbrush |
| Porcelaine 150 paints in scarlet 06, ruby 07, azurite 15 (purple), amethyst 13, bronze 28 (leaf green) and etruscan 12 |
| Kitchen paper towels |

VARIATIONS

If your palette of colours is very limited, why not paint all the flowers bright red to imitate poppies instead. They usually have four or five petals and similar centres. Use a photograph of real poppies in order to copy the leaves.

2 Now start painting the red flowers first, working from the outer edge of each petal towards the centre. Use simple, flowing brush strokes and avoid labouring over each flower.

3 Continue to paint the rest of the flowers with the different shades of reds and mauves, working quickly to keep the whole design fresh and spontaneous. It is best to allow the plate to dry for an hour or so before continuing with the leaves.

4 Imitate the frond-like leaves and stems by using the no 2 brush and the leaf green. We have not given a pattern for the leaves as they are simple to paint with single brush strokes. Fill in the white areas between the flowers, building up the density until you are happy with the result.

5 Finally, add the dark centres using the no 2 brush and the black paint. Start by painting the large central areas and then add a few random dots around each one. Allow the plate to dry for a full 24 hours before being tempted to bake it following the manufacturer's instructions.

HERB-EDGED FISH PLATTER

This elegant fish platter looks so good with its decorative border of garden herbs, but just one word of warning if you would like to copy it – do make sure it will fit in your oven first!

1 Wash the plate in hot soapy water. Trace off the pattern for the two herbs using a fairly soft pencil and cut around the tracing fairly close to the edge. Turn the tracing over and then tape it into place around the edge of the platter once you have decided the position of the herbs. Use a coin to rub gently over the back of the tracing in order to transfer the pattern to the platter.

YOU WILL NEED

Long fish platter
Template (see page 363)
Tracing paper
Soft pencil, 5b for example
Scissors
Masking tape
Coin
Porcelaine 150 paints in green-gold 31, amazonite 29 (dark green), bronze 28 (leaf green), azurite 15 (purple), petrol 22, olive green 27 and ivory 43
Fine liner brush
Old tile or plate, for mixing paints and to practise on
Small bowl of water
Kitchen paper towels

VARIATIONS

If you are feeling ambitious, why not edge the platter with a whole range of different herbs instead of just two. Use a reference book or fresh herbs for inspiration.

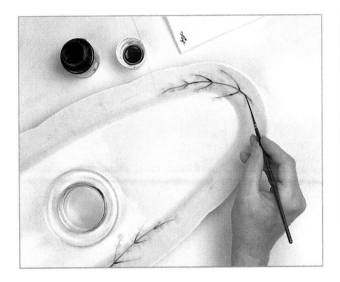

2 Paint the stems of the thyme with the green-gold using a fine liner brush. Use long sweeping movements for a more natural effect. It may be an idea to have a practise run on an old plate or tile until you feel sufficiently confident. The design can be as complicated or as stylised as you wish.

3 The thyme leaves are painted with a mix of the three greens and petrol blue to add a realistic look to them. Dip your brush in and out of the four colours without mixing them and this will give the natural effect of light and shade.

4 Now paint the stems, leaves and buds on the summer savory with the olive green paint mixed with a little dark green. Work quickly and freely for a painterly effect.

5 The flowers are painted with azurite and ivory, again not mixing the two colours together but simply dipping the brush from one colour into the other so that the flowers appear to have more depth to them. Allow the dish to dry for 24 hours, then bake following the manufacturer's instructions.

SPANISH-STYLE PLANTER

A few simple brush strokes are all that is needed to create this eye-catching planter. It is a free technique and the flowers are simply painted on at random.

1 Wash the pot in hot soapy water. This is such a free technique we have applied it straight onto the pot without prior marking. If you do not feel sufficiently confident, use a pencil to mark faint outlines of the flowers. The petals are made up of three brush strokes, each working from the outside towards the centre of each one with a no 6 paintbrush. Paint all the pink flowers first and then go back over them working more colour into the centre of each one. Allow the flowers to flow over the top rim. It is best to allow the pot to dry before moving on to the next step.

YOU WILL NEED

Ceramic pot
Template (see page 363)
Nos 6 and 2 paintbrushes
Porcelaine 150 paints in garnet 11, amber 36, peridot green 30, and mummy brown 39 (very dark brown)
Kitchen paper towels
Small bowl of water

VARIATIONS

Once you have mastered the idea of painting these flowers, you can make them larger or smaller depending on the size of your object. Scaled down, this would make a stunning set of coffee mugs and each one could be a different colour scheme.

2 Repeat the process as before but this time using the amber paint and fill in the spaces between the pink flowers already painted and go over the top edge as before. Again, allow the pot to dry before proceeding.

3 The background colour is also painted using the no 6 brush and the peridot green. The stippled effect is achieved by applying the paint with quick, short brush strokes. Fill in all the white areas between the flowers but remember that precision is not important with this style of painting.

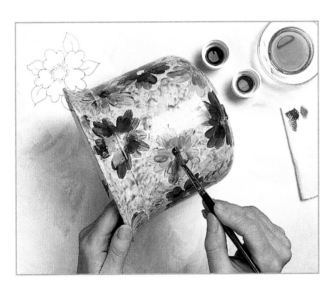

4 Paint the centres of the flowers by using the amber in the centre of the garnet flowers and vice versa. Use the no 6 brush and a stippling movement to give the appearance of stamens.

5 Finally, outline the petals of each flower using the no 2 brush and the dark brown. Use the template as a rough guide to paint the flower centres and then add a few leaves where there are spaces to fit them in.

FIFTIES-STYLE COFFEE POT

Reproduce the classic, simple lines and colours of this era with the sheer simplicity of this project. This elegant design also translates well onto plates and cups and saucers, so you could paint a complete set of matching china.

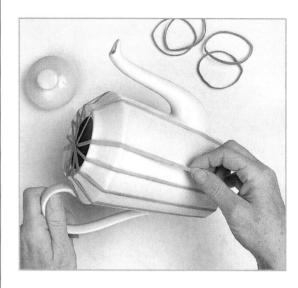

1 Wash the pot in hot soapy water. Then take the rubber bands and wrap them equidistantly around the pot as shown in order to create even vertical lines.

VARIATIONS

Paint coffee cups and saucers, milk jug and sugar bowl to match. Combining red and gold would be very festive with a holly leaf pattern substituted for the gold swirls.

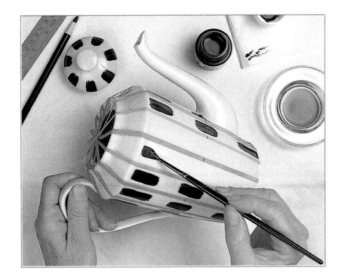

2 Mark the centre of each band with a chinagraph pencil. This will make it easier to position and paint the three black areas as shown. Allow the paint to dry before carefully removing the rubber bands. A hairdryer will speed up this process if you are impatient!

3 Paint more black areas between the first ones to create a chequerboard effect as shown and again allow the paint to dry thoroughly before moving on to the next stage.

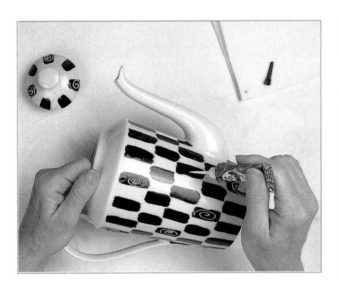

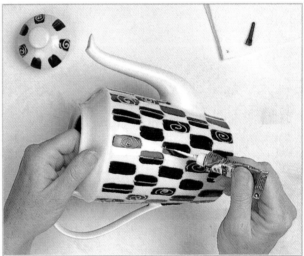

4 Use the outliner to apply the swirls to some of the black areas. It is a good idea to practise this on an old tile or plate first in order to perfect your technique. Have a piece of paper towel close to hand in order to keep the nozzle clean.

5 Now use the outliner to make vertical lines on some of the other black areas, remembering to leave some of them unembellished. Finish the lid too and allow them both to dry for 24 hours, then bake following the manufacturer's instructions.

ESPRESSO COFFEE CUPS

This simple, white set of cups and saucers in a traditional shape has been elevated to designer status with the addition of a little ceramic paint and some imagination. The dotted line in gold outliner provides the perfect finishing touch to after-dinner coffee cups.

1 Wash the china in hot soapy water. Before you start, it is a good idea to have a trial run at painting the scallop edging directly onto a saucer, as it is quite easy to do freehand with a little practise. Alternatively, use the scallop design as a guide and draw the outline with the chinagraph pencil onto the inner and outer rims of the cups and saucers as shown. Do not feel that you have to stick to the scale we have used. If you feel happier painting larger scallops, then do so but remember it will be more difficult to make them meet up neatly.

YOU WILL NEED

| Set of coffee cups and saucers |
| Nos 1 and 2 paintbrushes |
| Template (see page 360) |
| Chinagraph pencil |
| Porcelaine 150 paints in mummy brown 39 (very dark brown), esterel 37 (burnt sienna) and gold 44 |
| Porcelaine 150 outliner in gold |
| Small bowl of water |
| Kitchen paper towels |

VARIATIONS

Why not enlarge the design to create a matching dinner service? Experiment with different colour combinations too.

2 Next, using the fine paintbrush, carefully fill in the outline with the dark brown. Work around all the cups and saucers, remembering to fill in both the inner and outer rims of both.

3 Using the burnt sienna paint and the fine brush, paint the motif of a set of three lines with a central dot under alternate scallops. You will notice that this part of the design is mirrored to balance the depth of the cup, but not on the saucer.

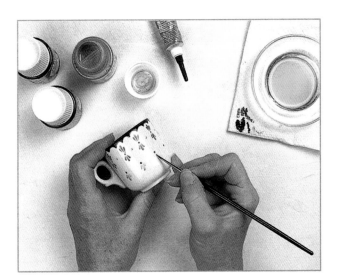

4 Continue to follow the pattern by adding the gold details to the cups as shown, again using a fine brush and steady hand.

5 Finally, using the gold outliner, add fine dots to the design to add another dimension to the surface. Allow the crockery to dry for 24 hours before baking following manufacturer's instructions.

TEMPLATES

The templates shown here are actual size.
They may be easily enlarged or reduced on a
photocopier to suit the size of the item you
wish to decorate.

Colourwashed cookie jar
(see page 308)

Barge-ware pot
(see page 310)

Jazz jug
(see page 314)

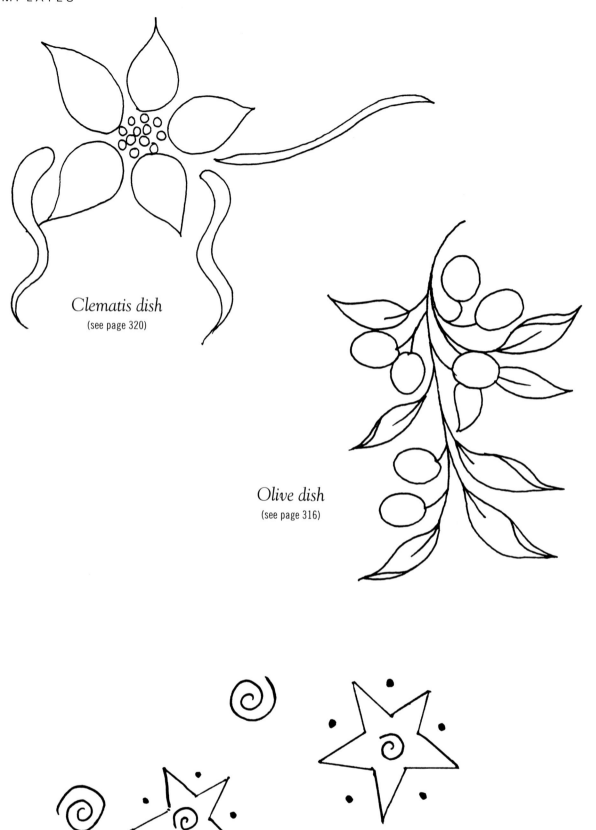

Clematis dish
(see page 320)

Olive dish
(see page 316)

Starry breakfast cup and saucer
(see page 324)

Floral finger plates
(see page 322)

Cherry coffee cups
(see page 334)

Espresso coffee cups
(see page 354)

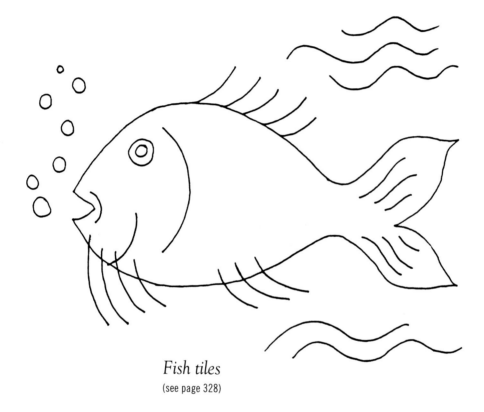

Fish tiles
(see page 328)

   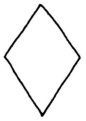

Playing card egg cups
(see page 338)

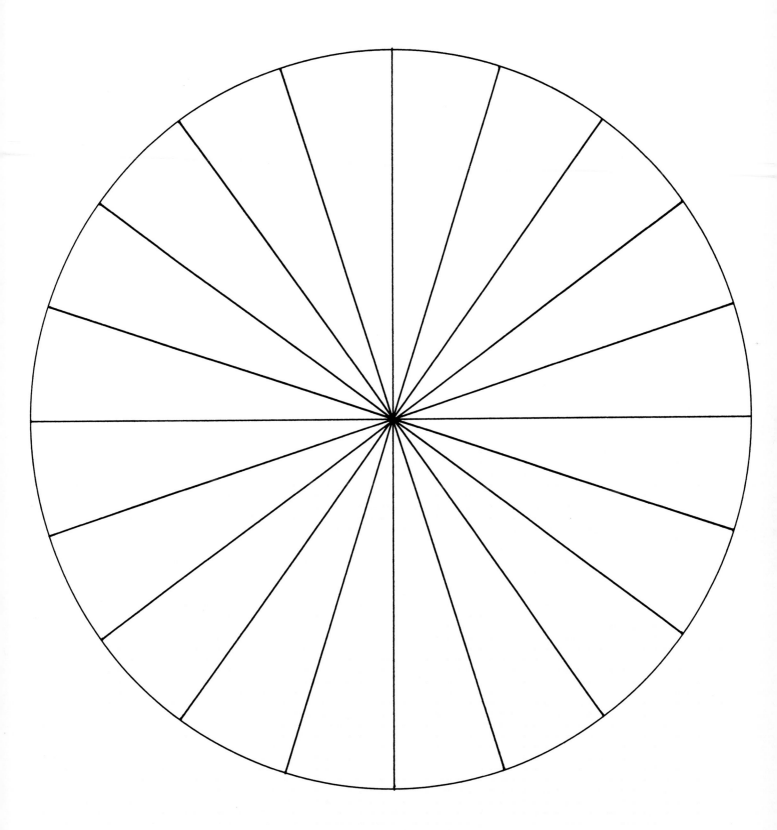

Chequered fruit plates
(see page 340)

Anemone plate
(see page 344)
Enlarge this template on a photocopier
to 140% to fit a plate with a diameter
of 28 cm (11 in).

Herb-edged fish platter
(see page 346)

Spanish-style planter
(see page 348)

GENERAL SUPPLIERS

UK

Cowling & Wilcox
26-28 Broadwick Street
London W1V 1FG
Tel: 020 7734 9556
Email: art@cowlingandwilcox.com
www.cowlingandwilcox.com/art

Craft Creations
Ingersoll House
Delamare Road
Cheshunt
Hertfordshire EN8 9ND
Tel: 01992 781 900
Email: enquiries@craftcreations.com
www.craftcreations.com

Fred Aldous
37 Lever Street
Manchester
M1 1LW
Tel: 08707 517 300
Fax: 08707 517 303
www.fredaldous.co.uk
(Suppliers of wide range of craft products. Mail order)

Homecrafts Direct
Unit 2
Wanlip Road
Syston
Leicester
Leicestershire
LE7 1PD
Tel: 0116 269 7733
Email: info@homecrafts.co.uk
www.homecrafts.co.uk

L. Cornelissen & Son Ltd
105 Great Russell Street
London WC1B 3RY
Tel: 020 7636 1045
Email: info@cornelissen.co.uk
www.cornelissen.com

Lakeland Limited
Alexandra Buildings
Windermere
Cumbria LA23 1BQ
Tel: 01539 488100
Email: net.shop@lakelandlimited.co.uk
www.lakelandlimited.com

Panduro Hobby
Westway House
Transport Avenue
Brentford
Middlesex TW8 9HF
Tel: 08702 422 874 (catalogue)
or 08702 422 873 (orders)
www.panduro.co.uk
(Mail order catalogue)

Specialist Crafts Ltd
Unit 2B
Wanlip Road Industrial Estate
Leicester
LE7 1PD
Tel: 0116 269 7711
Fax: 0116 251 7722
www.speccrafts.co.uk
(Suppliers of a wide range of craft materials. Mail order)

T N Lawrence
208 Portland Rd
Hove, East Sussex
BN3 5QT
Tel: 01273 260260
Email: artbox@lawrence.co.uk
www.lawrence.co.uk

Trylon Ltd
Wollaston
Northants
NN29 7QL
Tel: 01933 664275
Fax: 01933 664960
www.trylon.co.uk

SOUTH AFRICA

Art, Crafts and Hobbies
72 Hibernia Street
George 6529
Tel/fax: (044) 874 1337
(retail and mail order)

Art, Stock and Barrel
Shop 44, Parklane Centre
12 Commercial Road
Pietermaritzburg 3201
Tel: (033) 342 1026
Fax: (033) 342 1025

Bowker Arts and Crafts
52 4th Avenue
Newton Park
Port Elizabeth 6001
Tel: 041 365 2487
Fax: 041 365 5306

Crafty Arts
Walmer Park Shopping Centre
Port Elizabeth 6001
Tel: 041 368 2528

Crafty Supplies
Shop UG 2, Stadium on Main
Claremont 7700
Cape Town
Tel: 021 671 0286

AUSTRALIA

Lincraft Stores

Adelaide:
Shop 3.01, Myer Centre
Rundle Mall
Adelaide   SA   5000
Tel: 08 8231 6611

Brisbane:
Shop 237, Myer Centre
Queen Street
Brisbane   QLD   4000
Tel: 07 3221 0064

Canberra:
Shop DO2/DO3, Canberra Centre
Bunda Street
Canberra   ACT   2601
Tel: 02 6257 4516

Melbourne:
Australia on Collins
Shop 320, 303 Lt. Collins Street
Melbourne   VIC   3000
Tel: 03 9650 1609

Perth:
St. Martins Arcade
Hay Street
Perth   WA   6000
Tel: 08 9325 1211

Sydney:
Gallery Level, Imperial Arcade
Pitt Street
Sydney   NSW   2000
Tel: 02 9221 5111

NEW ZEALAND

Spotlight Stores
locations throughout New Zealand
Whangarei (09) 430 7220
Wairau Park (09) 444 0220
Henderson (09) 836 0888
Panmure (09) 527 0915
Manukau (09) 263 6760
Hamilton (07) 839 1793
Rotorua (07) 343 6901
New Plymouth (06) 757 3575
Hastings (06) 878 5223
Palmerston North (06) 357 6833
Porirua (04) 237 0650
Wellington (04) 472 5600
Christchurch (03) 377 6121
Dunedin (03) 477 1478
www.spotlight.net.nz

CARD SUPPLIERS

UNITED KINGDOM

Card Inspirations
The Old Dairy
Tewin Hill Farm
Welwyn
Herts AL6 0LL
Tel: 01438 717000
www.cardinspirations.co.uk

Craft Creations
Ingersoll House
Delamare Road
Cheshunt
Herts EN8 9ND
Tel: 01992 781 900
Fax: 01992 634 339
Email: enquiries@craftcreations.com
www.craftcreations.com

Cranberry Card Company
Unit 16, Dyffryn Business Park
Ystrad Mynach
Hengoed
Mid-Glamorgan
CF82 7RJ
Tel: 01443 819319
Fax: 01443 816316
Email: info@cranberrycards.co.uk
www.cranberrycards.co.uk

Falkiner Fine Papers Ltd
76 Southampton Row
London WC1B 4AR
Tel: 020 7831 1151

First Class Stamps Limited
Hall Staithe
Fakenham
Norfolk NR21 9BW
Tel: 01328 851 449
Fax: 01328 864 828

Paperchase
213 Tottenham Court Road
London W1T 7PS
Tel: 020 7467 6200
Phone for your nearest store

The English Stamp Co.
Kingston Road
Worth Matravers
Dorset BH19 3JP
For mail order phone
Tel: 01929 439 117

T N Lawrence
208 Portland Rd
Hove, East Sussex
BN3 5QT
Tel: 01273 260260
Email: artbox@lawrence.co.uk
www.lawrence.co.uk

The Stencil Store
Head Office
41a Heronsgate Road
Chorleywood
Herts WD3 5BL
Tel: 01923 285577

SOUTH AFRICA

Art Mates
Shop 313
Musgrave Centre
124 Musgrave Road
Durban
Tel/Fax: (031) 21 0094
Mail ordering service available

Artistea
18b Menlyn Shopping Centre
Atterbury Road
Menlopark, Pretoria
Tel: (012) 348 6121
Fax: (012) 348 6433
Mail order:
PO Box 25902
Monument Park 0105

Crafty Supplies
Shop 105, The Atrium
Main Road
Claremont, Cape Town
Tel: (021) 671 0286
Fax: (021) 671 0308

L & P Stationery and Artists' Requirements
65b Church Street
Bloemfontein
Tel: (051) 430 3061
Fax: (051) 448 3242
or
141a Zastron Street
Bloemfontein
Tel: (051) 430 1085
Fax: (051) 430 4102

Le Papier du Port
Gardens Centre
Gardens, Cape Town
Tel: (021) 462 4796
Mail order:
PO Box 50055
Waterfront 8002

Southern Arts and Crafts
Flat no. 5
105 Main Street
Rosettenville, Johannesburg
Tel/Fax: (011) 683 6566

The Craftsman
Shop 10, Progress House
110 Bordeaux Drive
Randburg
Tel: (011) 787 1846
Fax: (011) 886 0441

AUSTRALIA

Alderson Arts and Crafts
64-68 Violet Street
Revesby
NSW 2212
Tel: (02) 9772 1066

Craft Warehouse Shop
Campbell Street
Bowen Hills
QLD 4006
Tel: (07) 3257 1739 **Edgeworth Craft Supplies**
63 Edgeworth David Avenue
Waitara, NSW
Tel: (02) 9489 3909

Lincraft
Gallery Level
Imperial Arcade
Pitt Street
Sydney NSW 2000
Tel: (02) 9221 5111
or
303 Lt Collins Street
Melbourne
VIC 3000
Tel: (03) 9650 1609
or
Queen Street
Brisbane
QLD 4000
Tel: (07) 3221 0064

NEW ZEALAND

Gordon Harris, Art and Graphic Supplies
4 Gillies Ave
Newmarket, Auckland
Tel: (09) 520 4466,
Fax: (09) 520 0880

Studio Art Supplies
81 Parnell Rise
Parnell, Auckland
Tel: (09) 377 0302,
Fax: (09) 377 7657

CANDLE SUPPLIERS

UNITED KINGDOM

Candle Makers Supplies
28 Blythe Road
London W14 0HA
Tel: 020 7602 4031/2
Fax: 020 7602 2796
Email: mail@candlemakers.co.uk
www.candlemakers.co.uk

E.H. Thorne (Beehives) Ltd
Beehive Works
Wragby
Market Rasen LN8 5LA
Tel: 01673 858 555
Fax: 01673 857 004
Email: sales@thorne.co.uk
www.thorne.co.uk
(Beeswax candlemaking supplies)

Senses Candle Design Ltd
Unit 4g, Atlas Business Centre
Oxgate Lane
Staples Corner
London, NW2 7HJ
Tel: 020 8450 3255**The Candle Shop**
30 The Market
Covent Garden
London WC2E 8RE
Tel: 020 7376 4220

The Pier
200 Tottenham Court Road
London W1T 7PL
Tel: 020 7637 7001
Branches throughout the UK.

Websites:

www.waxworkshop.demon.co.uk/

www.wicksend.com

SOUTH AFRICA

Cape Town
Candle Maker's Deli
46 Marconi Road
Montague Gardens
Cape Town 8000
Tel: (021) 552 4938
Fax: (021) 551 4822

Crafty Suppliers
32 Main Road
Claremont 7700
Tel: (021) 61 0286

Durban
Art, Leather & Handcraft
Maple Road
Morningside
Durban 4001
Tel/fax: (031) 23 7948

George
Art, Craft & Hobbies
72 Hibernia Street
George 6529
Tel/fax: (044) 874 1337

Johannesburg
Southern Arts & Crafts
105 Main Street
Rosettenville 2130
Tel/fax: (011) 683 6566

Wax ën Wix
Shop 111 Heritage Market
Hillcrest
Durban 3610
Tel/fax: (031) 765 7623
(Offer candle making courses)

AUSTRALIA

Complete Candle Supplies
Shop 3, 401 Grange Road
Findon
SA 5023
Tel: (08) 8235 1434

Gift Ware Agencies
1 Tandy Cart
Duncraig
WA 6023
Tel: (09) 9246 9445

Norton Olympia Waxes
9 Francis Street
Wingfield
SA 5013
Tel: (07) 8347 2525

Norton Olympia Waxes
46 Renver Road
Clayton North
VIC 3168
Tel: (03) 945 6333

Pacific Petroleaum Products
1628 Ipswich Road
Rocklea
QLD 4106
Tel: (07) 3274 3140

Stacks of Wax
196 Harris Street
Pyrmont
NSW 2009
Tel: (02) 9660 001

The Wizard of the Wick Candle Co.
40 Trinder Road
Ashgrove
QLD 4060
Tel: (07) 3366 7003
(candle making classes)

NEW ZEALAND

Aglow Wax & Wix
Box 7000
Auckland
Tel: (09) 834 6000

Handcraft Supplies NZ Ltd
13-19 Rosebank Road
Avondale
Tel: (09) 828 9834

National Candles Ltd
PO Box 6024
Wellington
Tel: (04) 384 6806

Waxglo House
PO Box 19800
Christchurch
Tel: (09) 410 4727
Fax: (03) 084 4777

MOSAIC SUPPLIERS

Local DIY and hardware stores stock many useful tools, adhesives and other materials. Materials and equipment in this book may be obtained from the following suppliers, many of which will send orders by mail.

UNITED KINGDOM

Button Queen
19 Marylebone Lane
London W1U 2NB
Tel: 020 7935 1505
Suppliers of the buttons used in the Button Box on page 22.

Caesar Ceramics
358 Edgware Road
London W2 1EB
Tel: 020 7224 9671
Fax: 020 7224 9854

Creative Beadcraft Ltd
Denmark Works
Beaumond End
Amersham
Bucks HP7 0RX
Tel: 01494 715606
Mail order beads.

Edgar Udny & Co Ltd
The Mosaic Centre
314 Balham High Road
London SW17 7AA
Tel: 020 8767 8181
Extensive stock of ceramic tiles, vitreous glass, smalti and gold smalti plus mosaic tools. Importers and distributors of mosaics and tiles.

Evode Ltd
Common Road
Stafford
ST16 3EH
For technical advice
Tel: 01785 272727
www.evode.co.uk
Suppliers of Evo-Stik, 'Resin W' PVA adhesive and Araldite two-part epoxy resins.

Ideal Standard
The Bathroom Works
National Avenue
Kingston Upon Thames
Hull HU5 4HS
Tel: 01482 346461

James Hetley & Co. Ltd
Glasshouse Fields
London E1W 3JA
Tel: 020 7780 2344
Mail order suppliers of coloured glass

Mosaic Workshop
Unit B
443-449 Holloway Road
London N7 6LJ
Tel/fax: 020 7263 2997
Suppliers of marble tesserae cut to order.

Reed Harris Ltd
Riverside House
27 Carnwath Road
London SW6 3HS
Tel: 020 7736 7511
Fax: 020 7736 2988
Ceramic and marble tiles plus unglazed Cinca ceramic tiles from Portugal. Catalogue available.

Scumble Goosie
Lewiston Mill
Brimscombe
Stroud
Gloustershire
GL5 2TB
Tel: 01453 731305
Mail order. Suppliers of furniture and accessories suitable for mosaicing or painting.

Tower Ceramics
91 Parkway
Camden Town
London NW1 7PP
Tel: 020 7485 7192

SOUTH AFRICA

Art, Craft & Hobbies
72 Hibernia Street
George
6530
Tel. (0441) 74 1337
Mail order service available nationwide

Crafty Suppliers
32 Main Road
Claremont
Tel: (021) 61-0286
Fax: (021) 61-0308

Southern Arts and Crafts
105 Main Street
Rosettenville
Tel/fax: (011) 683-6566

AUSTRALIA

BBC Hardware
Head Office
Building A, Cnr Cambridge & Chester Streets
Epping NSW 2121
Tel: 02 876 0888
Branches throughout Australia

Camden Art Centre Pty Ltd
1880200 Gertrude Street
Fitzroy
Victoria
Australia 3065

Ceramic and Craft Centre
52 Wecker Road
Mansfield 3722
Queensland
Tel: 07 3343 7377
Branches throughout Australia

Ceramic Hobbies Pty Ltd
12 Hanrahan Street
Thomastown 3074
Victoria
Tel: 03 466 2522

Ceramicraft
33 Deeinup Way
Malaga 6062
Western Australia
Tel: 09 249 9266

True Value Hardware
15 branches, contact
1367 Main North Road
Para West Hills SA 5096
Tel: 281 2244

NEW ZEALAND

Handcraft Supplies Ltd
13-19 Rosebank Road
Avondale
Tel: 09 8289834

NZ Hobby Clay & Craft Co Ltd
1/80 James Fletcher Drive
Mangere
Tel: 09 270 0140

The Tile Company
782 Great South Road
Penrose
Tel: 09 525 5793

Trendy Trims Ltd
16-18 George Tce
Onehunga
Tel: 09 6344531

GLASS SUPPLIERS

UNITED KINGDOM

Fielders
54 Wimbledon Hill Road,
Wimbledon
London SW19 7PA
Tel: 020 8946 5044
Fax: 020 8944 1320
Email: shop@fielders.co.uk
www.fielders.co.uk
(Brushes and glass paints)

Panduro Hobby
Westway House
Transport Avenue
Brentford
Middlesex
TW8 9HF
Tel: 08702 422 873
(Suppliers of Pébéo paints. Mail order)

Philip & Tacey Ltd
North Way
Andover
Hampshire
SP10 5BA
Tel: 01264 332171
(Suppliers of Pébéo glass paints, including Porcelaine 150 and Vitrail. Telephone for your nearest stockist)

The Glass Painting Specialists
48 Coningsby Road,
High Wycombe,
Buckinghamshire,
HP13 5NY
Email: web@glasspainter.demon.co.uk
www.glasspainter.demon.co.uk

SOUTH AFRICA

Art Leather and Handcraft
Shop 107
Musgrave Centre
124 Musgrave Road
Durban
Tel: (031) 21 9517

Corner Arts and Crafts
52 4th Avenue
Newton Park
Port Elizabeth
Tel: (0431) 57 231

Cottage Craft
20 Pearce Street
East London
Tel: (0431) 57 231

Crafty Supplies
32 Main Road
Claremeont
Cape Town
Tel: (021) 61 0286

Mycrafts Shop
Aliwal Street
Bloemfontein
Tel: (051) 48 4119

The Craftsman
Shop 10
Progress House
Bordeaux Drive
Randburg
Tel: (011) 886 0441

AUSTRALIA

Arts & Crafts Corner
34 Mint Street
East Victoria Park
Western Australia 6101
Tel: (09) 361 4567

Boronia Arts & Crafts Centre
247 Dorset Road
Boronia
Victoria 3155
Tel: (03) 762 1751

Elde Crafts
76 Main Street
Hahndorf
South Australia
Tel: (08) 388 7007

Oxford Art Supplies
221-223 Oxford Street
Darlinghurst
NSW 2010
Tel: (02) 360 4066

Sundale Handcrafts
Shop 11
Logan Hyperdome
Pacific Highway
Loganholme
Queensland 4129
Tel: (07) 801 1121

NEW ZEALAND

Auckland Folk Art Centre
591 Remuera Road
Upland Village
Auckland
Tel: (09) 524 0936

Dominion Paint Centre
227 Dominion Road
Mt Eden
Tel: (09) 638 7593

P A Inkman Ltd
36 Douglas Street
Ponsonby
Auckland
Tel: (09) 638 7593

Studio Art Supplies
225 Parnell Road
Parnell
Auckland
Tel: (09) 377 0302

CERAMIC SUPPLIERS

UNITED KINGDOM

Pébéo UK Ltd
109 Solent Business Centre
Milbrook Road West
Milbrook
Southampton SO15 0HW
Tel: (01703) 901914
Fax: (01703) 901916
(*Suppliers of Pébéo paints including Porcelaine 150 and Deco. Telephone for your nearest stockist*)

F. Trauffler Ltd
100 East Road
London N1 6AA
Tel: 020 7251 0240
Fax: 020 7251 0242
www.trauffler.com
(*Plain white china by Apilco*)

Forsline and Starr International Ltd
P.O. Box 67
Ware
Hertfordshire SG12 0YL
Tel: (01920) 485895
(*Rubber shaper brushes*)

Fred Aldous
37 Lever Street
Manchester
M1 1LW
Tel: 08707 517 300
Fax: 08707 517 303
www.fredaldous.co.uk
(*Suppliers of wide range of craft products. Mail order*)

Specialist Crafts Ltd
Unit 2B
Wanlip Road Industrial Estate
Leicester
LE7 1PD
Tel: 0116 269 7711
Fax: 0116 251 7722
www.speccrafts.co.uk
(*Suppliers of a wide range of craft materials. Mail order*)

SOUTH AFRICA

Art, Craft and Hobby
72 Hibernia Street
George 6529
Tel/fax: (044) 874 1337

Art Mates
Shop 313, Level 3
Musgrave Centre
Durban 4001
Tel/fax: (031) 21 0094

Crafty Suppliers
UG105 – The Atrium
Claremont 7700
Tel: (021) 61 0286
Fax: (021) 61 0308

E. Schweickerdt (Pty) Ltd
Vatika Centre
475 Fehrsen Street
Brooklyn Circle
Tel: (012) 46 5406
Fax: (012) 46 5471

Liserfam Invest. Pty Ltd
P.O. Box 1721
Bedfordview 2008
Johannesburg
Tel: (011) 455 6810
Fax: (011) 455 5341
(*Suppliers of Pébéo paints including Porcelaine 150 and Deco. Telephone for your nearest stockist*)

Southern Arts & Crafts
105 Main Street
Rosettenville 2130
Tel/fax: (011) 683 6566

AUSTRALIA

Bellbird Hobby Ceramics
377 Newbridge Road
Morrebank NSW 2170
Tel: (02) 9601 8161

Brookvale Hobby Ceramics
9 Powelles Road
Brookvale NSW 2100
Tel: (02) 9905 0264

Ceramic & Craft Centre
52 Wecker Road
Mansfield QLD 4122
Tel: (07) 3343 7377
Fax: (07) 3349 5052

Ceramic Hobbies
12 Hanrahan Street
Thomastown VIC 3074
Tel: (03) 9466 2522
Fax: (03) 9464 0547

Elliot, Fay & Paul Good
31 Landsdown Terrace
Walkerville SA 5081
Tel: (08) 8344 4306

Francheville
1-5 Perry Street
Collingwood
VIC 3066
Tel: (03) 9416 0611
Fax: (03) 9416 0584
(Suppliers of Pébéo paints including Porcelaine 150 and Deco. Telephone for your nearest stockist. Please also contact for New Zealand stockists)

Mals Hobby Ceramics
3093 Albany Highway
Armadale WA 6065
Tel: (08) 9399 7746

The Craft House
51-55 Seymour Street
Ringwood VIC
Tel: (03) 9870 4522
Fax: (03) 9870 4788

NEW ZEALAND

Auckland Folk Art Centre
591 Remuera Road
Upland Village
Auckland
Tel: (09) 524 0936

Dominion Paint Centre
227 Dominion Road
Mt Eden
Tel: (09) 638 7593

P A Inkman Ltd
36 Douglas Street
Ponsonby
Auckland
Tel: (09) 638 7593

Studio Art Supplies
225 Parnell Road
Parnell
Auckland
Tel: (09) 377 0302

ACKNOWLEDGMENTS

CARD MAKING

This book is the result of my dedicated team without whom it would not have materialized! Much time, effort and patience has gone into the card designs shown in this book and I would like to take this opportunity to thank all my friends, family and colleagues for their support and wonderful encouragement.

Special thanks to all at NHP who worked with us especially Rosemary for her direction input and fingers, Anke for her card designs and Shona for the photographs. Chiu Mei and Nick Stephens need a mention for their tireless support and enthusiasm and for keeping us on our toes with their amazing organization. Thank you, Chiu, you are always an inspiration to the team and make things worthwhile!

Special thanks to my Mum for letting me use a glamorous photo of her and to both her and Dad for always being there.

Phil Wood for taking my photograph and more importantly for being the light of my life and believing in me and all my mad endeavours and keeping my spirit free.

Mandy Welch and Wyndham Hollis for their help with embossing, stamping and shaker materials from All Night Media.

Finally to my brother Steve for putting up with me and my moaning and my chaotic business and keeping it all in order!

CANDLE MAKING

Candles splashed with crystalline wax (pages 82 and 94): Candid Candles

Rolled candle (page 93): Martin Ridley

Candle dipped into ice-cold water (page 95): William Watson

Refillable candle (page 97): Ken Parsons of Spectrawax

Beeswax candle (page 108): Peter Kemble

Appliquéd candle (page 128): Jessica Payne

MOSAICS

By now you will have realized how much patience is required to make successful mosaics. This book is the result of a dedicated team. I would like to take the opportunity to thank all of my friends and colleagues who have been so supportive, particularly:

THE MOSAIC TEAM:
- Yvonne McFarlane, who commissioned this book and has helped and encouraged me every step of the way with great humour.
- Shona Wood, who did more than take the photographs so cheerfully and patiently. Shona's artistic eye was always appreciated.
- My assistant, Sylvia Bell, for her tireless help, for which I am so grateful.
- My dear friend Alan Welcome, for producing and marketing the mosaic kits so brilliantly as well as helping on this book.
- Rebecca Driscoll, Paul Hazelton, Liz Sims, Marilyn Wharton and Kim Williams, who each made mosaics for some of the projects and for the Gallery. In every case, their inputs were inspired and invaluable.
- Lady Davis, for allowing us to photograph her mosaics.
- Carol Stephenson, without whom our whole house (and me) would be in greater chaos than it already is.
- Joe Briggs, for dropping in on us whenever he felt like it.
- Rodney and Dinah Aird-Mash, for allowing us to photograph some of the finished mosaics in their beautiful garden in Broadstairs, Kent.
- My Mom and Dad, who never stopped believing in me and helped me whenever I needed it.

- My son and heir Thomas, for allowing me to steal some of his best ideas, long may his imagination continue to grow.
- My baby daughter Mollie, who entertains us all and lifts all our spirits.
- And finally, to my dear wife Margaret, for putting up with me and my mess for all these years.

THANKS ALSO TO:

Evode Ltd, for supplying Evo-Stik Resin W PVA adhesive and Araldite two-part epoxy resins; Scumble Goosie for lending the blanks for the fish table (page 174), bead box (page 182), button box (page 173) and the cat firescreen (page 174); The Button Queen, London and The Bead Shop, Portobello Road, London and Jane Churchill, Ideal Standard for the loan of the taps which are photographed with the Frog Splashback on page 206. Thanks also to Gideon and Jessica of the Upstart Gallery in Bevington Road, London W10 who have exhibitions of work by the best contemporary mosaic artists.

PAINTING GLASS

The authors and publishers would like to say a very big thank you to Pébéo, in particular John Wright of Pébéo UK and Carol Hook from Clear Communications Ltd, who have been so generous in their supply of paints, especially Porcelaine 150 and Vitrail, which we have used almost exclusively in this book.

Thank you to Clearcraft for their beautiful glass oil burners and to the Egyptian House who generously supplied us with a selection of their lovely coloured and recycled glass. Thanks to Shona for her patience, stamina and superb photographs and to Yvonne for letting us write this book! Thank you to the Cambridge branch of Emmaus, the self-help group for the homeless, for having such an abundance of glassware at incredibly good prices just crying out to be painted (we hope there is a branch near you).

PAINTING CERAMICS

We would like to say a very big thank you to Paul Sparrow of F. Trauffler Ltd who has generously provided elegant white china by leading French manufacturers, Apilco, for us to embellish. Thanks to Pébéo UK, in particular John Wright, for their abundant supply of paints and outliners and to Carol Hook of Clear Communications for her help. We were delighted with the rubber shaper brushes provided by Forsline and Starr as they are perfect for etching details in the paints.

Finally, to Tony and Jim for putting up with us, our mess, our moods and our mountains of china salvaged from every local bootsale causing shelves to sag and cupboard doors not to shut – thank you very much indeed!

INDEX